contents

one lord, one faith, one cornbread

EDITED BY FRED NELSON, 1941-

AND ED McCLANAHAN

ANCHOR BOOKS

ANCHOR PRESS/DOUBLEDAY

GARDEN CITY, NEW YORK

1973

ACKNOWLEDGMENTS

"All Girls Should Have a Poem" from *Rommel Drives on Deep into Egypt* by Richard Brautigan. Copyright © 1970 by Richard Brautigan. A Seymour Lawrence Book/Delacorte Press. Reprinted by permission of the publisher.

"A Few Words for Cannibalism" by Wendell Berry. Copyright © 1968 by Wendell Berry.

"To a Siberian Woodsman" by Wendell Berry. Copyright © 1968 by Wendell Berry, reprinted from *Openings* by permission of Harcourt Brace Jovanovich.

"A Letter to Ed McClanahan and Gurney Norman in California" and "The Contrariness of the Mad Farmer" by Wendell Berry, reprinted from *Farming, A Handbook* by permission of Harcourt Brace Jovanovich. Copyright © 1969 by Wendell Berry. Photograph of Wendell Berry by James Baker Hall.

"Dark by Four-thirty and Blowing From the West" by Karl Burton. Copyright © 1969 by Karl Burton.

"The Perry Lane Papers" by Vic Lovell. Copyright © 1968, 1969 by Victor R. Lovell. "Nymphet? Maybe. by Marty." Copyright © 1968 by the *Peninsula Observer*.

"A Kentuckian at the Wallace Rally" (Illustrations by Joan Larimore) and "Five" by Gurney Norman. Copyright © 1968 by Gurney Norman.

"A Correspondence" by Gurney Norman. Copyright © 1969 by Gurney Norman.

"Interruption" by Speer Morgan. Copyright © 1970 by Speer Morgan.

"Space Daisy" poems. Copyright © 1969 by Judith Quarnstrom. Illustrated by Jon Sagan.

"At the Center" reprinted with the permission of Farrar, Straus & Giroux, Inc. from *Moly and My Sad Captains* by Thom Gunn, copyright © 1961, 1971, 1973 by Thom Gunn. Also by permission of Faber and Faber Ltd. from *Moley*.

introduction

This collection of articles, poetry and fiction is taken from the *Free You* magazine, which flourished from 1968 through 1970 as the public voice of the Midpeninsula Free University on the San Francisco peninsula, one of the earliest and liveliest experimental universities.

The Free University began as a serious, Marxist-oriented challenge to the remote and ponderous educational style of nearby Stanford University, but its membership quickly swelled with repressed housewives, students, sexual revolutionaries, Haight-Ashbury evacuees, drifters, Maoists, artists, psychologists and psychotics, an occasional professor, and just enough curious souls straying in from the straight community to give it a twist of respectability.

Some of the original, more serious activists withdrew in the face of this confused onslaught of organized do-your-own-thingism, but enough stayed on to give the Free University at least the appearance of revolutionary teeth—an easy illusion to summon up, in the quiet, elegant communities near Stanford—as it combined its private classes with rallies, occasional sit-ins, flower-festooned rock concerts in public parks, and other fairly amiable public activities before falling back to its original posture, with fewer members and more militant leaders, as the Cambodian invasion ignited the Stanford campus in 1971.

The *Free You* magazine occupied the colorful and erratic middle period of the organization's life, growing rapidly from a mimeographed house organ to a full-size, fifty-page magazine with opulent color graphics and wide distribution outside the Free U's membership.

The magazine reflected the group's diverse membership and outlook: It wasn't quite a literary magazine, standing in proud, esoteric obscurity, but it wasn't quite an underground publication, shrill and self-conscious. . . . It was sort of, well, a sort of *Saturday Evening Post* of the left, a wild assemblage of fiction, fancy, and hard street-reporting sewn together under a common masthead in a monthly-magazine format.

Its editors held the magazine to only one enduring editorial policy, but it was truly revolutionary: Within space and budget limitations, the magazine printed any Free University member's contribution without first straining it through the editors' criteria for political or literary suitability. A simple-enough-sounding policy, but deceptive. It meant that a manuscript carefully coaxed by an editor from a Stanford creative writing student, or from an established writer, could be followed immediately by the volunteered philosophy of a newly liberated steamfitter from a Free U. encounter class. It meant a hundred flowers blooming noisily every month over the heads of a dismayed Free University governing body, whose liberationist instincts did noble, regular battle with that old, irresistible urge to rein in someone else's divergent opinions. It meant a rare instance of editors struggling to facilitate communication, not to stifle it.

It also added to the challenge common to all magazines, particularly small ones: establishing enough reader identification to have the magazine anticipated every month and bought and read in preference to the reams of other printed material competing for a reader's attention. The stories had built-in relevance; we added personality with strong graphics, consistent format, and an overriding sense of humorous self-perspective bannered by Wendell Berry's contributed motto: One Lord, One Faith, One Cornbread.

The magazine ended suddenly, changing as the Free University changed, evolving into a narrower, less-expensive tabloid newspaper to express the organization's new political realities. It was a loss of sorts, but it's easy to lament too much a magazine's passing. Magazines serve a need, but even as large and established a magazine as *Life* should be allowed a quick, natural death when the need no longer exists. The makings of a successful magazine—people and their changing ideas—remain free to fall together again into new forms, to serve new needs and opportunities. The pieces in this book represent the best use of our own opportunity.

For Robert S. Cullenbine:
Old Culley, who had himself sterilized for the
cause. No higher honor, no lower sacrifice . . .

highway 52 revisited

by ed mc clanahan

"Speak swiftly, and carry a big soft."   Ken Kesey

AUGUST 1968, the week of Chicago, and All Across the Linth and Breath of This Great Land (as the politicians on the teevee have been bleating all week long) there hangs a sulphurous cloud of suspicion and malevolence as foully palpable as smog, and here I am in what is very possibly the absolute worst place in the continental U.S. for a man of my persuasion to be during these trying times, just getting out of my mother's car in the parking lot of the Pennington Club tavern on Highway 52 in Manchester, Ohio.

Now Highway 52—at least the stretch of it I care about—runs along the Ohio River for about twenty miles in Brown County, Ohio, from Ripley through Aberdeen to Manchester. And the reason I care about it is that at Aberdeen there is a toll-free bridge from Maysville, Kentucky, my hometown; and since Ohio permits the sale of 3.2 beer to eighteen-year-olds, whereas in Maysville you can't even smell a bottlecap until you're twenty-one, that bridge to Aberdeen loomed as large in the landscape of my adolescence as the Golden Gate undoubtedly does for Marin County teen-agers. Southern Ohio has always known perfectly well why the good Lord in His infinite wisdom stationed it over there at the north end of the bridge, and in the days of my youth Highway 52 was fairly lined with taverns—the Top Hat and the Terrace Club and the Bay Horse and the Pennington Club and Danny Boone's Tavern and the Riviera Lounge and a dozen others—rank, musty, low-ceilinged places with puke in the urinals and Cowboy Copas on the jukebox and lighting feeble enough to allow a sixteen-year-old to pass for eighteen if the bartender wasn't too particular, as he almost never was. Some of those havens have long since given way to motels and Frisch's Big Boy Drive-Ins and the like, but a remarkable lot of them have survived pretty much unscathed by Progress. And the most unscathed of all is the scrofulous old Pennington Club, where I have been wasting my substance in riotous living off and on for twenty years or more.

To which purpose I now find myself, as I do every summer when I come back to Kentucky for a visit, about to sally forth into the Pennington Club once again. Ordinarily a happy moment for me, this, a moment filled almost to bursting with eager anticipation; nostalgic nitwit that I am, I can be moved almost to tears by the raunchy familiarity of such places, the sweet memories of high old times—especially when, as tonight, I'm stoned to the eyeballs on the two plump numbers of Kentucky Blue I've just done up, courtesy of an old friend I ran into in Lexington the other day.

But this year there are also a couple of other subtle circumstantial deviations from the norm—namely, this year I'm decked out in high-heeled Fag Store frootboots and a modestly mod over-the-collar bob and a droopy Mandarin mustache and round, gold-rimmed, lime-tinted spectacles, a set of accessories not likely to take the Best Dressed Barfly award in Pennington's, where the clientele's taste runs at its very dandiest to plaid sport shirts and brand-new blue jeans and wingtip oxfords, eyeglasses with tortoise-shell upper rims and steel lowers, and not the first sign of a facial hair below the eyebrows. Already my little affectations, modest as they seemed at home in Palo Alto, have won me countless wide-eyed stares on the streets of Maysville. It's the spectacles that do it, actually; if it weren't for them, the boots and even the hair and mustache would sneak by okay, I think; but the spectacles, representing as they obviously do a fairly substantial commitment of cold hard *cash*, seem to confirm what my other trappings merely hint at: *it's a hippie it's a yippie it's a commie it's a California crazy it's a fruitcake it's a freak!* Not exactly the sort of reception a sensible and prudent thirty-six-year-old-college-English-teacher-father-of-three would ordinarily choose to be accorded by the usual Friday night crowd in Pennington's—farmhands and highway construction workers and beer-truck drivers on a busman's holiday, all in all a bunch of very rough customers, most of whom would just as leave knock me on my California ass as look at me. In truth, would rather.

And as a matter of convenient fact, it just so happens I've got my regular old black horn-rims right in the glove compartment, put them there myself (if you must know) against just such a contingency as this. But what the hell, I'm thinking, if I really believe all the stuff I'm always claiming to believe about being straight with people, about *caring* enough about them to be straight with them, then I can't very well go slinking around in disguise, can I now? And anyhow I've always taken a certain secret pride in my supposed talent for turning hostility into curiosity into communication at California cocktail parties; so I really shouldn't cop out just because I'm faced with playing a tougher house. And if worse comes to worst—although I'm very likely the world's most inept fighter since Ethelred the Unready —I can manage to *look* fairly formidable to a not-too-discerning eye (like the song says, "I ain't big, jes tall, thass all"), and of course *they* don't know I can't fight, do they now?

So get thee hence, goodbuddy, get on with it. Into the breach. And suddenly there I am, sitting at the Pennington Club bar with a beer in front of me, sitting there amidst the neon murk and the beery blare of loud talk and laughter and Red Sovine on the jukebox and the heady reek of Lysol from the men's

toilet, and so far not a soul has uttered an unkind word. Couple
of suspicious glances, maybe, but nobody's bad mouthed me a
bit. All right then, I decide, sucking at my beer and gaining
confidence by the minute, so it was just paranoia after all, just
Kentucky Blue paranoia compounded by my own unseemly will-
ingness to think the worst of my countrymen. Clearly I owe them
an apology, perhaps a musical salute to demonstrate that, appearances to the contrary notwithstanding, I stand foursquare
with them against the barbarian hordes. Taking my beer along,
I leave my barstool and go over to the jukebox, plug it with a
couple of quarters, pick myself a nice bouquet of songs—Kitty
Wells and Buck Owens and Porter Waggoner and Johnny Cash
and several others—then make my way between the tables to a
booth over against the wall, where I settle down to drink my beer
and listen to Patsy Cline sing "I'll Sail My Ship Alone" and
watch a two-hundred-pound lady and her one-hundred-pound
boy friend play shuffleboard.

But no sooner have I set my head adrift in these familiar and
relatively tranquil waters than I become aware of some sort of
minor turbulence at my shoulder, a gentle but insistent jostling,
and I look up to see a kid (I took him for eighteen or nineteen,
though later I discovered I'd slighted him by half a dozen years)
standing there beside my booth, a hefty, husky fellow all decked
out like an archetypal Pennington Clubber from his blond crew
cut to his half-rim glasses to his plaid shirt all the way down to
his burnished wingtips (to tell the truth he was the model for
my archetype in the first place), standing there above me all big
and blond and burly, his cheeks so cleanly shaven they are as
pink as two slabs of raw tenderloin, standing there shaking my
shoulder ever so gently and grinning down at me like a cat eating shit—a repast which, *au contraire,* there's every reason to
suppose is precisely what *he* has in mind serving up to *me.* Already I can feel the old adrenalin commence to surge . . . but
for me that brand of fuel only works for running ("Whenever
they get his chickenshit up," a college drinking buddy of mine
used to sing, to the tune of "Clancy Lowered the Boom," "Mc-
Clanahan leaves the room-room-room . . ."), and flight is out

of the question just now, if only because my man has had the foresight to position himself between me and the door. So all I can do is return his grin with interest, meanwhile trying to make my own face say, silently, *Yeh? What can I do for you, Jack?* You know, an out-of-the-corner-of-the-mouth kind of look, not hostile yet, with just the merest hint of danger in it—a Humphrey Bogart kind of look.

"Hey, sport," he says, still grinning, "see that guy over there?" He points to a nearby table where in fact two guys sit watching us. But there isn't the slightest doubt which of the two he has in mind. The big one. The big, thick-necked, dark-haired lout of a kid who is even now smiling at me as amiably as if he is privy to my every secret qualm, and knows exactly how to deal such chicken-hearted trash as I. His smaller companion looks a bit uneasy, but he too eyes me the way he might something revolting he'd discovered on his shoe sole.

"I mean that black-headed one," the crew cut explains unnecessarily. "You know what he called you? He called you a fucken punk."

Well, here it is at last, hot-shot, I tell myself, *your big moment, your chance to become the first man to cross the Generation Gap on a tightrope . . . backwards.*

"Is that so?" I hear myself saying lamely. But to my surprise my voice seems stronger and steadier than I'd dared hope.

"Yep, that's what he called you, all right." He pauses as if reconsidering, then corrects himself: "No, wait now, I take that back. He just said you was a punk. *I* was the one that said you was a fucken punk."

"Oh, well, that's different then. That's a different story." Careful there, McClanahan, no sarcasm now, no patronizing. Patronizing will get your ass handed to you in the Pennington Club.

"So what do you think about that?"

"Well, I don't know, I guess he's got a right to his own opinion."

My championing of the fine old principles of democratic egalitarianism does not impress him in the slightest. "You know why

we said you was a fucken punk?" he demands, his grin slowly
metamorphosing into a sneer before my very eyes.

"Sure," I say, with every last smidgeon of good-fellowship I
can muster, "I expect it's because of this hair and mustache and
stuff. These glasses."

He shifts his weight from one foot to the other, looking just
slightly taken aback. He obviously hadn't anticipated a direct
answer, and it has put him just the tiniest bit off-balance. But
he plunges on.

"What you ought to do," he says, gesturing once again toward the other table, "you ought to go over there and tell him
you're gonna beat the hell out of him for sayin' such a thing as
that." When I glance up, the behemoth at the other table favors
me with an almost pitying smile and flips me a diffident little
two-fingered salute. Just letting me know he's still in the picture,
so to speak.

"Naw," I say, struggling to calm my jittery voice, "I don't
think that'd be too good an idea, to tell the truth. Because if I
did do it, then he'd probably just get mad and beat the hell out
of *me*. And then where'd I be, what good would all that stuff do
anybody?"

Again that fleeting hint of confusion crosses my interrogator's
visage, and I sense that I'm evidently still making the right moves,
that he'd been prepared for almost any reaction except what is
—somehow—still passing for relaxed candor. But he isn't about
to hang it up yet, not by a long shot.

"Hey, Emory," he calls above the din, "come on over here a
minute."

Emory rises and ambles toward us, growing taller and broader
by the step. He brings his beer bottle with him, carrying it by
the neck like a billyclub, despite the fact that it is still half full
of beer. A very bad sign, that.

"Emory," the crew cut says, "I was just tellin' this fucken punk,
here, that you called him a fucken punk. Ain't that right?"

Emory's grin widens. "Naw, Cecil," he says, "now you know
I never said he *was* a fucken punk. All I said is, he *looks* like a
fucken punk."

As well to take the bull by the horns; they're the nearest thing to handlebars I'm likely to find.

"Well," I tell him, "like I said, you're entitled to your opinion, I won't argue with you on that. But what I *am* just might be an entirely different thing from what I *look* like. You all ever think of that?"

"How's that?" Emory says, edging forward menacingly. "I mean, I reckon I know a fucken punk when I see one, by god . . ."

"Okay, maybe you do and maybe you don't. But I tell you what, why don't you all sit down here a minute and let me explain to you why I don't think I am one, and then if we have to have trouble, well, at least we'll have it over what I really am, and not just what I look like."

Hearing myself make the plea, I realize that if they do sit down with me it will mean the tide has begun to turn in my favor, and with that realization comes the first full knowledge of just how desperately I want this encounter to work out right. Because it will justify so much; already I can see in it the substance of a metaphor that will explain perfectly the directions my life has taken during the last few years, explain them not just to the world but to *me*. And it'd also be sort of nice if I could manage to survive this situation with my physical person more or less intact. So a lot is suddenly riding on what happens next.

Cecil and Emory look quizzically at each other, and for an instant my breath catches in my throat, and then to my relief and delight Emory slides into the seat opposite me, and Cecil, following his lead, sits down beside me.

"Okay," I begin, "now the first thing you ought to know is that I'm probably almost as old as both of you all put together."

"*Shit* you are," Emory scoffs, his disbelief dangerously reviving his baser impulses. It is not, I understand intuitively, that my appearance is notably younger than my years; rather it is just that Emory and Cecil haven't yet seen through the get-up to the man behind it, and it has simply never occurred to them that they might find back there a man who's reached the age of reason.

"Well, I'm thirty-six," I tell him quickly. "I could show you my draft card or something. I graduated from Maysville High School in 1951. So you figure it out."

"*Shit* you did!" Cecil explodes. "You mean to tell me you're from *Maysville?*"

"That's right. I live in California now, but I grew up right around here, in Maysville and Brooksville, over in Bracken County. What'd you think I was, some Cincinnati dude or something?"

"California?" Emory says. "What do you do in California?"

Far out, as we Californians say: Now they're asking for information, instead of making me force-feed it to them. "I'm a teacher," I tell them. "I teach college English."

"Shit you do!" Emory cries; but this time his scorn has been almost totally replaced by wonder. "English? What college?"

"Stanford University."

That one struck a nerve I hadn't expected to hit. "*Stanford?*" he says. "Sure enough? Wasn't they in the Rose Bowl one time or somethin'?"

"I could show you my faculty ID card, if you . . ."

"I went up to Morehead State one semester myself," he muses wistfully, "but I flunked out."

I see now that the game is almost over, and that a kind of limited victory is within my grasp. I could probably launch right now into a just-between-us-college-men talk with Emory, and get out of it all with a whole coat. But I'm feeling very much on top of the situation now, and there's a lot I haven't said yet. For a starter, there's one more speculation about me that I want to eliminate from their consideration. I mean the chance that they suspect I'm gay.

"One more thing," I tell them. "I'm married, and I've got three kids."

"Shit you do," Cecil sighs wearily, all the fight gone out of him at last.

"Right. So the way it looks to me, if you all want to believe

that a thirty-six-year-old college English teacher with three kids
is a fucken punk, well, help yourself, I guess. I mean, I pretty
much *know* what I am, and it just doesn't seem to me like it
makes much sense to go and fight over what somebody else
thinks I am, especially when I know good and well they're wrong
anyhow. There was a time in my life when it would've upset me
something terrible to be called a fucken punk. Because in those
days I *was* one, you see, and like they say, the truth hurts. But
that was a long time ago."

"Well then," Cecil begins, "how come you . . ."

"How come I wear this hair and glasses and stuff? Well, first
of all, I *like* them, you know, and I think everybody ought to
wear just about what they like to wear. I mean, if I'd come in
here tonight looking just like you guys, with short hair and all,
we probably wouldn't be talking right now, would we? Because
if everybody looks the same and thinks the same, pretty soon
there won't be much to talk *about*, right? In a way it's kind of
like teaching school, you know? And if you all don't mind my
saying so, I hope you learned something from it, I hope you
learned not to be quite so quick to judge people. I mean, you
make *mistakes* that way, that's why the wrong people are always
getting hurt!"

It is over, for once in my life I've made all the right moves
and I know it, and the knowledge is positively exhilarating. At
this moment I'd be entirely satisfied if Emory and Cecil would
tuck in their tails and go skulking back to their own table right
now. But this turns out to be one of those rare times when the
breaks just won't quit coming my way. Because just as I finish
my little sermon, up to our booth steps their forgotten friend, the
smaller fellow who'd been sitting with them at the other table.

"Come on, you guys," he says grumpily, "leave this poor
bastard alone and let's get out of here."

"Hey, Jim," Cecil says, "this here guy claims he graduated
from Maysville High!" Cecil evidently sees one last chance to
vindicate himself; if Jim, who is clearly something of an authority
on graduates of Maysville High, rules that I've introduced false
evidence, then we're right back where we started.

"Shit you did," Jim says flatly. "When was *you* ever at Maysville High?"

A bad moment. Nothing for it, though, but to ride it through and hope for the best. "I went there three years," I tell him. "I graduated in fifty-one."

"*Shit* you did. Because listen here, my name is Otis, and my brother Charlie . . ."

"Oh for Christ sake," I interrupt, laughing with the relief of recognition, "you're Jimmy Otis, you're Charlie's little brother! Hell, I *graduated* with Charlie!"

Of *course* he's Jimmy Otis! Little Jimmy-O whose brother Charlie was a basketball superstar and therefore the best guy in Maysville High to take along when you were going out cruising, looking for a little strange. Little Jimmy-O whose brother Charlie was—therefore—one of my most cherished friends in high school. Little Jimmy-O whose brother Charlie used to chase him home whenever we set out on those nightly expeditions. Little Jimmy-O! How could I have failed to know him?

But in my delight at this unexpected turn of events I've momentarily forgotten that Jimmy-O still doesn't know who I am. Even now, in fact, he's leaning across the table, peering intently at my face. Suppose he doesn't remember me? After all, it's been—what?—seventeen years since we've seen each other, and he was just a little kid then. . . .

"My name's Ed McClanahan," I say finally, searching his face for some reaction. For the first few seconds, nothing. Then, spurred by sudden inspiration, I take off my glasses; and as I lower them Jimmy-O straightens very slowly, raises his eyes to the cobwebby ceiling, and dramatically claps a palm to his forehead.

"Jee-zus Christ!" he cries. "Eddie McClanahan! Why you stupid sons of bitches, this guy went to school with Charlie! Why this here was one of the smartest guys in Maysville High School! He teaches *college* somewhere, ain't that right, Eddie? Why you stupid sons of bitches, this here guy is smarter than both of you all put together, and you all wantin' to *punch* him!"

And now Jimmy-O is pumping my hand energetically, and

my own grin is nearly splitting my face in the almost boundless
pleasure of this moment, and Emory is hiding his face behind
his hands in mock shame. "Hey, Cece," he says, peeking between
his fingers, "you know what you are, don't you?"

"Yeah, Emory," Cecil snickers. "I'm a fucken punk."

So that's it, that's all there is to tell, except that I spent the
next five hours or so getting roaring drunk with Jim and Emory
and Cecil, and that during those five hours I told them just about
all I knew about Vietnam and Chicago and spades and dope
and hippies—which, although it may well have amounted to a
good deal less than some folks know about those matters, was
nonetheless a good deal more than Jim and Emory and Cecil
had known about them prior to that occasion—and that for the
first time ever they actually *listened* to these heresies, and found
them a good deal less difficult to get next to than they would
ever have suspected.

And as I drove home, drunk and happy in the dawn, it came
to me, in the perverse form of what has to be the silliest pun
ever concocted, that the only real difference between my freaky
paraphernalia and, say, an Oxford don's cap and gown was a
difference in degree. But then, even as I giggled at my own
giddy wit, I was also struck, for perhaps the tenth time in the
ten years I'd been a teacher, by the full force of the revelation
that teaching is one of the very few things worth doing every
single time one is obliged to get in there and really do it.

the universal life church:

kirby j. hensley, preacher of good times
jon buckley

There was this old man who came down the road one day ordaining ministers, thousands of them. Denomination? Whatever you felt like preaching. Cost? Whatever you were willing to pay, usually pocket change, often nothing . . . legality? Absolute. Selective Service, and others with a vested interest in the extent of the clergy, were scandalized. You could even become a doctor of divinity (this was where the law finally intervened) with a little more work, a little Divine will.

We asked Jon Buckley, a talented poet, songwriter, musician, and hard-bitten investigative reporter, to investigate. Buckley returned a convert, performed several (legal) marriages and invested several more ministers on his own, including the entire Free You staff. (Editor McClanahan, in turn, later inducted Paul Newman into the ministry.) The Free University printshop was legally consecrated as a religious sanctuary. Buckley's marriages have lasted longer than the average.

I

WE CROSSED the flooded Tuolumne River, past mudbanks and trailer shacks, past pine board boxes—some empty relics and some occupied—past country that could pass for Alabama.

There were blurred visions of American Legion Halls, lazy pheasants climbing through murky skies, sliding sensations as the car swerved down the slippery mudflat that folks use for a road. A large red and white sign proclaims: *Life Church.* We parked and listened briefly to the silence that echoes at the end of a long ride.

Welcome to Modesto.

Hardly Vatican City. Country house, tacked-on church office, muddy footprints leading to a blast of warmth as the door is opened. We knock the earth off our boots and walk inside. There's an aura about the place that pleases the soul. The word is funky. Large U. S. flag spread-eagled behind the pulpit, tattered books, strewn boxes and collapsed folding chairs. And everywhere you look are stacks and stacks of mail; teetering on desk precipices, staggered up against walls, scattered on tables: letters exploding out of their envelopes.

"2,000 a day, yes sir, 2,000 a day."

Reverend Kirby J. Hensley, founder and president of the Universal Life Church, runs his hand fondly across the stacks and nods approval.

There's a dark-haired girl writing names and numbers in a big record book, two student types are typing, and Hensley is darting here and there around the room gathering chairs to sit on, a place by the window, and the phone—all in what seemed to be a single motion.

"Hello? Hello? Yes this is Rev. Hensley. What's that? Why, of course girls can be ordained, honey, never yet met up with a woman who didn't preach. Bye."

He's an exuberant little man in a dark rumpled suit; quick eyes set behind bifocals; long drawl; and the tongue of a master tale-teller. He's of that rare breed that can wrap words around you like a cocoon and let them trickle into your mind like drops of Southern Comfort.

Yet there's nothing to mark him as being different from a thousand other rustic preachers; nothing except for the fact Rev. Hensley is ordaining ministers at the rate of a couple thousand per day.

There's a gnomish quality about the man that revels in what he's doing, and what he's doing is simply consecrating everyone who asks, without question, thus bringing untold woes to draft boards, airlines, Internal Revenue and any other body that gives special consideration to the clergy.

But the Universal Life Church is more than just a pain to Selective Service. At the present time there are 20,000 ministers scattered in 1600 churches throughout the west—and further.

(Mark, our photographer, is hopping on file cabinets, muscatel taking its toll, searching for interesting camera angles.) Hensley pauses to direct some visitors to a good mechanic, resumes talking in mid-sentence. ". . . You know, boys, many people who come to this planet take a long time before they find their calling, but some of us are nigh driven into situations that set the direction for the rest of our lives."

He shifts mental gears and jumps to the nearby blackboard and begins to diagram the essential structure of world history. We group around near the flying chalk and listen.

"We start with a globe, with some people on it. And the people, being such, naturally develop a unity of existence, a kind of bond that flows in and around them. *But!* as time goes on we see the great dividin' and out of that one source comes two branches—the spiritual and the political. We've been fightin' that split for centuries, it's been the root cause of wars and devastations, but finally man (or some of us at least) is evolving to a point where the branches are coming back together. And when it hits, folks'll be happier, their lives under their own control and the spirit secure within themselves."

II

To speed this synthesis of spirit and politics, Hensley established the Universal Life Church in 1962 so that all men of whatever shade of religious belief might have the ultimate freedom of religion—the freedom to be your own priest.

Church dogma is contained within the simple statement that members and ministers believe in that which is right each according to his own conscience.

Although he can neither read nor write, Rev. Hensley dictated the articles of incorporation himself, and made the church just as legal as your local Catholic or Methodist congregation. Men—and women—of all ages and descriptions are being ordained on a daily basis, without price and without question. Many of the new ministers are establishing churches of their own. Much to the distress of various governmental agencies, not to mention the more orthodox faiths, the Universal Life Church and its founder are going strong.

Hensley rambles through long and intricate adventures, talking continuously in three streams about re-incarnation, his youthful catastrophes, and tales like: "Well, you know, we're always gettin' tests throwed in our way that change the course of life. There was this church out on the Loop in Chicago, kind of radical pentecostal if you know what I mean."

(We nod soberly.)

"Me and my wife was invited into this basement sanctuary and this preacher was going into froth over sin and damnation and people were lapping it up, just confessin' and moaning all over the room. It came my turn to speak and I thought, 'Now if I say what's in my heart, they gonna beat me up, but they won't let me leave without preaching.' So I got up and spoke and next thing there's six big men ripping half my clothes off and that minister is hollerin' that God told him to kill me for blasphemy and long about that time I started talking up a blue streak and hoping for a miracle (my wife was pregnant at the time) and it turns out that I kind of talked my way free. They even asked me to join the church, after the minister decided that God didn't want me to die after all. But it just goes to show . . ."

He looks quickly around at our faces and grins, ". . . people will kill you quicker over religion than anything else."

He leans back in his chair. We tilt back in ours: imaginary cracker barrels and pot-bellied stoves getting stuck in the crevices of my mind.

III

Reverend Hensley ran for President of the United States in '64 on the Universal Party ticket—he doesn't feel too badly that he lost.

"Media is the pathway, young fella, get it? *Time* magazine was down yesterday, articles are appearing in most papers— why, reporters just love being ordained."

(The Reverend Doctors Pierre, Buckley, Fabisch and Newman smile in approval.)

"When we get to a million ministers, why, every politician around will be scrambling to pat my back. But I'll tell you all something right now . . ."

He leans closer and I catch a familiar look in his eye—". . . I don't want to *talk* to that system, I want to *change* it!"

He jumps up again and begins to leap around the room.

"We're all just repeaters, that's it. Repeaters more than anything else. We learn how to get along by repeating what we've been told. Well sir, I can quote you the Bible from the first line of Genesis to the last line of Revelation and I can't even *read* it! My greatest discovery was that you can't just repeat other people's words all your life—cause I've got something to say and other folks got something to say, and by God we're gonna say it!"

In between phone calls and questions and yarns, he'd begun to dig around for something in the labyrinth of boxes and file cabinets. He finally emerged, grinning like a fisherman after a good day, clutching a stained, greyish book.

He opened it excitedly and thrust it at me. A musty odor, the kind you smell when you search through an old dictionary to find a forgotten word, flew up and engulfed my nose. He pointed to a place in the text and I began to read . . .

"Congress shall make no law establishing a religion or prohibiting the free exercise thereof . . ."

Hensley's voice doubled mine, gleefully sing-songing the words in obvious delight that the Constitution itself is on his side.

IV

A week after we were ordained, the District Attorney of San Jose issued a warrant for the arrest of Kirby J. Hensley for the "crime" of giving honorary Doctor of Divinity degrees, an offense against the California Education Code.

The forces of lawnorder had been chomping at the bit for months trying to nail something on the little minister. This time their efforts backfired and dumped a pile of roses on Hensley's lap.

"Think of the publicity!" he chortled excitedly to me over the phone, "Thousands more ministers! Every two hours there's another lawyer on the line offering his legal assistance—even *Newsweek's* coming over . . ."

He paused for breath and then: "Those jailers, why one of them told me to go to hell. *Told* me! They gettin' too used to kickin' poor old winos around. They've got their hands full this time, by God . . . the state's got no right to mess with any man's Divinity . . . I'll take it all the way to the Su-preme Court if I have to, all the way to the top!"

Knowing Rev. Hensley, he'll do it, too—

And he's got just enough balls to win.

". . . he said unto me, Thou must prophesy before many peoples, and nations, and tongues, and kings."—*Revelations*

The Message

"You know, when you find out who *you* are you won't need to find out who God is . . ."

". . . the laws of men are just an addendum to the natural law and therein lies a paradox—when you break the law of man you get punished, yet the unwritten law *rewards* you if you keep it . . ."

". . . things are falling into place—I say that heaven's when you got what you need to make you happy and hell is when you don't have it . . ."

". . . what's death? Oh it's just the lapse of memory from one life to the next. It's like tryin' to remember every single house you ever lived in . . ."

". . . the only thing that *really* separates men is knowledge . . ."

". . . the kingdom of heaven is a jig-saw puzzle—it's all here, all we gotta do is put it together . . ."

POSTSCRIPT: HOW TO BEAT THE RAP IN THE NAME OF NAZ

He's become somewhat of a local legend: able to leap vast legal hassles in a single bound, more powerful than a stack of bibles, capable of confusing the FBI itself with just a slash of his lightning tongue. Bishop Kirby J. Hensley, president of the Universal Life Church, illiterate caretaker of the Cosmic Giggle, has beat the rap that the San Jose power structure tried to pin on him—accusing the little preacher of dispensing academic degrees (doctorates in divinity) without a license, an offense against the California Education Code.

In a dizzying series of events, Hensley sweet-talked a San Jose judge into throwing the case out of court, popped up at Stanford during the height of the April 3rd movement, ordained everyone in sight, and vanished, showed at Foothill College and made a lightning pass through Palo Alto, promising to give thought to the idea of establishing his world center here on the mid-peninsula.

He is absolutely elated at all the publicity that the law has been throwing his way. The Universal Life Church now holds a flock of almost 100,000 ordained ministers, hundreds of chartered sub-churches, and a growth rate that is positively phenomenal. "A million ministers by 1970," Hensley told me in one of his serious moments, "yessir the time is just around the corner when every house will be a church and everyone who wants to can make his own religion—legally!"

Legality is something Reverend Hensley knows about. He believes that in some former lifetime he was a lawyer, as well as a minstrel show comedian, and judging from recent performances in various courtrooms, I'm inclined to agree with him. He uses the first amendment like a battle-axe to defend both his church and his person—and he uses it well.

The whole San Jose fiasco began when D.A. Dennis Lempert sent one of his minions, a police sergeant named Ralph Brune, to Modesto in order to "trick" Hensley into giving him a doctor of divinity degree, an honorary title granted by the Universal Life Church in recognition of a minister's good work in the field. Since Rev. Hensley naturally feels that divinity as well as ministerial status should be available to all people, without hesitation he ordained one of the few clergyman-cops since the Inquisition.

Then Brune busted him on charges of granting a degree without state approval, which brought the services of a deputy attorney-general into the act, and the three of them (Brune, Lempert, and the state attorney) took Hensley to court May 19th and suffered the consequences.

"Our Leader" (as Ed McClanahan fondly refers to the good reverend) has a wonderful gift for turning legal proceedings into three-ring circuses, with himself in the central spot as ringmaster.

The preacher took on his dissident church members (now including two state witnesses who'd gone to Modesto as private citizens, were ordained, and then offered their services to the D.A.) addressing them by their proper title of "Reverend" or "Doctor" asking them a few simple questions, and bringing down the house. The judge fell with it.

His Honor took the most logical course of action in this case. He measured the Incredibility of it all, looked at his watch, wondered briefly if that Old Time Religion had finally made a comeback, and threw the case out of his jurisdiction.

Then the real fun began. The way the System works is run roughly according to this maxim: "If we can't nail you in San Jose, we'll try in Sacramento." The State Attorney immediately served Kirby Hensley with a restraining order to show cause why the injunction shouldn't become permanent. That case will be up soon and the only one who is truly unconcerned is Hensley himself.

Our leader responded to this turn of events with just a bit of home-spun philosophy—"Well, Look at the Romans. They were the Establishment long before there were Republicans or Democrats, or Sacramento, or anything else for that matter. And they wouldn't admit that even *Christ* had a church! And then their empire fell apart.

"Of course, He didn't get anywhere till he got crucified . . ." (pause; he peers shrewdly under his bifocals)

". . . and I'm not ready for that yet. So I'll just give 'em one hell of a fight. Yessir, I'm gonna do a good job with the church, back up my ministers to the hilt, fight the good fight—and I ain't runnin'!"

And I believe him. He may not chase the money changers from the temple, but he's sure to run a few dis-believers off the premises.

the perry lane papers (I): the prologue

vic lovell

Vic Lovell, the first Co-ordinator of the Free University, was Ken Kesey's neighbor on Perry Lane in Menlo Park during the late fifties and early sixties, while both were graduate students at Stanford, and Kesey's One Flew Over the Cuckoo's Nest *is dedicated to him. Lovell is now a practicing psychologist in Palo Alto and a pioneer in psychodrama marathons, in the growing field of activist therapy.*

The Electric Kool-Aid Acid Test, Tom Wolfe's new book, explores a time of my life which is at once dead and eternal, over and here and now. It is the story of my old friend Ken Kesey, of Perry Lane, Menlo Park's one time hippy ghetto where I lived for six years, and of the Acid Test, the Pranksters, the Trips Festival, and the Hell's Angels.

Perry Lane was a one block long area in unincorporated Menlo Park, situated next to the Stanford golf course, just off Willow Road as you come from the Stanford Shopping Center, a block before you run into the place where Willow Road becomes Sand Hill Road and Santa Cruz Avenue turns into Alpine Road.

The Lane had a bohemian tradition which went back to Stanford's beginnings. In the late fifties and early sixties it was the only liberated ground in the Midpeninsula. We were proto-hippies when everybody else was a beatnik, and radicals and hippies hardly dared to appear in public, for fear of the hostility they would encounter.

We pioneered what have since become the hall-marks of hippy culture: LSD and other psychedelics too numerous to mention, body painting, light shows and mixed media presentations, total aestheticism, be-ins, exotic costumes, strobe lights, sexual mayhem, freakouts and the deification of psychoticism, eastern mysticism, and the rebirth of hair. We lived and loved and worked and suffered together with that agonizing closeness that comes from knowing that you have nothing but each other. In very serious jest we used to get stoned and recite, deadpan: "I pledge allegiance to Perry Lane, and to the vision for which it stands. One consciousness, indivisible, with liberty and justice for all." After which we would march around the dining room table, carrying American flags and toy guns on our shoulders, giggling with profound hysteria.

We loved pop art, with its bitter irony.

It all ended quite abruptly and very slowly, as all beautiful things must end in a nation which continues to try to be half slave and half free. My present commitment to the Free University is in part an attempt not to make the same mistakes over again. Our current demand for "turf" or liberated space is a good example. In late spring, 1963, a developer bought up a one half block area which was the heart land of Perry Lane, and gave us notice to get out. We demanded to be relocated, and there was a short hassle. He was surprised to find that we were famous. One summer morning, like any other morning on the Lane, we went outside to watch the sun come up, having dropped a good dose of acid about midnight and stayed awake all night laughing and loving. Only this morning there was a bulldozer in the back yard, squatting like an angry June Bug.

I sat in the street and watched, through glazed eyes, as my house was torn apart. Only the devil, I thought, could have the power to destroy something which had existed for so long. A profound insight came to me: *Somebody else controls my environment*. It was my first real bummer: after being in that place where nobody owns anything, not even themselves, where there are not even separate things to own, to be coming down for the last time on Perry Lane, to this.

Next time, I vowed, it would be different.

The greater part of Tom Wolfe's book is devoted to following Ken Kesey's career after the fall of Perry Lane. In my view, it shows what a fine line divides revolution from decadence. The Lane was a delicate balance of forces, and it never recovered. It ended with our solidarity gone, and it was only then that I realized what a strange and unusual thing it had been. We drifted apart like the characters in a pornographic movie run backwards.

It ended with creativity turned to distraction, ecstasy turned to psychosis, and commitment turned to nihilism.

It ended with Kesey busted, Kesey fleeing to Mexico, Kesey convicted and languishing in jail while Bill Graham got rich exploiting the thing that Kesey had created. It ended before that at the Watts Acid Test, to which the title of Wolfe's book refers. They blew the calculation by a factor of ten when they put the LSD in the punch, and had a mass freakout. One girl sat on the middle of the dance floor beneath the flickering strobe light shitting and pissing in her pants and screaming, "Who cares? Who cares?" and they put a microphone in front of her and turned up the reverb. Bob Cullenbine was there and he cried for a week almost without stopping, afterwards, because the only people in the world he had ever been able to identify with had turned into inhuman monsters before his eyes.

It ended before that at Berkeley when Kesey and the Pranksters showed up high on acid before the first VDC march and told everybody to go home and get stoned because what they were doing wouldn't do any good. I said that I would never speak to him again and I almost didn't.

It ended before that and it has never ended and I cannot write of it now without weeping.

a few words for cannibalism

by wendell berry

I MUST ADMIT at the outset that my purpose here somewhat astounds me. For I remember the days of my youth when I contributed numberless nickels and dimes toward the conversion of cannibals. In my fantasies of those days, in fact, I used to tremble for fear that the Lord would call *me* into the "mission field," where I would be eaten by the beneficiaries of my goodness. (The shepherd eaten by his sheep! Perhaps it is in the metaphor that most of the horror lies.) That it might be at least equally unpleasant to be killed before being eaten didn't occur to me for several years. I seem to have gone on the assumption that I would somehow be present at the feast.

Later, when I became a man, I re-examined the practice in the light of all I had learned, and to my surprise was able to find nothing much wrong with it. Indeed it seemed to me that the cannibals probably stood at the apex of civilization, rather than at its foot as I had assumed previously. I asked myself why we, who scarcely blink at the wholesale burning alive of families, should yet quail and sicken at the thought of eating those we have not only killed but cooked. Such fastidiousness, it seemed to me, was far more curious and eccentric than cooking missionaries, especially when I considered that the missionaries were usually killed beforehand.

These thoughts, I assure you, turned my head around so vigorously as to threaten the integrity of my neck. But as I hope to be an honest man, I was not long a defender of cannibalism before I became its advocate. Even supposing it to be a sin, cannibalism hardly makes a visible stain upon murder. It may, rather, be thought to mitigate somewhat the sin of murder by the virtue of frugality, for after all a dead man is meat, and meat is either to be eaten or wasted.

I would propose for a start—believing that reform should be accomplished by gentle phases—that as a curtailment to murder we should have a law requiring every murderer to eat whomever he has killed. It is not that a murderer would *necessarily* hesitate to eat his victim, but that a law *requiring* that the victim be eaten would tend to cause the prospective murderer to reflect a moment beforehand on the palatability of the prospective victim. And who knows but what in that moment conscience might be able to catch up and prevent the murder from happening? For my own part I am sure that I would hesitate to kill and eat certain of my enemies once I took time to consider that they have spent their lives sweating cool oily sweats in little offices, eating frozen pre-cooked dinners and sleeping with detestable women. The flesh of such people, I am sure, is spongy and foul to the taste. With such a law I foresee that our killing of one another—at present our major industry, not to say our way of life—might come to be governed by a sort of bag limit. In short, mankind might once again aspire to the decency of wild animals, which rarely kill more than they can eat. With patience and luck, we might even reach a new Golden Age when we would hope to emulate *most* animals, which do not kill their own kind at all.

who the hell is mario procaccino?

l. j. davis

MARIO PROCACCINO. The name calls forth the same kind of chill as the words "whitened sepulchre." I don't know what a whitened sepulchre is, except that I have always suspected it was a grave with a lot of bird shit on it. I don't know who Mario Procaccino is either (except that I think that, if you looked into his mind, you would see something that resembled a grave with a lot of bird shit on it) but I know how he comes on. Mario Procaccino comes on as round and hard as a beebee, and about as smart. No doubt the media has something to do with it—the last man on earth I would have wanted for a college roommate would have been some dumb fuck of a boy scout like John Lindsay; Mario I could have gotten drunk with and Indian wrassled. Sometimes I feel as though I've known them all my life, and I have the feeling that if I were to stick with Mario, there would be a nice concrete contract in it for me somewhere. The hell with the fact that I don't know anything about concrete, there would still be a nice concrete contract in it for me if I wanted it. That's the kind of a fella Mario is. He looks out for his friends. He also punishes his enemies. Otherwise there would be no reason to worry about him, but the spectacle of Mario Procaccino in command of the NYPD is enough to curl the toenails, because when Mario says he will punish his enemies, he means it. That would be one of the concrete contracts I might be getting, if I were a friend of Mario's.

I was at a party on primary night. It was largely for Republicans. Around here, Republicans are mostly WASP and largely from California. They were the kind of people who openly admit having voted for Richard Nixon, not once but several times, and God knows what I was doing in their midst (I was playing a pinball machine and getting drunk, actually). As the returns came in and it became clear that it would be Marchi and Procaccino, it was the first time, in polite company, that I have heard the word "wop" used when most people were sober. Not once, but all the time, like the shit hitting the fan: wopwopwopwopwopwop. That's the kind of year it's going to be.

I was thinking about these and other things yesterday morning, down at the liquor store where I work, when Leroy walked in and turned my thoughts in a new and more prosperous direction. Leroy is a white South Carolinian of some fifty years who once owned a third of a Japanese whorehouse and who, more recently, served as the chauffer for a Middle Eastern diplomat of great dignity, insatiable appetites, and a purse tighter than a bull's ass. Leroy is bald as a billiard ball and crazy as a bedbug. He drinks a lot of Gallo White Port and suffers from the total inability to differentiate experience. He doesn't lie and he doesn't cheat much, but everything that happens to him is pretty much the same as everything else that happens to him, and as a result he is either sort of boring to listen to or absolutely fascinating, depending on what kind of a mind you have. (The inability to differentiate experience is a common trait in politicians.) If Leroy goes to South Carolina, which he does every so often, he will tell you about every inch of the way, every service station they stopped at, how much gas they got, what he did in the bathroom and how much of it, what the attendant said to him, what he said to the attendant, how much he tipped him, etc. . . . Leroy is a great tipper. He is also a great hater. He hates Italians although he's married to one, he hates commie beatniks and tells me all about it, and he recently treated Chester, the black man who runs the dry cleaners on the corner, to a long story about how he was mugged by another one of them nigger bastards, and what we ought to do about them. Chester sort of stared off into the middle distance and every once in a while said something that sounded like "hee hee hee." Chester has known Leroy off and on for the last 15 years and occasionally employed him in the sort of jobs that he seems capable of doing, like mopping the floor and putting the shirts in plastic bags. Leroy's trouble is that he simply can't tell that there's any difference between him and us. He can't see that his wife is Italian or that I am a filthy commie beatnik or that Chester is not only very black but occasionally his boss. With fine impartiality, Leroy accepts us all as his equals. In his mind we are all cut from the same piece of cloth. He would make a good mayor.

I can see it now. On his first morning as mayor, Leroy gets up in his apartment on Wyckoff Street. He gets out of his pajamas and climbs into his underwear, putting the drawers on first, then the undershirt, finally the socks. Then he goes into the john and brushes his teeth. Then he uses the toilet and examines its contents. Then he shaves. Then he comes back into the bedroom and puts on his suit, pants first, then shirt. Then he goes down the stairs and gets into the mayoral limousine and is driven to City Hall with a short detour to Lavin's for a quick snort and to the liquor store for a couple of bottles of Gallo White Port. Finally, seated behind the massive desk in the sumptuously-appointed Mayor's Apartment at City Hall, he looks around and surveys the situation, wondering if maybe he shouldn't get up, paint some of the furniture or fiddle with the lock on the door to see how it's made. After a while the President of the City Council comes in and says, "Leroy, you're going a good job."

Power would not spoil Leroy. He would go about his day the same way he always does, except in a chauffered limousine. Then one morning, after he'd had his new job for a week, he'd come into the store for his Gallo White Port, and he wouldn't be wearing his suit. "Naw," he'd say. "It's too cold to go over there to work today, and it looks like it might rain. I called 'em up and told 'em I wouldn't be in today. They got any objections, fuck 'em. Goddamned Irishmen. I'm going home and paint some furniture."

I think Leroy is just the kind of mayor we need. I think he'd make a hell of a president, too.

a correspondence

gurney norman

Dear Brother Herschel,

I know you will be surprised to hear from me it's been so long. How I found out you was yet living and where was Otis Pratt is from there, who came to rent my upstairs apartment, a nice young Air Force man. He says he grew up within a mile of where your daughter lives in Knott County, that his mother is her neighbor and for you to tell her hello. I call it the Lord's miracle that He sent Otis Pratt to my house a messenger of the only good news I have had in many years. I pray to Him this will reach you and that you will answer and we will be in touch with one another again.

So its been many years since we were all at home together hasn't it dear Brother? I often think of those old days and wish I was back at home with my loved ones instead of sitting in this lonesome place by myself. Did you know I lived in Phoenix? I have lived here eleven years. My husband, Troy, bought this house with two apartments and one other with three apartments and moved us here in 1954 when he retired and for my asthma. Then the next year he died of heart trouble and Bright's disease so I have a mighty load to carry by myself. Troy had a boy and girl by his first marriage but they have forgot their old stepmother, and I never had children of my own as you perhaps know. It is lonesome in Phoenix and I breathe with difficulty, and my tenants are the only ones I see and they are not always friendly except Otis Pratt, a nice young Air Force man who the Lord sent to me and put us in touch again and oh I hope how soon we can be together, like we were so many years ago when we lived on Cowan Creek. Join me in thanks to God and write soon.

Mrs. Drucilla Cornett Toliver
Your loving sister

Rt. 1, Hindman, Kentucky
August 18, 1965

Sweet Sister,

Could not believe your letter at first. I thought it was another trick to torment me. I read it again, then had daughter Cleo read it to me to be sure it was true. A big surprise, to think for years I have a sister living after all.

Yes, many years have gone under the bridge since we were all at home together and so happy. Now everything is down to a final proposition it appears like. I have the gout and cataracts. My wife Naomi Pennington Cornett (did you ever know her? I can't think if you did or not) died last year. My younguns are scattered here and yon, except daughter Blanche who died and son Romulus who lost his mind. I live first with one then the other, but mostly daughter Cleo, the others don't want me much. Bad business to be amongst ungrateful children.

Arizona. A mighty fine place I hear. Your man done good by you to leave you so well off. I seen Goldwater on television one night, speaking right from Phoenix. He strikes me as a scoundrel but it showed pictures of fine Arizona country, the desert and the sunset on some mountains so peaceful and quiet, it sure looked like where I want to be. And I hope how soon we can be together sweet sister to keep each other company in these terrible times.

Your brother Herschel Cornett
Age 79 how old are you by now

August 23, 1965

Dearest Brother,

I am 72. I have asthma and artheritis, bursitis and awful high blood pressure. My fingers hurts now to write this letter and I hope you will be able to read it.

But you have a nice hand write, Brother. You always was a good scholar at Little Cowan School. I remember walking to school with you boys, and the way it set back against the hillside, the front end of it on stilts high enough to play under, and the way the willows and the sycamore leaned out over Cowan Creek, and wading the creek and the Big Rock we played on that had mint growing around it. I remember an Easter egg hunt at the school. And the fight you had with Enoch Singleton. I know I have forgot a lot of old times but I do remember that school very well and hope to see it when I get back to dear Kentucky.

Which should not be too long now. My houses are not fancy but they are buying up property right and left here and I have buyers galore to pick from. But I want to get a good price so we can afford ourselves a nice place together somewhere there in Knott County. Do you ever hear of any places for sale in the Carr Fork section? Who owns the old homeplace now? Maybe we could buy it back and live there again and be like we used to be so many years ago.

I look forward to meeting your Cleo, and all your grandchildren. You are so lucky to have grandchildren. I never did even have children, but I guess I told you that. Until I learned you were yet living I cried myself to sleep every night with only Jesus for my comfort. But now He has sent me you, and soon we will be reunited in His love, sweet brother.

In His Holy name,
Drucilla Toliver

August 29, 1965

Sweet Sister,

So much racket going on here I can't hardly think what to write. It is this way all the time in this house, no peace and quiet. Cleo won't control her younguns. They all promised me my own room before I moved in, but then never gave me one, it was all a lure and a trap. I turn the television up full blast to drown them out. After a while you don't hear a loud television but it is still a poor substitute for true quiet like you all must have out west.

The '27 flood got Cowan School.

A flood can come and get the rest of this place for all I care. Kentucky is all tore up and gone, Sister. Soon they'll flood Carr Fork and that whole section, including the homeplace, the government's doing it. You are fortunate to have your property. I used to have property, on Hardburly Mountain, two hundred acres, with a good stand of white pine, plus a well, dwelling house, barn and good-sized garden. But the strip miners got it all. I lawed the sons of bitches but couldn't do no good. So here I am stuck at Cleo's house, crowded up, no privacy, she can't cook, younguns gone wild, not enough heat, and they read my mail before I get it. (You be careful what you say!) Count your blessings in Arizona, sister, none in Kentucky to count. And keep your property, I'll be out there before long to help you run it and we'll get along good for ever more.

> Your loving brother,
> Herschel

September 4, 1965

Dear Brother,

You would not like Arizona. It is not green and cool here like Kentucky, and Phoenix is difficult of living. I can't tell you too much about Phoenix except that Carson Avenue is a terrible place. I've only seen the downtown part once, in 1956, when the Presbyterians took me down and back one day for a good deed, but it wasn't much then and I doubt that it's any better now.

I want to pick blackberries again, and gather chestnuts and see the laurel when it blooms. I never see anything on Carson Avenue except the motorcycle gang go by. Taxes are awful and the heat and when you call the water company it takes it a month to come, and you can't see television because of this sarcastic neighbor Mr. Ortiz who pranks with the electricity.

So I'll be home in a month or two, soon as I settle up my business. You look for us a place to buy. Get it in the country, pick us out a cove off one of those cool hollows and have laurel on it if you can. It would be good to live close to Carr Creek or Troublesome, or maybe even over on North Fork River. I'm not much of a fisherman but you always were, and I can cook fish, Troy always liked them. It would be handy if we could buy us a good house already built. But if you feel up to it, and some of your children would help, I'd like to buy a hillside with good timber on it and we could have us a house built out of our own wood, to suit us, and cheaper too. Wouldn't that be something? I'd like to be on the road to see people go by, nice Kentucky neighbors and kin folks. Last Sunday I was sitting on my porch and a motorcycle man yelled an ugly thing at me and upset me terrible.

And I didn't exactly admire your using bad language in your last letter, Brother. That indicates you might not be saved, but I pray you are, but if you aren't tell me the truth about it.

Sister Drucilla

September 11, 1965

Drucilla,

Don't come to Kentucky. I tell you this is a terrible place. The union has pulled out. No work anywhere. They're gouging the hillsides down, stripping and auguring. Ledford Pope's house got totally carried off by a mudslide. The streams are fouled, not a fish this side of Buckhorn Lake, not even any water to speak of except at flood time then there's more than anybody wants. The young folks have mostly moved to Ohio and Indiana to work, and them that's left have no respect for old people, they'd never help us build a house even if we had something to build it out of, Kentucky's timber has been gone since you have.

Coal trucks make more racket than motorcycles, and there's no air fit to breathe for the slate dumps burning. Sure no place for asthma sufferers.

I've seen the pictures of Arizona, and read about it. It sounds like all the old folks in the country are retiring out there but me. Damn such business as that, I'm on my way soon as I can accumulate trainfare. If you've got some extra to send me for expenses I'd be grateful to you, and make it up to you once I got there. I'll rent two apartments from you myself, I want me some room to stretch in. And don't worry about getting downtown. Me and you will take right off the first thing and see all the sights and visit all the retired people in Phoenix and go to shows and ride buses and sit around the swimming pools drinking ice tea.

Sorry for the bad words. Yes, I'm saved. I was a terrible rip-roarer most of my life, but 12 years ago I seen the light and give up all bad habits except cussing. I'm ready to give that up too but see no way to go about it till I get somewhere where there ain't so much to cuss about.

Your brother Herschel

September 17, 1965

Brother,

I'm not going to live in Arizona. That's all there is to it. You don't understand how it is here. Why do you not want me to come home? Are you making up all those bad tales on Kentucky, just to keep me from coming? I don't understand your attitude. A man that would cuss his sister would lie to her too, and the Bible admonishes against oaths and lies. I don't want to boss you but I'll not be bossed myself, and I absolutely will not stay in Arizona.

Drucilla Toliver

September 19, 1965

Sister,

You say you don't understand my attitude. Well I don't understand a sister that would have two fancy houses and yet turn out a suffering brother to suffer at the hands of mean children and a bad location. You talk like such a Christian. I say do unto others as you want them to do unto you and you're the one with two houses. I didn't cuss you. And I just wonder who is lying to who, for I have seen the pictures of Arizona and read of everybody moving there to retire and be happy. It sounds like you're all out there together plotting to keep me out. Well you won't get away with it and I have one question to ask: have you been getting secret letters from Cleo on the side? It wouldn't surprise me.

Herschel Cornett

September 23, 1965

Brother,

I still refuse to stay in Arizona, in spite of your insults, and I suggest you read The Beatitudes.

Drucilla Cornett Toliver

September 26, 1965

Sister,

You and Cleo think you can lure and trap me into staying here but you are wrong.

Herschel Cornett

September 29, 1965

Herschel,

You have turned out strangely is all I can say, unmindful of the needs of others, and if you continue to curse me we might as well forget the whole business.

Drucilla Cornett Toliver

October 2, 1965

Drucilla,

I have not cussed you, but I am about to get around to it. And Cleo and Emmit and Jenny and Sarah and R.C. and Little Charles too if they all don't hush their racket. If you don't agree to my coming there then you are right we might as well forget the whole thing, for I absolutely refuse to stay in such a goddamn hell-hole as this.

Herschel Cornett

October 4, 1965

Dear Herschel,
   Satan moves your tongue and I won't listen, or agree to stay here another week.

Drucilla Toliver

October 8, 1965

Dear Drucilla,
   Then we just as well forget the whole thing.

Mr. Herschel O. Cornett

October 12, 1965

Herschel,
   Suit yourself.

Mrs. Drucilla Toliver

---

all girls should have a poem

richard brautigan

the man who lost his race

jon buckley

Albert Lee Burton, in this age of black self-realization, is a truly humble man: a black supporter of George Wallace. Interviewed by a television reporter at the fringe of a George Wallace rally, he spread his arms wide in a sho'-nuff Bojangles pose and asked, "Would you expect the black buzzard to fly as high as the great, white eagle? Would you expect the catfish to swim with the trout?" Not sure of exactly what to expect, all considered, Jon Buckley investigated.

ALBERT LEE BURTON is a very unusual man. He spends the greater part of his time lecturing to radio and TV audiences, college fraternities, civic groups, former governors of Alabama, and other interested parties. He has only one topic: The inferiority of the Negro people to the Caucasian race. He is a card-carrying member of the Ku Klux Klan and the holder of an honorary membership in the Alabama State Troopers Association. During the last presidential campaign Burton served as part of George Wallace's Bay Area retinue, often acting as a bodyguard for the candidate.

Mr. Albert Lee Burton is black.

He lives in a pleasant house tucked into a fold of the Berkeley foothills. The interior looks like an old china shop and there's a gold framed portrait of a cocker spaniel enthroned atop the grand piano. The man himself wears a white-on-white shirt and tie, dark suit, and several rings, which he twists around his fingers when he gets nervous. He comes on like a successful undertaker or a highly polished used car salesman, and that's exactly what he is. There is a deceptive aura of ease about the man that belies at times the content of what his message to the world is—but probably it would be best to let Mr. Burton speak for himself.

JB: Mr. Burton, how do you view what's happening in the Black Revolution?

ALB: Well, it's a historical review of exactly what happened during the Reconstruction period in the U.S.—a friction-type situation that results when you put a primitive culture into competition with a highly evolved white civilization. It's impossible to mix the races—and I can prove it! Environmental factors like slums or schooling are of no consequence to the genetic process.

JB: Uh, what does that mean exactly?

ALB: Racial differences start in the womb and continue throughout life . . . now, take the catfish; you don't ask him to leave the swamp and swim with clear-water trout, now do you? And you don't take the buzzard and tell him to fly high with the eagle either. People shouldn't mess with the natural order and it's a natural fact that Caucasians and black folks are two different species.

JB: You spoke of environmental factors . . . where were you born?

ALB: In Oregon, 43 years ago; in a town where there were no other Negro families. People used to call me 'Big Nigger' . . . I was always taught to capitalize on my race. You see, life is a contest of adjusting to nature. The individual who is mentally prepared to do that in his physical activities, why, life becomes a game for him.

JB: Do you see your own life as a game?

ALB: In a manner of speaking. As long as you pay your dues, you got a right to play. Take the American Indian for example. He's just a proto-Mongoloid that wandered onto this continent by accident—but the white man, well just look at all he's done to build an admirable civilization out of this primitive land . . . he's paid the price for it.

JB: Then you're satisfied with the quality of American culture?

ALB: I'm *so* satisfied with our country. The most rewarding thing in my life was being born here in America, because I knew if I tried hard enough, I could fit into the socio-economic program that the white man had developed . . . It all has to do with education . . . Education prepares the individual to conform to the most admirable values of the surrounding society . . . that's why black people are still *nationals* and not *citizens,* because the Negro will not contribute to our economy and because he won't accept the white man's scientific educational principles.

JB: How would you feel . . .

ALB: By the way, here are some letters sent to me by former President Johnson thanking me for my lecture to his staff . . . it was Mr. Johnson that introduced me to Mr. Venable.

JB: Mr. Venable?

ALB: Yes, Mr. Venable is the Imperial Wizard of the Knights of the Ku Klux Klan . . . Are you registered Republican or Democrat?

JB: Umph . . . Johnson . . . Venable . . . hmmm . . . what?

ALB: Well, no matter . . . the Klan, you see, is a religious organization dedicated to preserving the natural law . . . violations of the natural law are what's causing most of this social unrest . . .

JB: It's interesting that you keep returning to the phrase natural law. What's your interpretation of it?

ALB: Well, from the Klan's point of view the white woman was evolved for the use, enjoyment, and continuation of the white race. It says here right in this book . . . Mr. Venable even described it himself to me . . . "anything that goes against pure racial breeding goes against natural law."

JB: What about the bloodshed and violence that organizations like the Klan use as tools of enforcing their point of view?

ALB: I don't take part in violence; I am a lecturer, not a gunslinger . . . but when the law moves too slowly to stop transgressions against natural law, or against civil disorder . . . then the police or the Klan should use everything at their disposal to fight it, as bloody or as violent as it may be.

JB: How do you feel about being black? Do you hate your race?

ALB: No, since I must identify with Negroes biologically and socially, I don't hate my race. But Negro life has nothing in it that I can admire and nothing in it for a better life. This chart here proves it. The Negro *must* accept white culture . . . your large Caucasian brain makes it inevitable . . . The black woman, for instance, has the smallest brain capacity per centimeter of any human type—even Jews.

JB: Jews?

ALB: Yes. The Jew and the nigger have one similar trait and that is that they are the result of indiscriminate breeding . . . they're simply biologically hybrid.

JB: How do you feel about the Nazi solution to the "Jewish problem"?

ALB: If you look at it closely, you'll see that the only thing Mr. Hitler did wrong was losing the war. If there is ever a civil war in this country, the Germanic stock will wipe out the Jews . . .

JB: What do you see in the near future?

ALB: I see permanent, geographic racial segregation as the only solution to our racial problems. Otherwise the Welfare System will allow the niggers to destroy the schools, since the schools can never be primitive enough to accommodate them. And after that, they'll destroy everything.

JB: Mr. Burton, do you feel inferior to me?

ALB: Yes, I do. Why else would I have to get all my education and information from your culture?

JB: Just one more question—how do your children feel about being black?

ALB: Children? Why, I don't have any. I couldn't stand the idea of bringing more little niggers into the world . . . There's too many as it stands.

*

As we drove back through the Oakland flats, back through "primitive" territory, my head slowly began to ease out of tangled gnarl of circular logic that Albert Lee Burton lives in.

We pulled away from a stop light where a young black man was standing. He nodded and casually raised his fist into the victory sign—it felt good to be back among the living.

interruption

speer morgan

Lucy . . . who was that? thought Nardo—that name which had blinked through the sleepless tedium of the night . . . Lucy . . . ?

Now at 6:00 in the morning, Nardo was relaxing in the bathtub. His eyes were empty, drained finally of the vigil beacon that had pulsed through the night. His hands which had sweated ice for the last twelve hours, curled happily dead in the water, and his steamed hair formed a wild sogpile halo which he could see reflected in the chromium faucet. Around him, new daylight warmed dull red walls, and steam caused old plaster to sweat.

This trip, his seventh, had begun at 3:00 the previous afternoon behind several hundred micrograms of "Pink" LSD. It had come on strong, a noisy blastoff that had lifted him into a room of bending shapes and wooden sounds. His alarm clock had TOCK-TOCK-TOCKED, as though made of Redwood trees; a radio announcer had echoed like a space monster through all his windows; the red rug in the Trip Room had puffed, floated, bled, congealed, and exploded.

Now, sitting in the tub, Nardo could remember the clock, rug, and radio announcer; but, strangely, nothing else. This had never happened on a previous trip. The records he had made of each of them on tape, film, and in his journal had jived perfectly with his memory of them. Nardo had one hour and twelve minutes of film of those last six trips; he had watched each trip several times: Images of himself—himself staring into the camera with a wet, stoned, open face, himself in clumsy distraction, stumbling over furniture, himself in foetal despair, himself tearing up a dictionary, himself leaping with energy, himself eating a can of spinach, himself ecstatically kissing the camera or superstitiously hiding from it.

He had studied each film carefully, and the tapes, hours of them, and the journal, dozens of pages replete with speculation on feeling levels, diagrams of states of consciousness and unconsciousness, mystic anagrams, records of stomach response to certain foods, color of bowel movements, relative effectiveness of different sleeping pills, descriptions of hallucinations, confessions of despair, haiku poems, abortive suicide notes, crayon drawings of mythological beasts, landscape paintings, political cartoons, and various other less easily identifiable manifestations.

Nardo had been farming all this information very carefully. He hoped to write a serious comprehensive description of the acid-state before medical school reconvened in the Fall. It would be entitled *One Mind Under Acid* and would include: (1) A philosophical justification for taking LSD centered around the poetry of Christopher Smart, the "body consciousness theory" of Norman O. Brown, a little-known fragment of a satyr play by Euripides, Laing's theory of apocalyptic madness, Jung's theory of the archetypal "night sea journey" (which he intended to buttress by explicating the symbolism of Beowulf's fight with Grendel's Mother, of Goya's drawings, and of a Hollywood movie from 1929 called *Tough Guy*), the confessions of St. John of the Cross, Professor Binkskey (of the University of Buffalo)'s analysis of Dr. Johnson's hypochondria, and Marcuse's theory of political liberation. (2) It would contain a detailed description, part one in clinical and part two in poetical language, of his own trips, and (3) a warning about the dangers of immature or unstable minds experimenting with acid, illustrated by the fatuous comments of some stoned teeny-boppers he had once observed at the beach. The book, when completed, would be six or seven hundred pages long.

But right now he couldn't remember anything beyond the first few minutes of the last trip. He sat in the bathtub, eyes unfocused, dawdling unconsciously with his floating penis, trying to recall some thread of experience that would open up his memory. The rug levitating . . . the announcer booming . . . Lucy . . . the clock . . . Lucy? Who was that? Nardo emerged from the tub, dried his rosy skin, got a Rolaid from the medicine cabinet (his stomach was still sour from the trip), and went into the kitchen for a bowl of cream of wheat. But even that didn't aid his memory. After breakfast he was still jittery and confused.

He went into the Trip Room and checked the camera: Yes, all twelve minutes of film had been taken: and the tape: It looked as though there were only about five minutes or so of recording: and the journal: A few pages . . . He glanced through them: There was a giant circle in red ballpoint on the first page; in the center of the circle was the word "STOMIK" in crabbed, shakey letters. On the second page was a poem printed in block letters:

LUCY IS FAT
LUCY IS A RAT
LUCY WILL BE HERE IN SECONDS FLAT.

Nardo lit a cigarette, puffed hard, and turned the page.

LUCY CAME
WHO IS TO BLAME?
LUCY WILL BE HERE TOMORROW AGAIN.

This was gibberish to Nardo—but also somehow disturbing. He took a pencil, inscribed the date in the margin of the page, drew an arrow to the poem, and wrote: "Gibberish, but disturbing."

Perhaps the tape would explain further; he turned on the recorder and sucked his cigarette while it rewound; he paused, exhaling windily, then punched "Play."

"Head series, number seven," whispered his voice. Long pause. "Listen!" Another pause. "I think she's horney, that's what. But

I can't imagine how her voice is getting into my room like that.
Calling like a spook, for what? An egg? Jesus! Maybe she's in
the room next door . . . Couldn't be; she has no friends. It must
be coming through the building somehow—through the pipes?
Yeah! Wow! Listen to her . . . She must be in the bathtub
downstairs, so it's like coming out of my steampipes or something . . ." The next couple of minutes of the tape are wordless,
but with a close breathing in the speaker. Nardo is impatient
with it; he grinds out his cigarette and lights another. "Hey now,
let's not get too wrapped up in these whispers—I'd freak. It is
essentially a comic situation, after all. Picture it: A four-hundred
pound leviathan in a tiny old-fashioned bathtub, whispering.
. . . I'm coming up, I'm coming up. . . . Shit! He-he! I never
even paid any attention to her before. What does she do in the
bathtub so long? Is she trying to steam off the fat? Whisper off
the fat . . . Goddamn, play with it, Nardo; don't listen, just
play with it boy . . . What would old Willie Faulkner do? Con-
struct a fucking baroque sentence, I bet: As if perhaps her words,
the vibrations from her throat, carried not only the empty signal of her distress, foundering turtle that she is, stuck tight in a
tiny bathtub which is not even big enough to sink in, a whispering monster in a miniature enamel ocean, whose words are so
heavy in my head that I must conceive of them as molecules and
not waves—molecules straight out of her insides, not symbol of
fat but fat itself, transformed by the alchemy of her grief into
something that can be expressed through the pipes of this big
old lonely motherfucker of a dormitory . . . oops, slipped into
the modern idiom . . . (Nardo sucks on his cigarette; he is
pleased by the articulation. It showed that he was finally learning
to 'function under acid,'" learning to play with hallucinations
rather than taking them seriously.) ". . . Well, o.k., so we'll
introject Burrough's imagery on Faulkner's syntax: '. . . sprouting invisible globules from her stomach, from all her stomachs,
from the deepest one down there under nineteen tons of viscera,
where there must be solids—whole chickens, heads of lettuce,
chunks of beef, scoops of unmelted chocolate ice-cream, tangles
of spinach, globs of crunchy peanut butter—and liquids—Coke,

iced-tea, Stag beer, mineral oil, water, beef gravy—and gasses—sulphur dioxide, nitrous hydrochloride, carbon monoxide, whole farts—all clashing together in primal chaos, as though she were a volcanic earth mountain in new genesis . . . With maybe little troglodyte devils hopping around with rusty pitchforks shovelling piles of food; smoothing it into an even mash; with dripping, gurgling, spurting sounds echoing off the pock-marked, acid-burned walls and green and red reflections of light from stinking, sputtering fusions of waste material—all gathered together, this cosmic garbage pile, to rumble up through her other stomachs and channels, to be subtleized by her larynx, and sent whispering through the cold air and iron pipes of this lonely old motherfucker of a barn. . . .'" The voice ends with a breathless shudder, drained of playfulness, and that is it. The tape is finished.

Nardo was even more confused than before, but nervously elated. There *was* a basement apartment in the building; perhaps he had been thinking of Wordsworth's Lucy. Anyway, that didn't matter so much. The source of hallucinations were always hard to trace. The amazing thing about this one was its nature, not its source: First, it was audial instead of visual, which was pretty weird—the first he'd had at any rate. Whispers in the pipes! That sounded like real schizophrenia instead of just acid vision, real "body-consciousness," "haptic harmony," honest-to-God invasion of Ego by Shadow. He was getting closer to the Source, closer to the *mysterium conjuntiunus* of light and dark, yin and yang. And he had treated the vibrations, wherever they came from, in a totally emotive fashion. The talking had obviously been bravado to cover up real feeling, response to the vision. It was too much.

But also a little spooky. Perhaps he had taken more than one pill. He went to the refrigerator, got out the bottle, and counted —no, he'd apparently only taken one. And out of one pill had come "Lucy," a five-hundred pound delusion, a grotesque *anima* calling to him. It was like some kind of weird reversal of Jung's theory. The *anima,* the female element inside himself, should have appeared as an attractive figure, as a filmy, *sfumato* blonde in flowing white robes—but instead she had arisen as a giant ogre, as a smothering glob of fat, whispering the warning that she was "coming Up." Obviously, this meant that she was somehow threatening to him, that her arrival presaged some dire psychic reversal.

Nardo took the skim milk out and chugged—to calm his stomach. It was nervous and irritated, almost as though he were still on acid. The next step was to develop the film, which would take hours in his primitive darkroom. He was clumsy, spilling chemicals and mis-threading film, as he set up the baths and began running the film through. The darkness seemed heavy and close around him. He bungled his way through the procedure, fitfully speculating on the implications of a threatening *anima*. Jung, or somebody, had once interpreted a monster-*anima* as a reflection of a past experience with a female figure which was smothering or frustrating—overprotective momma or something. But this simply wasn't the case with him. His mother hadn't been uptight, toilet-training had been un-traumatic, and as to girlfriends—well, he'd never been close enough to a girl for her to be "smothering" or "frustrating."

The film, he kept hoping, would perhaps hold some further clue about the fat lady, although he couldn't remember when he had turned on the camera.

It was noon by the time he finished. He went to the kitchen for another big chug of milk and some crackers while the film hardener dried. In a few minutes he had the film threaded on the projector and a sheet hanging against the wall in the trip room for a screen. He was ready for the first showing:

"Ten, nine, eight, scrabble-blip, three, two, scrabble, blip-blip," there he sat, at the desk, listening to the tape recorder: ". . . whispering through the cold air and iron pipes of this lonely old motherfucker of a barn . . ." The tape stops; Nardo looks toward the camera, addresses it: "Well, there you have it. First she sings in the bathtub and then she comes up for an egg —but you could tell by her face that she wasn't really looking for an egg. Or baking a goddamn cake. Why would she have giggled like that: He-he! I'll give you a piece. Ugh! Freaky bitch! I mean like she must have known that I was on a trip. You can tell by looking at my goddamn eyes that I'm tripping. Look!" Nardo stands up and scrambles over the top of his desk, narrowly avoiding knocking the tape recorder onto the floor; he stands directly in front of the camera, his face a blur. "Here, see, you can tell by looking that I'm tripping. Balls! There. . . ." The focus is adjusted, and his face looms clear. ". . . Now. How would you like it if you were like stoned out of your mind, and a goddamn seven-hundred pound monster from the Black Lagoon busted through your door and came waddling in, asking for a . . . for a what? for an egg! As though she needed an egg! Damn! One more egg and she's gonna split the seams, explode, destroy her big miserable self. . . ." Nardo's face goes from anger to blankness. He stares stupidly into the camera for three minutes, then assumes a look of cunning. "I know what she was up to. She came in to invade my head; to flub up my peace and quiet; to get me off on a sympathy-for-big-fat-and-lonely-people trip. Well no, by God, I won't take the bait." Nardo readjusts the camera. Wow! I'm functioning, thinks Nardo, observing his careful handling of the camera—functioning, by God, under acid, turns, walks to his desk, and picks up the remote control camera switch. "That would be about the stupidest thing I could do—or anybody could do—to have sympathy for a five-hundred-pound-egg-bummer. . . . And she said she was coming back tomorrow with a piece of her goddamn cake!" Nardo's face slips into a mask of abstraction; he stares at the floor. After several minutes, an expression of resolve comes across his face. Full into the camera, and with heavy sententiousness, he says: "I could by God write a lampoon against the fat egg-bummers of America." With a flourish he flicks the remote-control switch, and there is a moment of slow dying in the motion of his tongue emerging to lick dry lips and his arm coming down with the switch—

—Then, white space, blip, he's on again, this time sitting at his desk, picking up a pen, and saying to the camera: "Observe. I am writing a polemic against fatso and all that she represents. . . ." He applies the pen to the page, draws and scratches

flamboyantly, then gets up from the chair, giggling at his production. "Hee! I've captured the goddamn essence of her. . . ."
He comes around the desk toward the camera. "See, here she is.
Hee! Just like I saw her when she came trundling through my
door." He stares at the picture, losing himself in it for a moment,
then turning it, blurry, then adjusted, to the camera. It is the
circle with "STOMIK" written in the center, held steady for a
moment, then blurring, disappearing—

—White space, blip, he's at his desk again, this time in poor
focus. His facial expression is inscrutable, and his voice sounds
far away: "It's so hot under these lights . . . stupid camera . . .
I'm not sure . . ."

—Then, white space, blip, still blurred, he says: "How can you
be sure of anything, even big fat egg-bummers? . . ."

—White space. Wow! thinks Nardo, all this cutting is just like
a real movie—technique like never before! blip, on again, loud
voice crackling in the speaker: "She's like BIG, man, like HUGE
for Christ's sake . . . RE-AA--AAll," the voice dies slowly—

—Then, suddenly, he is standing in front of the camera, focused, shoulders slumped, holding the switch in both hands. He
looks up slowly, revealing a flaccid, tear-stained face. He gasps,
sobs gently, motionless—then cries his shoulders into convulsion.
Wiping his nose with his arm, crying some more, then wiping
again, he blubbers barely distinguishable words: "How cud I be
tho detaged—how cud I sid ub here like some kide of fuging god
interbreting her poor fuging stobach? Oh shid, too mudch, too
fuging mudch!" He cries again, then tapers off into sniffing, sobbing, and hiccupping. "Poor Lucy, Poor fad fucging Lucy—hic!
All alode, Snfff! in her blubbery shell, fugck! Hic! Too mudch!!
Hh-hh-hh-huhhh! Snffff! Hic! I'll love you, Lucy, if dobody else
will, hh-huh-huh! . . ." Nardo goes on crying for a few more
minutes, then slumps back to his desk and sits down. He stares
at the journal, then, noticing the camera switch, turns it off—

—White space, blip, on again, now with his face washed, his
hair combed. He says to the camera: "It is seven hours later. I
am finally coming down and can see my folly. It has all been
display. I am sorry for it. I am going to try to write some truth

in the journal. All the rest of this trip has been wasted." He begins writing, at first slowly, occasionally shaking his head and muttering, then faster, nodding and saying "yeah, yeah . . . ain't it the truth . . . no shit!" The film thus ends—with Nardo in the heat of composition.

Before the reel of the film had stopped spinning, he had picked up his journal and located the passage; it was two pages (of scribblings) past the "Lucy" poem he had read earlier. In neat handwriting, almost like the kind he had written in junior high school, it said:

1:00 a.m., Aug. 1: Dawn of a New Day
Dear Lucy of the Basement,
        You don't know it, but you are the cause of my most recent salvation. My antics since your arrival have been absurd. They arrived finally at a sob-sister effusion of self-indulgent bullshit, a phony catharsis, a monument to masturbatory emotion; it makes me sick to think about it.

Sure, an eminently successful trip: My head expanded to infinite capaciousness, opened up to exquisite vibrations of human sympathy; my compassion extended; my vulnerable soul infused with a tragic vision; the saltiest tears from my eyes. Oh poor Lucy! Oh poor mankind! Only I, alone in this apartment, realize the sadness of your lives! Only I can suffer for you loneliness!

Shit.

Waves of sympathy and sorrow bouncing through my skull, interfering with each other, amplifying, picking up extra strength from my pathos-programmed brain; crying a full faucet-load of sympathy-and-sorrow tears out of my eye-ducts, down my neck and chest, into my bellybutton, back up through my tear recirculator and out my eyes again: A Roman fountain spurting the same water over and over again. Freaking on my own variable lag of sympathy; suffering the eerie sound to multiply geometrically in my skull, winding me up into a tightly twitching amoeba gobbling my own pseudoped of sympathy.

I am sorry I regarded you as an emblem. Forgive me for abstracting. I would not have done it in a normal mood. I look forward to your coming up when I am straight, so that I can respond to you as a person rather than a fake entity for false sentiment.

Love,
Nardo Hearne

Nardo read the passage again, with growing excitement. He went into the bathroom and splashed his face with cold water, slapping his cheeks more vigorously than usual. After drying, he looked at himself in the mirror. "Amazing," he told himself. "Positively fucking amazing."

Back in the Trip Room, he sat at the desk, stoked up a cigarette, and turned on the tape recorder: "August 2, the day after the seventh trip. I am now fairly unstoned and am amazed at the records of this trip. It moves from hallucination through ethical confrontation to resolution. The conjured *anima* is grotesque, but she leads to a whole succession of ethical rebirths. The mythical experience, the recognition of the Female inside me, sparks the further image of suffering mankind; I move from cynicism through self-indulgent pity to honest sympathy and love. . . . Thus, from the initial vision of a fat lady coming to borrow an egg—*egg*, think of it! The egg, which in certain genesis myths symbolizes the primordial chaos out of which arises creation—so, dig this, what she came to elicit from me was nothing short of a new creation—obviously a *new creation of the self*. And the bathtub business—how perfect! Images, says Coleridge, arise out of the watery depths, the vast ocean of the unconscious—so how do I rationalize an ocean? By making it a bathtub, of course. Incredible. And from this "delusion of a fat lady," as a stupid Freudian would call it, came a progression of ethical stances from the most adolescent and cynical to the most realistic and humane; from Falstaff through Dostoevski to Sartre.

Think of what this means: From contemplation of the forms within comes ethical growth. Shelly was right. Plato was right. Jung was right. Freud was full of crap: We must *not* extirpate the contents of the unconscious, but must encounter it, deal with it, incorporate it into our ego-conscious.

This is the confirmation of all that I suspected. I am ready to write my book."

Nardo switched off the recorder and went to the kitchen for something to eat. He was almost too exhausted and excited for food. This whole thing had been such an incredible trip, such a heavy dose of the truth, that it left him dizzy with ideas. He opened a can of tomato soup and put it on to heat, forgetting to add water. He sat at the kitchen table and began scribbling on a paper towel:

"Encounter with Self=Encounter with World

Descent into Underworld (Lucy from basement) precondition for Actualization.

Chaos to Cosmos

Lucy=Proserpine"

He heard a knocking at the door just as the smell of burning tomato soup awakened him from his thoughts. "Balls," he muttered, moving the soup from the fire and fishing the empty can out of the garbage. "Just a minute!" As he filled the can, there was another knock. "Who is it?" he asked, irritated. Probably the landlady coming around for the rent. That was perfect: Here he sits pondering his new-born socio-mytho-psychic Philosophy of Life, and the landlady comes around for the rent. "Philistine," he muttered. "Interrupting my opus with comic reversal—piss on ya, as Descartes would say." He mixed the water slowly, trying to think of some way to put her on; she was such an officious old crone.

He finished mixing, went to the door and flung it open suddenly, to freak her a little bit . . . but there was no one there. He looked down the hall and could see no one. As he started to close the door, he saw it on the floor—a large, luscious slice of chocolate cake carefully centered on a white paper plate. Nardo hesitated, then quickly closed the door. He went into the bathroom, turned on the tub water, shut and locked the door.

the man who turned on the here

robert stone

"I will stand on your eyes, your ears, your nerves and your brain and the world will move in any tempo I choose." MAR-SHALL MCLUHAN ON THE *Modern Archimedes*

ONE CLOUDY DAY last October, a muscular young man wearing a cowboy hat and carrying a guitar walked up to the U. S. Customs and Immigration Station at Brownsville, Texas and looked uncertainly about him. He was obviously somebody's hard-times cowboy and they had not treated him right South of the Border.

"How long you been in Mexico?" asked the Customs man.

"Too damn long," the cowboy said.

He was Singin' Jimmy England, he explained, and he had been down there to play a little old country music gig and damn if the Mex's hadn't laid him out and cleaned him. Hell no, he didn't have no papers. He didn't have no money neither. Why, he didn't have nothin'. 'Cept (pat, pat) his geetar. Yep, the women and the margaritas and the streets of Matamoros had laid Ole Singin' Jimmy low and all he wanted out of fortune was into God's country and then home to good old Boise.

Boise, yessir, that's where he was born. Boise, Idaho.

Thus, her maternity stirred, the Republic reclaimed a bruised offspring and Ken Kesey "freshest, most talented novelist of his generation" creator of a New Esthetic, diabolist, dope fiend, and corruptor of youth passed the brown bank of the Rio Grande to his native soil.

He had not been in Mexico overnight to play country music. He had been there since the previous January and he had gone there concealed in a truck after being arrested for the second time on charges of possession of narcotics.

Kesey is sitting in the garden of the Casa Purina when Des Prado bounds through the adjoining lumber yard crying "Battle Stations." Des Prado is a young man of vaguely Okie origin who gives the unmistakeable impression of having spent a great deal of time on Highway 101. He has also done some time in the can, along with one hitch in the Navy and one in the Marine Corps, so he can shout "Battle Stations" with professional zest. And, indeed, something like a combat situation seems to be developing.

There is a dapper Mexican lurking in one of the bungalows under construction across the road. The Mexican is equipped with an elegant and complex camera and is covertly taking pictures of the house and its occupants.

One of the Pranksters has seized a camera which is even bigger than the Mexican's and is pretending to photograph *him* although there is no film in the Prankster's camera. The Mexican lowers his and looks thoughtful. He is about thirty, casually dressed in the style of the Mexican tourists who regularly come down from Guadalajara to vacation on the Colima coast.

Kesey sits tight in the yard, a baseball cap pulled low over his eyes. There is a possibility that the man with the camera represents the press but it is more likely that he is a policeman or an advance man for the American bodysnatchers.

Babbs and George walk across the road and hail him. He is now making awkward conversation with the Indian laborers who are building the bungalow. He will not look at the Americans or reply to them. The Indians are clearly embarrassed at the turn things have taken. Some of them have removed their hats.

The camera man answers no questions in any language. After a while he gets into a white Volkswagen parked down the road and drives off. It is the same car that has been seen regularly on the road.

The siesta hour passes tensely. Everyone has assembled at the main house for desultory speculation on the stranger's intentions. A few optimists express confidence that he will turn out to be a journalist but this is not the prevailing opinion. Kesey leans against one wall sipping Coke. Every now and then he looks out the window.

When siesta is over Kesey looks out of the window again and sees that the man with the camera has come back. He has come directly to the house and is standing before the door looking about him with an amiable expression.

Kesey turns and walks into a room where Faye is making Prankster costumes on a sewing machine. They exchange looks, say nothing.

Two or three Pranksters go outside to say hello. One of the Pranksters who goes out is Neal Cassidy of song and legend, the companion of Kerouac and Ginsberg in the golden days of Old San Francisco. He has been a sidekick of Kesey's for years, functioning as chief monologuist and Master Driver for the Acid Test. Now, without a word (which is a most unusual *without* for him) he walks into the road and constructs a little brick target. He has been carrying a six pound hammer in his belt for days, and he begins to throw his hammer at the target with a great deal of accuracy and control. The dapper Mexican watches Cassidy's hammer throwing as though he finds it charming. Three other Pranksters are standing around him and they are all taller than he is. Babbs is much taller than he is. He seems to find this charming as well.

He has learned English during the siesta.

"Well," he says, "I guess you guys were wondering what I was doing out there with the camera."

Cassidy continues to throw the hammer but now he accompanies the exhibition with a rebop monologue. When there is no one else around Cassidy practices his routines with a parrot named Philip the Hookah. Philip and Cassidy discuss automobiles or books of current interest and since Philip is rather a non-verbal parrot Cassidy does most of the talking. Occasionally, the question arises of what to do with a parrot who will talk like Neal Cassidy. Kesey suggests that it would make an Ideal Christmas Present.

"Um yass, quite indeed," Cassidy says, retrieving his hammer. "Quite a set-up, yaas, yaas. Bang, bang, bang," he sings, "bang, bang, went the moto-sickle."

The dapper Mexican tells an astounding story. He is from Naval Intelligencia. He is looking for a Russian spy, whose description is incredibly like Kesey's. The Russian spy is spying on the coast of Mexico. Occasionally, Russian ships appear off the bay and they flash lights to him. Russian spies are Commies, the man explains, and mean America no good. The Pranksters are Americans No? Ah, the man likes Americans very much indeed. He hates Russians and Commies. Might the Pranksters assist in investigating this nastiness?

Ah, now the dapper Mexican sees musical instruments lying on the porch. The Pranksters are musicians are they not? He seems to find this charming, as well. He is watching Cassidy's hammer from the corner of his eyes.

And how long have they all been in Manzanillo?

Kesey stands in the room with Faye and the sewing machine. Faye continues to stitch costumes for the forthcoming Manzanillo Acid Test while Kesey looks through the blinds.

Faye Kesey is a woman of great beauty, the sort of girl frequently described as "radiant," possessed of quiet vivacity and a dryad's grace. It is said that the meanest cops refrain from giving Kesey's handcuffs that nasty extra come-a-long twist once they've seen Faye. Fourteen years ago, she and Ken were steadies at Springfield High and they have come a long way together since. Her name was Faye Haxby, she was a dreamer and she was of the legendary and heroic race of women who, appearing delicate and fragile as ice cream swans, were yet prepared to accompany some red-eyed guzzling oaf over frozen passes and salt flats, mending axles, driving oxen, bearing children and nursing them through Cholera. Faye has never driven oxen, although she can be a handy mechanic, but she has come over some strange passes in some funny mountains and, with Kesey, she has been out in all the weathers.

Faye leans forward over her machine for a look at the man with the camera, smoothing out the colored cloth on the table before her.

Kesey watches the Mexican intently trying to gauge his size, weight, intelligence. He does not know what will happen or what he will do. There is a little song he likes to sing, a cowboy style ballad called Tarnished Galahad. It has that title because a judge in San Francisco so referred to him when he disappeared and Mountain Girl remained in the coils of the law.

> *Down to five pesos from five thousand dollars*
> *Down to a jungle from a five acre home*
> *Down to a dope fiend from a prize winning scholar*
> *Down to the dregs from the lip-smacking foam*
> *What used to be known as a promising talent*
> *What folks once called a real likeable lad*
> *Now hounded and hunted by the police of two countries*
> *And judged to be only a tarnished Galahad*
> *Tarnished Galahad did yore sword get rusted?*
> *Tarnished Galahad—there's no better name*
> *Keep arunnin' and hidin' til the next time yore busted*
> *And locked away to suffer your guilt and your shame.*

He accepts the turns of the outlaw game but he does not want to go to jail. He is not the type.

Just beyond the doorway, the agent with the camera is still talking Foreign Intrigue. When his conversation with the Pranksters lags, he revivifies it by asking questions.

Now it is Babbs's turn to be uncommunicative.

How about him, the agent wonders. Does he play a musical instrument?

Babbs nods his head affirmatively.

The agent looks him in the eye. In order to do this he must bend his head backwards and stare almost straight upward.

So, the agent says, Babbs prefers not to talk. He prefers simply to watch? He wants to just listen?

Babbs nods and scratches his nose.

Cassidy is still performing the hammer throw. Babbs belches.

The Mexican agent smiles the grim smile of Montezuma. But he does not go away.

Inside the house Faye sews and Kesey watches. It is now a year and a half since the night when several varieties of law enforcement officers, human and canine, dashed into his house in La Honda to arrest him and thirteen of his friends on charges of marijuana possession. The cool Mexican operative outside is only the latest in a long procession of agents, D.A.'s, sheriffs, snoops, troopers, finks, commissarios and detectives who have peopled his fortunes since 10:30 PM on The Night of April The Twenty-Third, 1965.

Kesey recalls finding little piles of cigarette butts and Saran-wrap on the hillside across from his property several times during the weeks preceding the raid. He had, he says, taken all possible precautions against being accused of marijuana possession. Nevertheless on that night, the officers struck. Kesey says that he, Mountain Girl and Lee Quarnstrom, a former newsman, were painting the toilet bowl in the bathroom when Federal Agent William Wong sailed through the door, clapped a Federal Agent lock around his neck, and commenced to beat on him. (The bathroom at Kesey's was, and thanks to the simpatico sensibility of the house's present owners, remains a remarkable pop composition. Much painting and pasting was done on it at all hours.) The police maintain that Kesey was trying to flush his marijuana down the toilet.

A fracas ensued, police guns were drawn, an alleged attempt was made by one of the Pranksters to grab a deputy's service revolver. The occupants of the house were collared, busted, and taken away. Faye Kesey and the Kesey children were off visiting relatives in Oregon at the time of the arrest.

Ken Kesey has always maintained that the bust was queer.

"We'd been warned by 3 people to expect a bust that Saturday night," he says. "Not a bad trip if you're expecting it. You can set up to film and record the cops' frustration. You can even have your lawyer forewarned. But some way, they boxed us and showed up a day early. They blew our cool for a while, I have to admit. I'm in the bathroom with Mountain Girl and Lee. Page is standing in the bathroom shaving. Other people were out sewing, working with tapes, wiring and like that.

"Suddenly I got a guy beating on me from behind and chaos all around. Babbs snatches him off me onto Page who falls on his back in the tub. Then follows the whole search, question, banter and looking ceremony. Other events happened that I tell no more because they have been so often sneered at as likely stories from one side—or nodded at as "what else can you expect from those bastards" from the other. Like the business of painting the toilet; beautiful double edged paradox. One side: Okay, but why would you just happen to be painting the can—the most likely place for a man to be disposing of contraband just when the cops busted in?

"Other side—Okay, but if they were watching and waiting for the best chance to make a good case wouldn't they wait for the most incriminating scene to bust in on? And this I believe is the true price of justice—the amount of time wasted justifying."

The net took Mountain Girl, Mike Des Prado and Neal along with Kesey and various other Pranksters and the "contraband" assembled by the arresting officers ranged from "one disposable syringe" to "one Western Airlines bag" and included one pint jar and two and a half lids of grass in addition to "marijuana debris."

One of the principals in the first Kesey arrest was Agent William Wong of the Federal Bureau of Narcotics, the officer whose flying tackle opened the Battle of the Bathroom. Agent Wong, who is no longer with the Bureau, was then working as

Federal liaison officer with the San Mateo County Sheriff's Department Narcotics Division. Wong seems to have become convinced that Kesey was, in addition to being a novelist, a dealer in both marijuana and heroin on an international scale—in any case he seems to have conveyed this conviction to officers of the county. Just how the Federal presence was introduced into the case is a question which no one involved feels quite able to answer. Some local detectives remember a story that Wong had been working on a heroin case in the area and had come to believe that Kesey was connected with it. Kesey's lawyers aver that Wong told one of the girls he was grooming as an informer that he believed it was Kesey's practice to lure girls into his house, get them "hooked" and then sell them into prostitution.

According to a San Mateo officer, Wong as Federal liaison man would frequently drop by the bureau to "bullshit." The Great Raid seems to have developed from one of these "bullshit" sessions, more or less as a law enforcement caper. And there are persons officially connected with the legal apparatus of San Mateo County who feel that Kesey's prominence as a novelist and "nonconformist" was not wholly unconnected with the zeal with which his arrest was sought and obtained.

According to the affidavit submitted by the police to obtain a search warrant, Agent Wong was working "undercover" in the North Beach area of San Francisco. In what must be imagined as a low dive frequented by twilight figures without hope, he chanced to overhear the following remarkable conversation.

First Male: Hey, man—did you hear?
Other two persons: What?
Said First Male: At Kesey's. La Honda, man—a swingin' pad!
Other two persons: Yeah! Yeah!

The said persons continued to address each other enthusiastically in this manner; the connoisseur will recognize their frenetic mode of speech as the argot of the so-called hipster. Agent Wong, who doubtless does a great deal of listening, seems to possess a gifted amateur's ear for dialogue for here again the imagination takes wing. One pictures the Agent, inconspicuous as hell; perhaps his hat brim is pulled low across his countenance, perhaps he counterfeits the stupor of narcosis. In the next booth sit the said persons—and, man, you *know* how they look. They wear berets and sandals, the girl has stringy hair, and like all three of them are carrying a set of bongo drums.

In any case, as the incident is rendered in the affidavit, the first male conveys to others, in the colorful speech to which he is given, intelligence which Agent Wong interprets to mean that Kesey is going to have a party at which dope is served.

Kesey, whose point of view is admittedly subjective and who is perhaps overly given to regard comic strips as vehicles of contemporary reality, professes to believe that this conversation never took place. He holds that Agent Wong lifted the whole number from a recent installment of Kerry Drake.

After relating the Agent's North Beach adventure, the police affidavit goes on to record the alleged statement of a coed who reportedly admitted to officers that she had been "furnished" with marijuana by Kesey and the account of a surveillance mission during which the police encountered several persons who appeared to be under the influence of a "narcotic, dangerous drug or other stimulant." The document also records the police belief that Kesey was a drug dealer on the evidence that "said Ken Kesey has written two books one dealing with the effects of marijuana and one with the effects of LSD, namely *Sometimes a Great Notion* and *One Flew Over the Cuckoo's Nest.*"

The point seemed to be that Kesey was so confirmed a dope pusher that he felt able to devote his spare time to enriching the literature of narcotics, perhaps with an eye toward drumming up a brisker business.

Signatory to the affidavit and a participant in the raid and arrest was Deputy Sheriff Donald Coslett, a pleasant, crew-cut young man whose office is decorated with assorted buttons of the kind favored by youthful narcotics offenders, examples of psychedelic art, and a Ken Kesey for Governor sign. Deputy Coslett is what might be termed a "head buff" and it is fitting that he should be such for he is assigned to Narcotics Division of the

San Mateo County Sheriff's Department. At the time of Kesey's arrest he had served some ten months on and off as a narcotics officer and attended a Federal training course for Narcotics Officers. As a result of his training and experience, the Deputy has evolved a simple method for detecting probable violation of the narcotics laws.

"Whenever you get a person who has a Bohemian type house," he declared, "weird paintings on the wall, nothing made out of coat hangers hanging from an oak tree, and people around banging the bongos all night—nine out of ten somebody's blowing grass."

It has been a year and a half since Kesey bolted and now they are back. The Mexican with the camera means he has been found or is about to be found.

Kesey peers through the window, thinking of Lenny Bruce. (Bruce was *courted* to death," Kesey says. "He got tripped out on the law as though that would help him.") Kesey will not let them court him to death. He will do something they do not expect, something super-heroic.

Babbs and the Mexican walk off down the road together. Kesey waits a few moments, borrows someone's hat and goes outside cautiously. One of the Indian workmen in the bungalow across the road makes the sign of the Slit Throat and smiles sadly. Kesey waves.

He walks down the road, his shoulders thrown back, his pace determined. With the postman's whistle around his neck he looks like a soccer referee on the about to make an unpopular decision.

A friend walking with him remarks that this latest of cops is pretty cool. Kesey agrees. The cop is very cool, he has talent. The thing would be to fuck him up.

"Remember the Casablanca routine?" the friend asks. "Humphrey Bogart? Claude Rains?"

"What was that?" Kesey wants to know.

Kesey's friend does the Casablanca routine. Claude Rains is a Vichy policeman. Humphrey Bogart is Rick, the owner of Rick's. He's in trouble with the Vichy police for his suspected Warner

Brothers Allied sympathies. ("Why did you come to Casa-
blanca?" asks Claude Rains. "For the waters," says Bogart.)
Rains is urbane but puzzled. ("But there are no waters here.
We are in the desert.") Bogart tells him: "I was misinformed."

"Yeah," Kesey says.

He looks around, surveying the quiet beach. When they come,
he thinks, they will materialize out of the sand, they will scamper
down from the palm trees, they will emerge from lidded baskets
holding tommy guns. Perhaps they will have dogs again.

When Kesey was arrested for the second time, it was on a
rooftop in North Beach. On that occasion, fortune dealt Kesey a
slice of whacked-out reality exceeding the most freaky delirium
he had ever dispensed at the acid test. He was so impressed with
it, that he decided to compose the event into a scenario.

It was the night before the Trips Festival Acid Test. Kesey
and Mountain Girl were free on appeal bond and plotting the
doings. They got together on the roof. Someone didn't like the
sound of falling gravel and called the cops.

The cops went up and found a cellophane bag of grass near
their reclining mattress. Kesey attempted to fling the bag off the
roof. One of the policemen attempted to prevent him and a
wrestling match ensued; Kesey, having been an All-American
wrestler at good old Oregon U, looked like a winner. The other
cop thought everything was happening too close to the roof and
drew his gun. The match ended with police in possession of their
evidence, and of Kesey and Mountain Girl.

It was at this point that Kesey decided he had detected a
trend. A short time later, his Acid Test bus was discovered abandoned near the hamlet of Orick, in far northern California. Inside the bus was an eighteen page letter which began: "Last
words. A Vote for Barry is a Vote for Fun. Wind, wind send me
meee not this place though, onward . . ."

The letter proceeded to convey Kesey's respects to the principles in his life and career and went on "Ocean, ocean, ocean,
I'll beat you in the end. I'll go through with my heels your
hungry ribs . . ."

As Kesey speeded south toward the border, he might have heard what Tom Sawyer heard on *his* disappearance, for the press lost no time in firing cannons over his wake. Everyone seemed to believe him a suicide except those who had heard otherwise and this category included practically everyone concerned. All agreed it was a Prankster's Prank.

"Hey," Kesey calls to the people in the house. "Where'd they go, Babbs and the Mexican?"

"Up the road," someone says. "They went off to the Hawaiian joint for a beer."

Things have taken a Prankster-like turn. The agent has not arrested anyone but instead he has gone with Babbs to an elegant Polynesian style roadhouse. Kesey looks around and sees the margin of reality widening.

"All right," he says. "Let's go do that Casablanca thing."

The Mauna Kea is quite the right place. It has thatch and palm trees, it has little tables with coconut candle holders. It has a bamboo bar behind which there is a tank of gorgeous tropical fish and a fat bartender who wears a loud sportshirt. Continental music purrs from the leafy loudspeakers. There is even a beaded curtain to glide through.

The Mexican agent has bought two beers; he and Babbs are sitting at the bar, sharing a small plate of spiced shrimp. Kesey waits before the beaded curtain and measures the scene.

He will be Humphrey Bogart. The Mexican agent is no Claude Rains, but he will do for the smooth foreign cop. Kesey eases through the beadwork, slicing it with the edge of his hand.

Babbs and the Mexican agent are now on speaking terms; the agent is buying beer and telling stories, presumably Mexican naval yarns. He looks up with interest as Kesey joins them on a stool.

"Hi," says the agent, "how are you?"

"Well, just fine," Kesey says.

Babbs introduces him as Solomon Grande. The Mexican's name is Ralph.

"Grande?" he inquires, "Grande? What is that? French?"

"American."

"Fine, fine," says Ralph. He is quick to buy another beer. He seems in a mood to drink beer, himself.

"A guy in Sinaloa," Ralph declares, apparently resuming an anecdote, "one time swears he's going to kill me. He believes he's more man than me and that he could do it. One time I'm in the office and the chief says to me—you know what? Old whats-hisname in Sinaloa wants you to come see him. He wants you to be godfather of his child.

I say good—I'll go.

The chief says man, you're crazy. He wants to kill you.

I say he can try.

I went. I'm godfather of his child. Now he's my compadre. He was going to kill me. He's my compadre now."

"Huh," Babbs says. "Was he in trouble with the Navy?"

"Naw. He was a big dealer in marijuana. We sent him up."

Kesey frowns. "Marijuana, huh."

"Yeah. You know about that? Marijuana?"

"Yes I have heard of it," says Kesey. "But I don't believe it's as much of a problem in the States as it is down here."

"Is that right," the agent asks. He is very cool indeed. "But I thought it was."

Babbs and Kesey shake their heads furiously.

"No, no," they assure him. "It's hardly any problem at all."

More beer and more shrimp arrive. Someone else pays for it and the Mexican agent is much put out. He is sensitive about his salary.

"So you investigate dope taking, too," Kesey asks.

"Sure." He goes into his pocket and produces a badge emblazoned with the rampant eagle and struggling snake. He is a Federale, and his badge number is One. He is agent Number One.

"Numero Uno," Kesey says. He looks at the badge.

Babbs whistles softly through his teeth.

"Do you have a license to kill?" Babbs asks.

Agent Number One cocks his head in the Mexican gesture of fatality.

"Sure," he says. "Sometimes people try to escape."

Someone buys another round of beer. Agent Number One seems to grow very angry.

"Don't do that again," he tells them. When that round is over, he buys the next.

He tells them that at the office they call him El Loco. They call him that because he takes on the cases that no one else wants, the cases you really have to be tough to handle. It was he, he informs them, who followed Lee Harvey Oswald through Mexico City. In Puerto Vallarta, he met Elizabeth Taylor in the course of a secret investigation.

"There was an American who was one of the movie company stooges," Number One recalls. "He tells me that it's impossible for me to see her."

He leans forward almost snarling into Kesey's face.

"I told him—you—don't tell me it's impossible!"

Babbs and Kesey nod in spontaneous approval.

"By the way," the agent asks, "have you ever been in Puerto Vallarta?"

"No," Kesey says. "And I've always regretted it."

"You'd like it," Agent Number One says. "It's beautiful."

There is a short pause as everyone sips their beer and takes a reality break.

"By the way," Babbs begins . . . he commences to tell outrageous stories involving Russians and people who appeared to be Russians whom he has encountered in and around Manzanillo. There have been many. Sometimes it has seemed that there were more Russians than Mexicans about.

Agent Number One receives the intelligence soberly. He keeps saying "Wow!" and seems always about to write something in his book. Kesey joins in telling of *his* encounters with Russians.

"Wow!" Number One says. He tells them that this information will set one hundred and fifty Federal agents in motion.

"Wow!" Babbs says. "A hundred and fifty!"

"Sure," the agent says.

Des Prado comes in to the bar and the Federale buys a final round of beer for everyone.

Kesey and Babbs present the agent with one of their Acid Test cards. Number One looks at it incredulously.

"Acid?" he inquires. "Acido?"

"Sure," Babbs says. "We say that if you can stand our music then you've passed the Acid Test."

"Wow!" the agent says.

They walk outside and stand in the sun beside Number One's white VW. There will be an Acid Test at their house on Saturday, the Pranksters tell him. He is invited. If the hundred and fifty other agents have nothing special to do that evening, they are invited as well.

Agent Number One looks at them strangely and says he will try to make it. Also, he has one favor to ask. Might he take their picture? For his collection. He already had Elizabeth Taylor's.

Kesey shrugs, confounded. Why not? Babbs, Kesey and Des Prado throw their arms about each others' shoulders and strike superheroic pose. The agent, all business, photographs them.

He gets in his car and Babbs climbs in beside him. They are going for a drive so that Babbs can show him all the places where Russians have been seen.

Kesey and Des Prado walk back down the road to the house and sit down outside.

After a while Babbs appears, grinning.

"What a great cat!" Babbs says. "How about that guy?"

"Definitely a man with something going for him," Kesey says. "Definitely."

five stories

gurney norman

1.

I HEARD this one as a news item on the radio a couple of summers ago. A woman was driving along one of the LA freeways when she felt an attack of epilepsy coming on. She took a pill but somehow it didn't work fast enough, so she pulled over to the side, stopped her car, got out, and fell to the pavement in a fit of convulsions. It happened that not far behind her in the line of traffic was a well-meaning man who, seeing the woman in distress, stopped his car, got out, and ran to give the woman aid. Thinking that she was suffocating, and worried that she was going to hurt herself, gyrating in the gravels, he lay down on top of her and began to apply mouth-to-mouth resuscitation.

This scene was observed by yet another well-intentioned man not far behind in the line of traffic, who was certain that an innocent woman was being raped by a mad-man right there on the LA freeway. So he stopped his car, grabbed his flashlight, ran to the writhing couple and proceeded to beat the man viciously over the head.

The court action was, to say the least, complex.

2.

One time in Arizona there was an old prospector who hadn't had any luck in 50 years. So one day he unloaded all of his equipment—which included a few sticks of dynamite and some fuse and blasting caps—and piled it all next to a big rock. First he put down the dynamite, then his tools, his grub, and his bed-roll. His burro carried a kind of saddle, so the old prospector placed it on top of the pile, then sat on it. Holding his burro closely by the reins, he lit the fuse and blew self, animal and belongings right out of this world.

3.

Last Spring I was working part-time in a warehouse in East Palo Alto, making about twelve dollars a day handling steel. Three or four other guys worked there too, lonesome down-and-outers trying to get enough money to drink on, or get some gas for their cars. It was hard work, for not much money, but most of us were philosophical about it. The only one that wasn't was an older fellow whose name I think was Lon.

It wasn't that Lon was bitter. He'd been doing twelve-dollar-a-day work most of his life, and he was used to it. Lon was just disappointed. The day before he'd gone to the employment office, and, praise the lord, they'd found him a soft, inside job in Redwood City that paid twenty dollars a day. Lon didn't have any money to buy gas with, so the next morning he set out for Redwood City on the bus. Only, he was daydreaming so heavily about what he was going to do with all his money that he rode right on by where his job was. By the time he back-tracked and finally showed up about mid-morning, the company had already hired somebody else.

His dreams of glory gone, Lon came down that afternoon to help us handle steel.

4.

Last Spring there was a hippie who tried to hitch-hike through the Kentucky mountains. In Letcher county he got in a car with a couple of fellows who were drinking beer and cruising around for the afternoon, and when they invited him to pal around with them, he thought, why not?

So they drove around, drinking, yelling at the girls, having a good time, as young men with a car and beer will do. They were driving kind of fast, naturally, a little too fast to suit a young state trooper who was also out cruising around that afternoon. He chased them a few miles, pulled them over, and, seeing that the boys were drunk, decided to take them all to jail.

The hippie and the boy who wasn't driving went along peaceably enough. They got in the trooper's car. But the other fellow was a little harder to deal with. When the trooper told him to get out, he got out all right, brandishing a hand grenade, threatening to blow them all up if the trooper didn't turn his buddies loose. It isn't clear who did what next, but the upshot of it was that the fellow pulled the pin on the grenade and threw it while the cop dived for cover blazing away with his pistol. The grenade turned out to be a dud, but the bullets weren't. Several of them hit the boy in the chest and killed him.

It turned out that the hippie wasn't really a hippie, either. He was a Marine, absent without leave, hitch-hiking, seeing the country. I'm not sure what finally happened to him.

5.

As late as the age of eleven, Wilgus Collier still had a bed-wetting problem. The only way he could control it was to get out of bed in the middle of the night and go outside and relieve himself. He even had his own alarm clock to get up by.

One night Wilgus was so sleepy he didn't hear the clock until its final ding. He managed to get outside okay, as if in a dream of the sweet outdoors at night, to pee. But he was so groggy that instead of going back inside the house to bed, he got turned around and wound up rattling the doorknob of the wash house, where his paranoid Uncle Emmit had been barricaded in almost three months now.

"Who the goddamn fuck hell is it!" screamed Emmit, going for his shotgun.

But the boy was so far gone he didn't hear, he only stood there on the bottom step, rattling the old loose doorknob.

"You crazy bastards, I'm going to kill you if you don't get away. I'll count to three. One!"

But Wilgus didn't hear.

"Two!"

Wilgus didn't hear.

"Three! BLAM!" The blast ripped out the whole top half of the door.

But fortunately, it missed the boy entirely. It didn't even scare him. Wilgus thought it was all part of his dream.

It scared Emmit though, the worst he'd ever been scared in his life. It scared him to find out how really crazy he was. It scared him to think his nephew might have been killed, and it scared him to think what the consequences would be when the others heard about what he'd done.

But as it turned out, Emmit didn't have to be afraid. His old parents heard the blast, but they were too sleepy to worry about what Emmit was shooting at this time. And the boy Wilgus proved himself a loyal comrade. He didn't get excited. And he didn't tell any of the others what had happened. For ever after that, Emmit and Wilgus had a special secret between them. And for ever after, Emmit always knew there was at least one person in the world that he could trust.

tears for robert oppenheimer

geraldine daesch

ONE AFTERNOON in Dr. Foster's waiting room I was looking at an old *Life*. There was a picture of a young man's face—cold, closed, hard and ugly. He was twenty-two years old and was being tried by court martial for an orgiastic civilian killing in Viet Nam. He was from Lazarus, Indiana.

I knew that town. The bus used to stop there on its way to Indianapolis. I don't think I ever saw such a sad town any place.

The bus would go along smoothly on the highways, through the quiet, unimpressive countryside and then it would turn into Lazarus and creep along dingy streets and cross railroad tracks and make elaborate round the block detours. Then it would stop and the driver would get off and load and unload things for a long time. It always made me nervous, even though common sense told me it would get to the city on schedule, and even though I can't remember ever having anything urgent to do in Indianapolis.

Mostly the people who got on at Lazarus were the kind of defeated tragic types you see in big cities. I remember a palsied old man with one leg and a paper sack of clothes, and a fat woman with an idiot child and two dead chickens in a shopping bag. Once an ugly girl got on who was so nervous I thought she must be running away.

On the corner next to the bus station was a poor looking bar with a neon sign that said "Lazarus' Dive." It was the kind of dreary pun that only Bible reading Indiana would understand. It always made me feel a little sick, the thought of drinking beer there, because, maybe erroneously, I associated Lazarus with leprosy.

The *Life* story was a good piece of writing in the style of *Life*. The horrible details of the killing were contrasted with the quiet of the little town where the killer grew up. The bewilderment of the parents was described. Townsmen were quoted, "Lyle was always a good boy." "Went to Sunday School every week." "Won a scout merit badge." "Had a real nice girl." It described the flag flying proudly in the town square above the Civil War monument and cannon. I often wondered why more Indianans didn't become murderers, faced as they are day after day by these inevitable phallic symbols of death.

I remember one December night. I had been Christmas shopping in Indianapolis. It was very cold and from time to time a little sleet would be scattered against the bus windows. I had been sad all day. I hadn't bought Mark a gift and I wasn't sure I would see him that holiday. The night before I had seen a movie at the University about the making of the atom bomb. A lot of it was devoted to Robert Oppenheimer. There were snapshots of him as a student at Goettingen, and newsreel clips of the Manhattan Project years and an interview with him as an old man. I thought he had the most beautiful and the most corrupt and tragic face I had ever seen. It had haunted me all day. I wanted to write him a letter and tell him how beautiful and how terrible his face was. I almost did, but he died before I found out where he could be reached, so I wrote a memoriam poem instead. When we stopped at Lazarus and I saw the Christmas lights strung in the window of that dreary saloon I started to cry. I turned my face to the window so the other people wouldn't see, though I really wanted someone to notice. I wonder now if someone had asked me why I was crying if I would have had the courage to say, "For Robert Oppenheimer."

I turned the magazine back to the page that bore Lyle Breck-hardt's face and looked at it. It was not beautiful or tragic at all. I looked up around the waiting room with its pale blue plastic couches and Klee prints. The clinic was supposed to be a community service thing, but mostly the patients sitting there were University genre—nervous young men pushed by the draft, sullen girls with long hair who read "Summerhill" or anxious young wives who had probably put their husbands through graduate school and then realized they were outgrown.

I had a vague feeling that there was some relatedness to all these impressions coming together in my mind. I felt that the Lazarus people would have been contemptuous of us sitting there, waiting for someone to probe our psyches, and in a certain way I felt contempt for us too, but I knew that though we might be suicidal we would never kill Gooks for the hell of it.

I sometimes wonder if Lyle Breckhardt was sentenced, and to what. I never saw anymore about his case, but I never cried for him.

amphetamine annie at the rock festival

patty fogel

WE PACKED a lunch, bought some fresh fruit and drove out to the San Francisco Rock Festival being held on the Alameda County Fairgrounds on the East Bay. Going up we smoked extravagant filter-tipped joints—doped-up mentholated Newports and plain old dope-stuffed Marlboros. The sun was shining, the radio blasting. Everyone was happy this Sunday morning to be stoned and driving away from school.

Before we even got within a mile of the grounds we had our first premonition that this was not going to be a perfect day. The landscape as far as the eye could see was carpeted with cars. Not cars in parking lot rank and file, but cars spread out chaotically, the fender of one car intersecting the bumper of another, cars in ditches, on hills, around trees, halfway up trees. In places it looked as if the cars were parked with some notion of leaving an exit lane, but a short way down the open way would be closed off by another group of cars at crazy angles.

The air was gray with smoke and dust. The smell of dope was

so distinct that it came as a surprise to see the lines of police-men stretching around the fair grounds. All of them had their professionally blank faces on. They showed no reaction at all to the parade of strange people going through the gates.

These festival goers *were* strange. There were, in this crowd of 20,000, very few of the mellowed, seasoned, old time heads that had been around a couple of years ago at similar gatherings in Monterey. As a matter of fact there weren't many people there over the age of fifteen, and the ones that were older looked as if they'd driven over from the Elvis Presley outdoor double feature; they came straight out of James Dean's *East of Eden*. A small number of grisly looking Hell's Angels completed the older set. The teeny boppers outnumbered the pompadors, bee-hives and Angels by a huge margin, but a lot of the teenies might have had pomps had they been born a couple of years earlier. We saw fourteen-year-old boys with their affectionate pimply-cheeked girlfriends sliding bulging baggies from one tight pocket to the other just obviously enough so the kids sitting next to them would see. They all held their cigarettes between the thumb and index finger. They all had mean frowns on their young faces. No one seemed to be listening to the music—which, of course, was difficult to do anyhow, considering the size of the audience and the distance from the stage.

The musicians had changed too. No more gentle Airplane songs, no delicate Beatle types. The era of soft drugs seemed to be fading along with the music and dress and demeanor of psy-chedelia. The featured groups at this festival were the Canned Heat and Steppenwolf—both are Eastern city bands that play tense, tough rock. Their images fit their sound. The band mem-bers are all ugly as shit; they work at looking mean and ugly in the Hell's Angel's tradition. No women in these bands: No acid meanderings. No soft marijuana highs. Amphetamines now. Amphetamine Annie—the chick whose brain is boogied to bits by five years of Speed. Her song is a warning but also a celebration of deliberate, joyful self-destruction. These new songs no longer suggest a temporary move out of the world, an escape allowing for the possibility of re-entry, but breathtakingly fast movement toward death.

What shook me up so much about this crowd of 20,000 was that it was suicidal and mindless, as if it had been duped into self-sacrifice by some omnipotent but mysterious social force. It wasn't afraid to destroy itself and wouldn't hesitate to take the rest of the world with it; there was no sense of restraint about this crowd. Fortunately, no one at the festival seemed imaginative enough or nihilistic enough to address the crowd in other than musical terms, but there was an undercurrent of easily evokable violence waiting to be tapped. 20,000 bored kids wanting something to happen so that they could participate in whatever it was.

You might argue that any crowd that huge and packed together becomes threatening. But I've been in college football crowds three times that big and haven't even entertained a thought about ultimate destruction. Of course in a situation like that the players perform a destruction ritual, exorcizing and civilly channeling a crowd's tendencies toward violence. I was also part of crowds in Chicago during the Democratic convention, though those were not so large. There the violence was also out front. It wasn't just the crowd itself generating it. Violence was happening all around, and people had to think about it, if only to keep their heads in one piece.

But at the Alameda County Fairgrounds all was submerged, underground and unconscious. The music wasn't loud enough or exciting enough to hold the attention of the crowd and there was little individual inspiration for creating one's own happenings. Everyone sat around waiting and things gradually began to happen.

Part of the fair grounds is a race track and the whole area in the middle of the track in back of the stage was blocked off from the crowd. Before you walked onto the grounds there seemed to be lots of policemen, but once inside, upon the presentation of a $5.00 ticket, the police were few in relation to the numbers of the crowd. There were, however, five or six mounted policemen. One skinny boy jumped a fence and ran out to the middle of the track. This gave a mounted policeman a chance to race his giant police horse at full speed out to accost the fence jumper, who just stood out there waiting for him. The crowd booed the cop at great volume, but nothing else happened.

The crowd was also keeping an eye on the gate crashers on both sides of the grandstand, cheering whenever one or two got through. Once someone could climb over the fence or squeeze through a closed gate, the police didn't dare follow him. As the concert went on and the more popular bands began to play, a whole mob of gate crashers started pushing against the tall fence. In a kind of physical climax coinciding with the musical climax of the Canned Heat's set they pushed down the fence entirely and streamed in. The stands went wild.

All this was warm-up for the real catharsis of the day. The Hell's Angels in attendance seemed to be waiting the most impatiently of all for some action. They were not satisfied with the inconsequential events that had happened already (inconsequential in terms of actual violence, blood and guts) so they staged their own happening. Five of them started beating the shit out of two older looking (19 or 20) guys for some unknown reason right in the densest part of the crowd. Some of the heroic police on horseback must have seen what was going on but just couldn't seem to get their horses' asses over there. Within two minutes the Angels had the two guys unconscious but they kept stomping on them and kicking them in the balls and head and stomach. It seemed necessary, inevitable that there be some sort of obscene blood rite to complete the movie of the day. Everyone around me was standing on their seats, transfixed. For once during the day there was silence. The crowd down below formed a small arena around the scene and in the first row were about five chicks who were looking on with benign smiles on their faces.

Then from somewhere in back of where I was now sitting down, sick in the stomach, there came the most bloodcurdling, heart stopping, unexpected scream, a scream intensified and amplified and framed by the silence—one isolated and perfectly distinct scream. I whipped around to see who it was, expecting to see a crying girl, a fainting girl, an hysterical girl, but there was no girl or boy like that at all. Everyone was still calmly watching, smiling, enjoying the action. The scream was a joke, a disembodied sound, a scream from a human mouth but divorced from human consciousness. It expressed no emotion. It was a meaningless scream that made a fool out of anyone who thought it was genuine.

We left a little after the Angels split up and disappeared into the crowd. Maybe these 20,000 kids knew what they were doing after all. Maybe theirs was the best way to endure the world around them. How mindless could that solitary screamer have been? Nothing during the whole day—not the Canned Heat dressed as Hell's Angels, not the Angels themselves, not the clouds of dope smoke that hung in the air all afternoon, not the crowds of dopey teeny boppers, not the officers of the law on horseback—nothing brought home so unavoidably as that scream, Amphetamine Annie's scream, the feeling that there was no future, that ghastly feeling of hopelessness that enclosed and enveloped the 20,000 festival goers along with the fences, police and dusty air. We waved good-bye to the faces in the lines of cars still arriving as we drove away, trying to leave the whole afternoon behind us like the lunch we gave to the three pubescent ladies that had been sitting next to us.

the abysmal baptismal

max crawford

BUBBA BADGETT, the assistant evangelist, gathered everybody who had been saved or wanted rebaptising under the windmill tower and tried to weed out those who just wanted a free swim, an operation calling for the sort of tact Bubba didn't possess. He reported to the evangelist a number half again as large as they had expected after the service, itself quadrupled their earlier estimate. Bubba wrung his hands because he knew what a bad mood baptising too many people put the evangelist in. It had been the plan, before Altus, to someday let Billy Rose do all the saving and Bubba all the baptising and though, after Altus, Mary Rose had scotched the idea it looked now as though they might be forced to implement it. They looked around but neither man could see the evangelist's wife. "And to make it worse," wailed Bubba, "that bigun wants to be rebaptised. What can I say to him?"

"What bigun?" said the evangelist slowly.

"Him," said Bubba and pointed into the milling crowd beneath the windmill. "The deacon's boy, Hubert."

"Oh, you have got to be joking, Bubba," said the evangelist and turned his back to him. "Why he's the deacon's son. He don't need rebaptising. Don't bother me with these details. I couldn't dunk him in a hundred years. He should know that."

"But what am I going to tell *him?*" said Bubba desperately.

"Tell him he should have been a Methodist," chortled the evangelist and started walking off. "Tell him to go get sprinkled."

Bubba went back to the crowd under the windmill and Hubert told *him* he was getting rebaptised whether the evangelist liked it or not. All Bubba could do was find the largest gown for Hubert and save it back. He went in to the wellhouse and rummaged through the bale of baptismal gowns and found the largest and stepped out into the blinding light. But he had lost Hubert in the pushing crowd. He could hear the evangelist calling his name and he had yet to run the first batch of girls into the wellhouse. He finally had to give up and throw the gown back inside. Hubert would have to make do with whatever size turned up.

The crowd hadn't even settled down yet when the evangelist had his first bad moment. Wearing hip boots he playfully tested the water with his toe and when no one noticed that he vaulted over the tank's side into the water. Only no one had told Rose that the tank was recessed, that it was twice as deep as it appeared from the outside. For a second the evangelist stood waist deep in the water, holding his breath and waving his arms around. The evangelist glared back at the round of laughter. His hip boots dragging like lead, the evangelist slogged to the center of the tank and asked everyone to bow his head. At a signal Bubba lifted the first girl over into the water and she sighed and gasped and giggled and tried to keep her gown, which was loose and tied only in the back like a surgical robe, from billowing too much away from her short, white, diagonal legs. The evangelist gently motioned her toward him and one baby step at a time, she finally made it, serious and trembling as she reached the churchman. He patted her and whispered for her not to worry. In turn she whispered her name in his ear. Then Rose said the words: "Mary Jane Tilding, do you accept Jesus Christ as your public Saviour, so help you God, the Son and the Holy

Ghost?" And she went down perfectly, her feet remaining on the bottom, and came up nicely wet all over.

For a while all the baptising went like this: as graceful as a dance, the evangelist swooping the light-boned girls into the water and then, without even trying it seemed, pulling them back onto their feet. The girls, shivering, hair stringing and gowns no longer very concealing, thanked the evangelist with a big smile and splashed back to the wellhouse to change clothes and tell how they had opened their eyes under the water and seen Jesus. Bubba stood arms akimbo at the wellhouse door pretending he wasn't listening to what was going on inside.

"It kind of reminds me of that famous queer doing the tango," said one farmer and spat in the tank. And as he did he saw a shadow slide beneath the spittle, pause, and glide off. "I didn't know Mack kept catfish in his tank," he said to the next man.

"Just one," said the second farmer. "Keeps one big one as a pet. Calls him Buster, I believe. But I would've thought he'd taken him out for the baptising. I would've thought that not even Mack was dumb enough to leave him in."

"It would seem the hell like it," said the first man and spat again but now no shadow glided beneath. He shook his head.

Billy Rose had finished with the girls and as he waited for them to clear out of the wellhouse and Bubba to run the ladies in, he strode around, his hands above his head, smiling and waving and joking and having conversations with the spectators. One of the ladies called him over to the side and gave him a sip of lemonade and wiped his brow. The evangelist was enjoying himself when he saw Bubba lead the first lady out of the wellhouse. This woman looked four times bigger than any of the girls. Despondently Rose trudged back to the center of the tank and Bubba helped the lady trip over the side of the tank and fall flat in the water. There is nothing more discouraging than baptising somebody already wet. The evangelist's arms grew tired just watching the woman beat waves as she approached him. He went through the same procedure, getting the name, saying the words, and then dunking the convert; but now it was different, the joy had gone out of it, he mispronounced the name, mumbled the words and, the life having fled from his arms, almost had to kneel to get the lady completely under and then back up again. And the next, though she was twenty pounds lighter, was no easier. If each lady after the first hadn't been impeccably dry Billy Rose would have sworn Bubba was running some of them through twice. But finally, with the evangelist, except for his hat, as wet as any of the converts, Bubba indicated that the women were over. Which meant that the battle was all but won, there usually being two or three times as many women converts as men. The evangelist told Bubba to hold up for a while and went over to the side of the tank and took a camp chair and placed it in the water and sat down, only his head and shoulders showing above the surface. He was that tired. But the water washed over him and Rose felt twice as strong, twice as ready to go on when Bubba opened the wellhouse door and by mistake let two men out and into the tank. Rose was trying to see who they were when Brother Knox stood on a car bumper and raised his hands for attention.

Knox announced that these two men as boys had been saved together and first baptised together in this very tank and that today at the powerful preaching of the evangelist Billy Rose they had come to the conclusion that no better time lay before them to rededicate their lives to Christ together and be rebaptised together. He went on to say that Cull had almost gone so far as to dedicate his life to missionary work with Lottie Moon along the Amazon, but that that hadn't been decided upon yet, and that Hubert had come to feel a powerful internal movement to preach. The young preacher hoped that today's baptising might do the trick and get them on their way back to God. Billy Rose couldn't appreciate Knox's flattery. He grimly motioned Cull to step forward. But Hubert pushed his friend out of the way and butted forward.

The evangelist fidgeted with experimental handholds on Hubert. Two around the neck? Two around the waist? Or one in the left armpit and one on the buttocks? No, maybe a fistful of hair with the right as the left arm encircled the waist. Rose could not decide; they all seemed insufficient for Hubert. He had about decided there was simply no way he could get the fat man down let alone back up, when Hubert announced he was as ready as he ever would be. "I realize you are ready," whispered the evangelist irritably. "I am letting the spirit fill up."

"Well, hurry up," said Hubert. "This outfit is drafty and my feet are getting cold. What was that I just stepped on? That felt like a fish I just stepped on."

It was probably my foot that was too numb to feel it, thought Billy Rose as he grabbed the nape of Hubert's neck with one hand and the front of his gown with the other. He pushed backward with all his might and winked at Hubert: if he would just fall backward he, the evangelist, would surely get him back up. Hubert rolled his eyes and locked his knees and didn't look convinced. Rose reached up and grabbed the short hair on Hubert's head and pulled and pushed at his chest but only moved him backward a few inches. With the congregation growing impatient, Billy Rose began to fear complete disaster. He would be the laughing stock of the revival circuit. If he wasn't already. No sir, he decided, my fortunes have changed. This had been the perfect revival and nothing was going to ruin it now. "Are you ready to go down peacefully, Hubert? I can do it with or without you," he hissed.

Hubert's eyes still rolled. He shook. "I think I want out of here. I think there's some kind of animal fishying around down there between my legs!"

Rose saw he had no choice. A few moments more and Hubert would be bolting from the tank. He could see the story in the *Baptist Standard:* "Dry Convert Flees Baptism." "Hold your nose, Hubert, you are going under," the evangelist said and reset his hands at Hubert's neck and gown and, while pushing and pulling as before, kicked the deacon's son's feet out from under him. Hubert went down without a whimper. All the evangelist had to do now would be reach down and lug Hubert out. If so far everything had gone exactly as planned, he couldn't imagine the rest going differently. But, before retrieving Hubert, as he turned to view the astonished crowd, he noticed a soggy white cloth in his left hand. He shook it out. It looked just like a baptismal gown. When Hubert burst gasping to the surface, the evangelist sadly saw that it *was* a baptismal gown. Choking and rubbing his backside, Hubert grabbed it back and threw it around his waist. "You ripped my gown off me. You tried to drown me. I think I'm bleeding. Get out of the tank, Cull. I'm telling you, it wasn't worth it."

The evangelist stayed in the tank and Bubba sent out another man, the only other, who was baptised with no problems. But after that the evangelist completely lost heart. He returned with the man to the wellhouse and stripped off his hip boots and changed into dry clothes. He hadn't been able to look the deacons in the eye. His career as an evangelist was now finally ruined. He was so blue that the fact that the collection money had already been divided up could not cheer him up. Perhaps Mary was right, perhaps he was too old for this foolishness, this traipsing around the hinterland when so many fine, solid churches were crying out for preachers with his experience. It was a thought. He told Bubba to go on and finish baptising the boys. He sat for a while alone in the wellhouse after they had changed into their gowns and gone.

eric nord now

fred nelson

1

THE MOST that can be said for Los Gatos is that it's there, exactly where is known only to the surveyors and the mapmakers, a sort of elbow in the homogenous body of apartments, tracts and freeways, always more freeways, that forms the San Jose end of the San Francisco Bay. There actually isn't even much bay that far down; it peters out quickly and most of what's left, like anything else around, is slowly being staked out and industrialized.

Los Gatos—or rather San Jose, it's all the same—is prototypical of the Sixties America, mourned by many and created by all. Like every urban sprawl across the country, it has been inevitable since the first Spanish missionary came up the coast. It's still inevitable, and when it can reach no farther it will grow taller and thicker, and even less visible in the haze of monoxide which is growing across the valley. Los Gatos is the product of the hurtling life style of the twentieth century. All of man's work, his mobility and his growth have resulted in towns like Los Gatos; it's fashionable to put down a suburb like this, but the very fact of its being there and everywhere, while much a part of monstrous accident and headlong inadvertence, makes it the reward, a desired reward, for the work of many.

It's not so bad when you get down into it. There's a sameness and it's crowded, but if each man had the individuality and room he deserves there wouldn't be *any* land left, an ecological disaster that would make Los Gatos seem like an oasis. Los Gatos isn't virgin beauty but it isn't a slum, either. The homes are safe shelters, warm, new and convenient. Most of them have lawns, there really are trees if you slow down and look for them; and the property, in its little bits and pieces, is actually *owned* by people who worked for it and treasure it.

The decor, generally, is straight American plastic, as derided as the houses but just as personal to the people who live there. There's a sameness, again, but this, too, is inevitable in a nation of 200 million people all wanting the same things. There's the All-Electric Kitchen, and the kids and pets tracking it up. The TV set sits squarely in the living room, maybe another in the bedroom. Things are never quite all put away, but it's neat and, above all, comfortable. The lawn and patio are too small for strenuous use, but they're pleasing and not too much work. There's a mortgage, perhaps, and maybe some neighbors you know, maybe not. There's a commute to work and back, but it could be farther. There are friends—yes, these people have friends, real friends—over on Saturday night, a washing machine inside the back door and two cars with no place to put the older one because that side of the garage needs cleaning and there's really no place to put all of *that*.

Above all, this is culture, the American culture, the life-style that typifies the people. This is what's there to be rebelled against, if you've a mind to.

Blossom Hill Road looks like all the rest of it—better, actually; while it's partially apartments, big, pink and ugly, it's bounded occasionally by a receding hairline of orchards—and runs through most of it, from Cupertino, through Los Gatos, on into San Jose, though nobody knows for sure just where the boundaries are. The uniform style here is neo-chalet but the rest is typical, the good and the bad. The homogenous American culture. And there in the middle of it all, right there on Blossom Hill Road, with the not-too-big-not-too-small lawn, commuting neighbors, half-cluttered garage and a TV set in *his* living room, sits Eric Nord, Big-Daddy-of-the-Beatniks Eric Nord, the bohemian of the headlines, the Rebel.

2

Eric Nord was so much the hub of a universe—many of them, actually—and the product of so many headlines and contemporary legends that when you finally do confront the man—yes, sir, the *real* Eric Nord—right down there on Blossom Hill Road you're put so far off guard by his almost totally-withdrawn shyness and quiet decency that you can't possibly think back and build the scene-that-was around him again. Eric is real, what he thinks and believes are real, so you're left wondering how much of the *scene* was real, and how much of it was stories created by their own headlines.

Eric really is Big Daddy: he stands nearly six foot nine and must weigh over three hundred pounds—not fat, just big. He moves delicately for his size but you know for sure when he's in the room; walking down a North Beach street with him is an adventure. He looks like a character actor and really is, although that part of his life has been obscured by everything else people have built around him. But that's what Eric's all about, after all: he's there, doing his thing of the moment, and things happen around him.

He's tweedy and bearded; he wears just barely big enough cloth caps and his hairline, at 50, is receding slightly, but at that height few notice. His native Rhineland barely shows in his voice, diluted by sheer softness. For all his notoriety, his manner is reserved and offhand.

Nord was born into a prominent German textile family, but his mother was American. His parents divorced when he was four, and he spent his earlier years shuttling between German boarding schools and Florida, leaving Germany for good with the rise of Hitler in 1936. He finished high school in Long Beach, California and began odd-jobbing in southern California when his family's fortunes were wiped out by the American and German depressions. His first experience with the stage was with the Hollywood British School of the Theatre, under the direction of Douglas Fairbanks, Jr., but for the most part he spent the Forties as a government contractor and Marin County land developer.

There was no plan, and Eric wasn't fully settled into a commercial life. At one time or another he was an art gallery employee and a bordello decorator, and the theatre still drew him. But he was on his way, at the moment, down the road to Los Gatos that most people were taking. He had most of the trappings, including, as he remembers, "a wife, three children, tract house, debts, the whole bit." Eric was Establishment. But you've got to notice Eric, and when he dropped out everybody knew it.

3

Eric dropped out, bounced through the San Francisco Municipal Theatre and landed in the cavernous basement of Columbus Tower, a long-defunct 1920's nightclub which he reclaimed and offered to North Beach as the Hungry i. Eric's intentions—and talents—are not commercial, and the club began as an uncapitalized attempt to give his fellow theatre people a place to go after their earlier after-the-show hangout had burned down. Just Eric, some "kids from the theatre" and some old, worn furniture and some comfortable decorations. Those were the days before North Beach was a public action spot and Eric dismissed most commercial amenities including, and this particularly attracted the authorities, liquor and entertainment licenses. "Everything in society," he will tell you, "is so punchcarded—don't fold, bend, mutilate, spindle and the like—I don't believe in licensing, taxes or any of that jazz, and I'm not so uptight about money that

I have to charge people. If they can't pay for it, they shouldn't be denied."

The entertainment was impromptu and informal, and included at one time or another most of the litany of "name" performers the Hungry i is credited with having discovered. "Folksingers, calypso dancers—we didn't go in for comedians at that time," Eric recalls. "We had beautiful sausage, Monterey cheese, lovely San Francisco French bread. The atmosphere gave you a floating feeling." Commercialism intruded, however, as Nord's ubiquitous theatre associates moved on and he was left with the lease. His fame grew as he hassled the law over licenses and tried such ploys as running the "i" as a membership club—along the lines of the Moose and the Elks, he claimed, but free to anyone who couldn't afford it. Eric the developer-turned-bistro owner began appearing in the press, particularly under the aegis of Chronicle columnist Herb Caen, an opera buff who began frequenting the "i" after shows. Then came that ultimate, awful badge of success, the city's one sure sign of recognition that you're really "in," the Gray Line Night Life Tour, plying the streets between Finnochio's and Bimbo's, now rumbling and whining into North Beach and dumping its cargo of conventioneers and old couples from Iowa into the cavern under Columbus Tower, into the Hungry i. The press had discovered the "beat generation," and offered it to the public like an abandoned child.

4

Despite its being so much in the public domain North Beach has its own history, private and personal to the people who live there. It was never altogether typical, not since the city's Barbary Coast days, but the neighborhood had much in common with low-rent immigrant sections in many large port cities. The neighborhood is largely Italian but lies hard by San Francisco's Chinatown. These cultural identities still endure, interspersed among the topless joints and remaining coffeehouses, choked in by tourist traffic. New arrivals from the old country still come off the boat there to stay under the wing of their established uncles and brothers. The streets were lined with old Italian bars that never did much business and with family restaurants, back-through-the-bar-and-up-the-stairs-to-the-left affairs that had maybe ten chairs, a few old posters, oilcloth on the tables and heaps and mounds of the incomparable food they served back home, all supervised by mama herself. (The restaurants still exist, pushed back further into the cultural core, and well worth the search.) The streets were a family scene.

The low rent in the district, as in New York and Chicago, has always been attractive to artists and other low-income intellectuals, and they've mingled unpublicized with the Italians for generations—always a real contrast, with a quiet mutual acceptance. By the Fifties the bohemian population had grown large enough to be a substantial neighborhood subculture in its own right. Cultural immigrants swelled this force daily but their lives and affairs remained private and secure right down to the moment the press and public, much as they later overwhelmed the lazy Haight-Ashbury, descended in force in search of a scene to be made, and standing right there in full view was Eric Nord. No, you couldn't miss him.

And North Beach became, in his memory, the meeting ground of the "intellectuals and the pseudos." What brought the pseudos in? "How many thousands of people," Eric asks, "read Herb Caen who would like to tune into something, who aren't prepared, who haven't the facilities? The "i" was a happening, a place where anything, everything or nothing could happen—play chess, drink wine, get thrown out—a beautiful, subterranean thing. We made people who drifted in feel at home."

The overrun "i" soon became too much for Eric ("the great quantities of smoke were bugging me—I don't smoke, myself") and in 1952 he sold the "i" for $800 cash and $800 equity (he still hasn't collected on the latter) to Enrico Banducci, the "i"'s celebrated Bandooch, once a child violin virtuoso and then the Hungry i's all-around waiter-helper and bankrupt owner of Enrico's Fine Foods on Bush Street. "I'm not uptight about money," says Eric.

5

With that settled, Eric was married again and off to Guatemala on a safari to colonize hundreds of virgin acres as a would-be Guatemalan citizen. The caravan's arrival coincided with armed revolution, and by the end of 1952 Eric was back in San Francisco, broke, divorced, and into the old neighborhood again. During his brief absence, however, what had already been a fair-sized river of tourists and reporters had become a veritable flood—everybody, *everybody* had come on board for the action, or for what they thought was the action, or at least for a vicarious titter. The "i" was thriving to all appearances, and new coffee houses dotted the streets to feed the bohemians and amuse the tourists—Miss Smith's Tea Room, the Bread and Wine Mission and most famous of all, the Coexistence Bagel Shop, where Eric chose to drop back in and become the nexus again.

He ran the shop with a verve. "I wasn't really part of what had grown up during that year," he sighs, "but when big old me came along, people identified, because I like to associate with a free type of people who aren't uptight, who can just sit down over a cup of coffee and philosophize, or pick up on some chicks or some jazz or whatever's happening. I didn't particularly have a lot of friends, but people felt comfortable around me to do their thing. I was permissive, maybe . . . . sort of the 'big daddy' thing . . . . without scolding."

Eric was also permissive in an interracial sense, invoking upon himself a great deal more private controversy than even the newspapers provided. He set up housekeeping in a loft in the produce district, 10 minutes' walk from North Beach, which became notorious as the Party Pad (again unlicensed,) simply Eric's place, inevitably crowded, reported on and raided. Eric was variously charged with running a disorderly house, running an illegal dance hall and contributing to the delinquency of minors, but none of the charges stuck. While being at Eric's became fashionable, the private pressure was enormous, particularly due to the early rise of the black-is-beautiful ethic

among the bohemians. "There were few open complaints, because the race business was a hot potato even then. But if some
dowager's daughter admitted that she'd been at Eric's pad dancing with some Negroes, you knew damn well there'd be some
reverberations at City Hall."

"By that time," he recalls, "the power structure was grasping
at straws to get me out of the way—it was Clean City. Mayor
Christopher—Crusader Chris—tried to clean out the brothels,
the after-hours places—everything had to be sterilized, pasteur-
ized, homogenized and authorized." All this comes with no
irony—a shrug, a smile, even a chuckle. Eric walked his own
road, secure in his own morality. One of his finest hours came
the night he and a large group of comrades invaded downtown
San Francisco, a la Gray Line, in a "Squaresville Tour" of the
city, celebrating his being charged with contributing to the delinquency of a 16-year-old girl.

Those charges, too, were dropped. The law, Nord remembers,
handled him "pretty much tongue-in-cheek, like they used to
have pleasant relations with gangland, except I never paid off.
They enjoyed notoriety as much as anyone; they still want to
get into camera range during demonstrations."

6

"The 'beat generation' thing just happened to me," says Eric
Nord, "people dropping out, going for values—I was just there,
part of the scene." And as the scene became completely overrun
and began to dissipate, Eric moved on again.

The new destination was Venice, California, a boardwalk
community on the beach, sandwiched between Santa Monica
and Pacific Palisades. The new scene was the Gas House, again
the target of outraged sections of the community and clearly,
in his every waking reminiscence, Eric's favorite.

"They knocked down the Party Pad, so we went down to
Venice and found this building—it was built like the Piazza di
St. Marco in the other Venice—columns, gingerbread. We got a

cheap lease and renovated it—Ward Kimball of Disneyland laid out the decor. It was a cultural center, a real one, the grooviest thing I ever had. Beach, boardwalk, kids' art classes, leftwing Pacific Ocean Park Democrats, *marvelous* light shows years before the current fad, bongos, Shakespeare, discussions, a kids' zoo in the window and a sort of subsidy for the resident artists and writers (bankrolled by Los Angeles criminal attorney Al Matthews.) Almost like the Last Supper every night."

"We enjoyed putting people on, on camera," he laughs, recalling the publicity which inevitably attended this operation, too, and which eventually led to the downfall of the Gas House at the hands of the Venice Civic Union—"a bunch of veterans' organization-based types, down on everything except their own way of life—their own thieves, winos and old whores were OK with them. We had a renaissance going there, at least six galleries. Now they're gone, and all that's left are their own liquor stores, girlie mags, American Legion beauty contests, flags, politicking . . . really disgusting. Highrises, blocking the ocean now. I can't stand to look at it." The vision does more than anything else to put emotion in Eric's voice. Not anger, and not really very much disgust, but a sadness. A little for himself, a lot for everyone.

Then more of the same. Another coffeehouse, this one in Provincetown, Massachusetts. Florida, then back to North Beach in charge of Mike's Pool Hall, an island of salami, beer and quiet in a sea of topless shows. A safari to Hawaii, turned back this time by pneumonia, then to Los Gatos to settle and recover. Los Gatos, the American product, the American style, the end of the long path of progress. Eric took his own road, but he's home, now, in Los Gatos.

7

North Beach is still there, just as it always was, but much has disappeared and scenes have changed. The Italians haven't changed, and probably never will. The artists are still around but just aren't looked at as much. The beats have been pushed out of the headlines by the flower children a few miles south (who've had *their* turn, now, to be vandalized by tourists and swallowed whole by the popular culture) and pushed out of the center of North Beach by the topless emporiums. The tourists are still there, pouring out of Gray Line buses faster than ever. Breasts are everywhere.

The sidewalk cafe in front of Enrico's Coffee House (another Banducci product) sits in the middle of it all, precariously. In the middle of *that* sits Eric Nord, alumnus, frequent visitor, sometimes with old friends, sometimes alone unto himself, enjoying, watching, remembering.

The Coexistence Bagel Shop is gone, there's a clothing store there now. "Everything I've ever started," sighs Eric, with a soft, wry look starting across his face, "has either been filled in or torn down. I always looked for low rent districts to start out in . . . I hated to get so commercial that I had to support a landlord."

The Bread and Wine Mission is gone, now a laundromat. The Minimum Daily Requirement and Enrico's, both of which Eric helped open, remain. The Coffee Gallery and a few other spots still operate on upper Grant, away from the neon and the noise, serving people who really want them. The Gas House is gone, now a parking lot. The Party Pad is gone, as is Mike's.

The old "i" is gone. It extended under Columbus Street, and when the street was rebuilt and filled in in 1959 it moved across the way to its most famous location on Jackson Street. *That's* gone now, too, wiped out with a small Filipino colony in the path of urban redevelopment. The new Hungry i is a $500,000 palace ("a small opera house," says Eric) in a newly-renovated corner of Ghirardelli Square.

"I hear Banducci finally admitted he owes me that eight hundred," Eric murmurs. "He realizes he screwed me a little, and he enjoys it . . . I let him . . . what the hell . . . he sees me as a prodigal stepson and feels kindly to me. He owes hundreds of people . . . he's always on the verge of being closed up." All this with amusement, not vindictiveness. The new "i" he says, "has been thin ice from the beginning. It has great overhead. . . . they're even turning off the electricity, and the waiters have to pool their resources to keep the place open." Eric helped open the new "i," and never has received his last check. "I'm not up-tight about money."

8

The scene continues, the *real* scene that exists in the lives, the aspirations and the memories of people. So much has changed, but Eric Nord looks out from Los Gatos and sees consistency.

Hippies are a new force, but not to him. It goes far, far back, to the beats, the old bohemians, the existentialists, the nihilists, the "angry young men," the intelligentsia of the 20's, "clear on back to the stone age." He looks out from Enrico's watching the scenes pass: "People have always gotten tired of tight collars, tight suits, tight shoes, colorless, drab lives, inheritances of false values, stupid values of religion and war sanctioned by religion, legalized stealing among the wealthy while the poor cat stealing bread does time for the rest of his life . . ." His voice is soft, but so easy to hear. "The hippies of today are much more of a threat to the establishment than they ever were. They're more in number, and there's a new militant element which was lacking before."

But what can happen, what can really change when the rest of society just plugs along, reacting to all this with either hostility or a kind of smothering acceptance that overlooks whatever reality is there, while aping the style?

"It amuses me. Society copies dress—berets, turtlenecks, all black and the like, but dress has no value. The more it's accepted, of course, the groovier. If socialites accept part of us, there may be some converts. We survived ourselves, though . . . the society pages played us all over, but we weren't pawns . . . remember the gypsies entertaining socialites but really hating them." (Images of rock bands playing for today's debutante parties, grabbing daddy's fat check and making it out the back door with the debs.)

Watching the street, one last thought, a burst: "Topless. Nudity is beautiful, but not exploited, horrendous nudity, seedy, seamy, a gin-mill atmosphere looking for tourists to take for $1.50 a drink to see stuffed plastic titties on some old whore—I don't know of one with any taste."

9

So there's North Beach, and there's Los Gatos, and there's Eric Nord, and the contradictions and the consistencies elude. He's stayed with the theatre in occasional film and television roles but that's activity, not life. He's had many loves. He's made many scenes and has been made by them. "I'm not a leader. I was just there, part of the scene."

There will be more. Eric dreams now of an art colony, a living group of artisans, all contributing from the ground up, incorporating modern architecture with the earth, the rocks. How will it be paid for? There'll be someone, there generally has been. "I'm always open to new things. The American Sunbathing Association is colonizing the island of Angola, in the Bahamas. I have no particular direction except living to the fullest, enjoying life." The government is trying to unload an entire village near Mt. Shasta—dreams of a "survival village," and Eric has Free U. attorney Jim Wolpman looking into it. A course on "Mind Unfucking" in the Free University.

Is there a scene already going now, the really ultimate scene, reaching out in the directions he wants? He smiles, "I'm looking all the time. If I knew of one I'd be there," and in time he will.

the moratorium in little rock: the day the toughest marine met the hard-rapping preacher

richard wyman

JOHN YANCEY rises with his notecard of notes. And if the minds of the young audience are reflective they will remember the fifth grade Landmark book, *The Marines*, with the last chapter "John Yancey: The Toughest Marine Who Ever Lived." An image forms of the book's finger-stained cover (for it was a welcome relief from all the horse stories): an immaculate Marine in a sandbag pit clutching a 30 caliber machine gun. The bullet belt is feeding and the muzzle is flashing, yet the soldier's face is not grimaced, but rather pleasantly excited and not unlike the expressions on the faces of children in the G.I. Joe section of the Christmas toybook.

The book elaborates Yancey's wounds in Korea. He had been shot in both public and private parts and still remained on the front. He had run through his ammunition and then charged the little yellow commies swinging his empty B.A.R. as a club and cursing them for not shooting him dead. As he confronted the peace Moratorium however, only two of his battles were evident: the extreme attrition age had laid upon his face and the deep harness Bourbon had forced upon his voice. Yancey cupped his solitary notecard in his brutal palm, staggered forward on one lead-filled leg, and made a quick motion toward his eyes with the palm.

"Power grows out of the barrel of a gun."

Well now I done heard that before at other places, I thought.

Yancey placed his hand into his tweed coat pocket and throwing his head back to catch the historic light once shone upon his comrade Douglas MacArthur, repeated "Power grows out of the barrel of a gun. Chairman May-O says that. I used to listen to the greatest man I ever knew, a Colonel in the U.S. Army. He had gone on this Long March with May-O; when he finished marching that 6,000 miles, he told me right then that May-O could take over any amount of land he set a mind to. Me and him and three others got together to stop May-O, but the Colonel died of many simultaneous wounds."

To illustrate Mao's saying, Yancey outlined with one hand a rather long gun barrel while he used the other to raise the stock to his shoulder. As he repeated Mao yet a third time, his forefinger curled in the air and jerked the ghostly trigger.

I searched the assembly hall containing at most one hundred people for the faces of my high school students. My eyes rested on several: a history student whose paper on Vietnam had consisted of nonsensical phrases copied from *Colliers Encyclopedia* although I had risked my job supplying him with anti-war material, a lovely girl with a strange tinge of English accent who had commented in her assigned autobiography that her father blackened her eye over her views on the war, a student from 5th period English who as a matter of self-destruction never wrote an assignment or allowed himself to be tricked into entering a discussion.

Not the best of my students, I sighed, for I had become something of a priggish intellectual during my confinement in Little

Rock these last two years. I was seized by a compulsion to make the students realize my presence. A strong urge swept over me to prove myself and my discipline to them by virtually deluging John Yancey with Vietnam history. Yet at this time there was probably not a hawk in the audience other than the aloof crew-cut gentleman in dark glasses who sat near the exit balancing a gray felt hat on top of his walking cane. Possibly he was with the FBI, but on the other hand, perhaps he was an extinct specimen of a Little Rock Communist. So Yancey was the lion being fed to the Christians today. I become uneasy at the martyrdom of a lion because it unleashes the bloodthirsty side of the Christians.

"So in Vietnam, the United States is just planting its power in the barrel of a gun," Yancey continued.

A reckless wildfire was beginning to burn through my disguise, my facade, my cover. For two years I had evaded the war draft by public school teaching. Behind me lay a multitude of statements of intricately devised double meanings which satisfied school superintendents that I was what I was not. My papers contained scores of perhaps overly elaborate plans designed to force my students down a mazeway of truth without plaguing me with the deadly mark of a misfit subversive. I became schizoid and successful at this exercise. The small town superintendent accused me of administering a lewd test on the *Canterbury Tales* in which the mind of the Beta Club Queen was raped into describing Harry Bailey's answer to the Summoner. Yet my politics were never questioned.

A high school student with shoulder length blond hair rose, firmly positioned himself in his gym shoes, and challenged John Yancey. "Mr. Yancey, the government's been a straight out fake, I mean you know they lied when they said all that about the war thing."

Yancey leaned one gnarled ear over the lectern out toward the audience, "Would you repeat? There's a bullet caught in this ear."

"How truthful do you think the government has been?"

"Lord bless you young people. I thought the government was

telling the truth during Prohibition, and when I bought my bath-tub gin I found out different."

"You're off the point," I yelled and felt the series of vibrations from my diaphragm run through my windpipe to my throat which demanded other loud words to quench the tremor.

Yancey slowly moved his eyes toward me, the heavy lids bleeding ennui. "Yes sir, soldiers fight, and the governments lie. And a man gets damn angry when he's lied to. So I understand why you are all here in these black armbands. Let me be straight. We're not over there to take care of those Asian people. We're over there taking care of ourselves. I wouldn't give one American life for a starving Asian. Because a man who is starving can't see any value to life."

The degenerate militarist was still on his feet. I had noticed reporters leaning against the door frames in the rear of the auditorium. I would seal my fate in newspaper quotes, and yet I languished to cut into Yancey with comments on the French colonialism, Bao Dai, Diem, the bomb tonnage.

The dramatic baring of my real and authentic self was post-poned yet a moment longer as a black man rose to question Yancey. This was the strongest polarity in the room. White radicals seemed to hold their breath in uncertainty whether the black militant would do what he was supposed to or would turn and condemn them all to a revolutionary grave. I well knew how little contact my most political students experienced with the part of town east of Broadway. The peace movement in Little Rock was still characterized as an eccentricity among the children of doctors and lawyers.

"You say that a man belongs with a gun when it is time to protect myself. Shouldn't black people get guns to protect themselves right here in this city?"

"Sir, if I was of the black color," Yancey answered, "and living in America, I'd be a general in the Black Panthers before nightfall and be glad to die on the streets."

Raising a clenched fist, the black man shouted, "Black people have a right to warfare in the white prison."

Yancey continued, "The one right any man has by birth is

to start a war for his own benefit and security. Since as you see I am a white man, I'd be glad to die on the streets shooting Black Panthers."

This was a rare objectivity John Yancey possessed. Yancey did not think in patterns which would have led him to consider waiving his right to warfare. In considering this, my eyes fell upon Sheila Sparks in the seat opposite my aisle. She was a first period student whose lank figure offered my mind a manner of diversion through the period. She gave a perfect sense of being a passive receiver of pleasure with a heightened sensitivity to the possibilities of pleasure. I had students who vied for my recognition and flattered my authority. But she was not among them. I had students who were troops in the long march for position in America. But she was not among them. Sheila Sparks wanted no part in the long march; for the flux of history had made her nerve endings extraordinarily sensitive to pleasure, and therefore she had passed beyond the need for conflict in war or social struggle. Gunfire and shouted slogans would have screeched upon her consciousness as the sound of an air raid siren in the midst of murmurs during intercourse.

"Let us say," Yancey suggested, "that you have outfitted yourself a fine house on a large piece of real estate. Fine wines are stocked in your cellar. Hand carved furniture lies in your living room. Around your property is a wall to protect your fine possessions. One day you are looking out your window and you see a man crossing your wall to come and kill you and take your possessions. You watch him and he comes a bit closer. The longer you watch, the closer he approaches. My question: At what point, my young friends, are you going to do something?"

"Black people will do it now . . . now . . . Now," shouted the black student as he rose and sat down for punctuation.

The political cortex of my brain was pounding as I spoke, "Mr. Yancey, you must consider whether the possessions of the United States can be best defended by walls and guns, or negotiations with the people who are on the far side of that wall. If we enrage the world, a wall becomes useless as well as any attempt to kill all who come against us."

John Yancey left his position behind the massive lectern to confront the evidence with his full body. Perhaps he believed that all people knew the positions and qualities of his scars as well as himself. Perhaps he believed his broken body was hallowed and would not be defiled by dissent. Finally, perhaps he expected for a moment to settle this conflict with the peace people as he had with the Korean Kommies, by simply bellowing until they could not bear his spectacle and retreated. Yancey glared at me as he said, "Sir, wouldn't you stop a man from stealing the very rewards of your long day of effort?"

"My Lord didn't."—A new voice from the rear portion of the hall, not a Southern voice, a clipped and exasperated tone. "He was dying, and they threw dice for his clothes, and it didn't bother him."

I turned in my seat and my gaze followed the man. *Jesus Christ, a long-tall-hard-rapping-chain-smoking-slang-spewing-anti-war-man-of-the-cloth.* I had not laid eyes on one since I last drove to San Francisco for a Joan Baez meeting in the Glide Methodist Church near Fillmore. He wore a black armband around the sleeve of his mackinaw covering the clerical collar

and vest. At all times he displayed two cigarettes while he was talking, a lighted one in his right hand, and an unlighted one in his left. Intricately he worked his cigarettes to an advantage by jabbing the rhythm of his words at Yancey with the unlighted one and then drawing on the lighted one with such intensity that the room kept silence.

"My stomach curdles at you." The sweep of his accusing hand did not stop with Yancey, but continued its course to include myself. "I came wearing a black armband to place myself in community with you. And I have been made to sit through discussions of the best means for protecting property. I am not a real estate man. What interest do I take in your ideas about walls? My only property is my life, and it is made worthless when other lives are wasted in defense of my own."

The high school students on the front row were turned toward his voice, and he was obviously carrying them in assent for some raised their hands in the sign of the spread fingers and some softly murmured "Awllll right now." Among them (I could not deny) were those who sat throughout my history class unmoved by the factual content of American treachery and brutality which I laid before them as a feast to nourish their ardour. Excitement ran through those who earlier this week refused to expend energy in a four page comparison of Diem and Thieu. I felt a seething hostility toward this man's easy way with their passions.

John Yancey did too, for he bawled, "And what will you make do for a church when the Communists board up your doors?"

"I don't need a building, I just need people, and there are plenty of them to come by."

As he spoke his answer, this preacher would charge Yancey by walking rapidly down the aisle only to reverse himself with his final word so his back blunted Yancey's return.

"How will you get people to believe Jesus when propaganda is spread all around?"

"I won't teach them by killing them in his name."

"You won't teach them at all after the Communists come because you're the first kind of person they'll kill against the wall."

"That is all that I expect. A violent death does not exempt me from concerning myself over the quality of my life as long as I may possess life."

This acceptance of the idea of death without a final barrage of gunshot into the faces of the oppressors outraged John Yancey, "And sir, you would let us all be killed to serve your ideals."

"I would be killed as only my Lord Jesus Christ was killed, because he could do no other in answer to his love for the world."

"And, sir, I love the members in my family and would not see them killed," roared Yancey.

"I cannot love the members of my family by killing the members of other families."

"Father, I sincerely wish you could have spoken with some of the men I knew who died for this country in the several wars recently past."

"My Lord died for no country, and yet for every country."

These fiery men of God possessed a divine obstinacy. Had they been present at the Reformation, and the Inquisition as well as at this Moratorium? The intricate rationality which I practiced would have fared with him no better than John Yancey's sentimental militarism. Now my students were moving under his words as they had never moved under mine. The girl of erotic vibrations I have earlier mentioned was standing and forcing her question upon Yancey: "Mr. Yancey, sir, will you try to explain why 42% of those who die are black soldiers?"

The figure was considerably wrong, but *why not say 92%? We're all among friends here. The government people allow themselves their fabrications, and at our get togethers we have our exaggerations.* A glimmer of pleasure shone from Yancey's scarred face. I felt certain he had suddenly found occasion which called upon his war record. Whenever he had run for minor office, he had so often printed a full page montage of clippings overlaid ribbons, his old bayonet, a grenade, and Presidential letters. ARKANSAN SHOWS HOW IT'S DONE.

"You can tell by this old body of mine," Yancey said, "that I've been wounded eight different times and might be becoming a bit short tempered. But I've learned a truth from the bullets in me—a casualty (and I don't see the justice in assigning a color to a dead man) is simply a man who couldn't stay alive."

"My Lord chose to die." The preacher was pacing, pivoting, and talking once again.

"And the Communists would choose to see all the Christians die."

"I would be killed rather than kill in the name of my Lord."

"The Communist state don't make room for the Lord."

"My Lord doesn't gain souls through the weaponry of this country."

The rhythm of the exchange between the soldier and the preacher remained as constant as if they were not creating their sentences, but merely reading aloud to one another what I have written here. Once begun, no valid resolution concludes their dialogue. This time John Yancey will not make a final assault toward the preacher swinging his weapon above his head and yalloooing for blood. YANCEY'S BOTTLE AND CORK is the most stylish and profitable liquor store to be found in the Little Rock suburbs. Nor will they converge at some distant point unseen by them and me. Yancey has too often won against death ever to comprehend dying upon a cross; the preacher ascribes far too much significance to the cross to consider shooting himself free of it. So they go on for infinity. Occasionally, at odd moments I find them.

"If you are killed, how will the world know what you believed?" roared Yancey.

The preacher made several rapid punctuations in the air with the unlighted cigarette and said, "They will know precisely by my dying."

highway

matt deweling

AL TRACKEN picked his nose with his left hand, the right thumb sticking up above the road as a car back seat empty arrowed towards him. The grill licking up the air panting the hungry machine, while its driver the man staring doped forward at the distant horizon heaven, appeared to fix on the bugs spattered the windshield. His wife, Al guessed hoping she'd run off with a hairy cock—but looking at the man and then looking into her iron womb mouth and detergent ad eyes—, his wife had everything over control with her map tucked between her legs and her body in tension relaxation—maybe move once or twice an hour—and the man, he almost, he *did* shoot a quick glance at Al but remembering his wife out of the corner of his eye, focused again on the horizon bugs spattered. The moving monster shoot passed in a mock display of power. Al already drop his thumb and took a look at the bugger on his left forefinger nail. "I'm still alive" he said as another huge machine slopped over the road ignoring his thumb goosing the heavens.

Lo, ahead on the highway a car with manufactured flowers glued all over. His thumb grew relaxed, the lowerlip curled up nodding knowledge. The promise car approached a hand came out the window with a V sign growing on it, as the gas eater shot past down the way he might someday go. "Fucking, Fucking, Fucking V sign."

A few inches of sun later a car slowed down, stopped actually up ahead, and, as Al grabbed his bags and mind-wandered up the road, the car smoked off without him amid imagined laughter. Al, Al cursed picked up a rock as the car zoomed ten stones-throws away. "I'll wait til the sun's over that barn, then take ultimate action."

Couple years ago Al writes a sign saying "I'm the good samaritan" but the ride was a web of silence on the awful abstraction, so he flagged down cars and did now til his pride beckoned him not to jump out of the way. Another same metal cunt and tame cock again in a shiny new sucker scooted up the drive, Al leaned out and spit splat on its windshield. A shocked face, a turn of the head backwards to see what thing could have blarred the air-conditioner drone, then, yes the windshield wipers swung into action.

"She-it" screamed Al Tracken, messenger of the Hun, breast fed, school trained, mind fucked then back again, "shit shit shit. I can read their self-regenerating shit. I must I see escalate my counter offense," he thought and smelled the beauty of his armpit. "The sun commands above the barn that from this robot wilderness shall rise one that smells grossly of hair and snot." Breathing in the air inflating his chest expanding in honest anger, growing like a wonder bread commercial, he, casting away the pebble meant for the next windshield, ripped up a boulder, smashing it with fire crushing stopping busting smoking the once zooming vehicle that attempted to pass him by. There, there it lay sprawled on its back, wheels faintly moving which another smartly chosen rock of destruction put an end to.

Mushrooming high above the trees, his puny clothes a shred on the distant ground, he stood in nude splendor, flexing Atlas like, an Atlas who had taken too much shit. The first cop car was squashed underfoot, the second picked up and cast into the Gulf of Mexico. Then striding majestically, spitting towns into a flood, farting hurricanes, off he went letting his feet step freely.

St. Louis loomed ahead as he glanced out over the Atlantic, growing at a fantastic rate, hands brushing away clouds, toes finding the mississippi gutter, stopped a moment, crouched to shit on the great metropolis. Then, hair aflame hands outstretched, chest beating against the winds, cock pulsing a jet of sperm arched over the land, eclipsing the sun, drowning the monuments of Washington.

The spinning earth knocked him backward, falling, his back thundered against the rib of the Rockies, his head resting in the surf at Santa Monica. Up again he rose, head reeling dizzy. "I've got to get off this fucking ball" he only knew, watching his toes trying to get a hold on. He jumping to the moon, danced across Venus Saturn Jupiter Pluto as stepping stones out of the solar system disappearing beyond the stars.

at the center
thom gunn

1

What place is this
              Cracked wood steps led me here.
The gravelled roof is fenced in where I stand.
But it is open, I am not confined
By weathered boards or barbed wire at the stair,
From which rust crumbles black-red on my hand.
If it is mine. It looks too dark and lined.

What sky
        A pearly damp grey covers it
Almost infringing on the lighted sign
Above Hamm's Brewery, a huge blond glass
Filling as its component lights are lit.
You cannot keep them. Blinking line by line,
They brim beyond the scaffold they replace.

2

What is this steady pouring that
                    Oh, wonder.
The blue line bleeds and on the gold one draws.
Currents of image widen, braid, and blend
—Pouring in cascade over me and under—
As one all-river. Fleet it does not pause,
The sinewy flux flows without start or end.
What place is this
             And what is it that broods
Barely beyond its own creation's course,
And not abstracted from it, not the Word,
But overlapping like the wet low clouds
The rivering images—their unstopped source,
Its roar unheard from being always heard.

What am
        Though in the river, I abstract
Fence, word, and notion. On the stream at full
A flurry, where the mind rides separate!
But this brief cresting, sharpened and exact,
Is fluid too, is open to the pull
And on the underside twined deep with it.

3

Terror and beauty in a single board.
The rough grain in relief—a tracery
Fronded and ferned, of woods inside the wood.
Splinter and scar—I saw them too, they poured.
White paint and the overhanging sky:
The flow-lines faintly traced or understood.

Later, downstairs and at the kitchen table,
I look round at my friends. Toward light we move
Like foam. We started Choosing long ago
—Clearly and capably as we were able—
Hostages from the pouring we are of.
The faces are as bright now as fresh snow.

                                    LSD, Folsom Street

This ballad is included in notes which Kesey jotted down during the last few hours of his four and one-half-months confinement on marijuana possesion charges. *Cut the Motherfuckers Loose* is also the title of a mixed-media book he has worked on intermittently since they cut the m——r loose.

cut the motherfuckers loose

ken kesey

Drunk tank full to overflowing
Motherfuckers wall to wall
Coming twice as fast as going
Heads get big and the tank gets small.

Dominoes slapping on the table
Bloods playing bones in tank next door.
Bust a bone if you be able
Red Death stick it good some more.

Three days past my kickout time
Ask to phone but don't got the juice.
And crime times crime just equals more crime
Cut the motherfuckers loose.

SHERIFF OFFICE

50.00

-6-65 ID 43115

IV

SHERIFF'S OFFICE
SAN MATEO CO.

1-6-65 ᴰ 43115

V

Will I make the Christmas kickout?
Will commissary come today?
Will they take my blood or take my good time?
Or just rip my guts away?

Some snitch has found my fucking outfit.
They've staked a bull up at the still.
They've found the pot sprouts I was sprouting
At the bottom of the hill.

They've punched my button, pulled my covers,
Blown my cool and ruint my ruse
They rehabilitated *this* boy
So cut this motherfucker loose.

And the fish that angles for the bull.
Let him off his heavy rod
And you that suckers the gavel banger
Cut him loose from playing God.

Back off from Johnson all you peace freaks
So he'll back off from Vietnam
Cut loose the squares, cut loose the hippies
Cut loose the dove cut loose the bomb.

You the finger on the trigger
You, the hand that weaves the noose
You, you hold the knife of freedom
Cut all the motherfuckers loose.

ECLIPSE
ONE NIGHT LAST WEEK,
AS THE SHADOW OF OUR WORLD
SLID ACROSS THE FACE OF THE MOON
I STOOD WITH MY ARM FULL OF JADE, MY FATHER'S ELDEST
THE CREATER OF NEW THEOLOGIES.
WE JUST HEARD THE NEWS ABOUT THE NEW MARTYR:
I WONDER HOW THE PEOPLE FEEL,
IN BERKLEY AND IN PALO ALTO...
HERE ARE MEN WHO DRIVE THROUGH TOWN
WITH THEIR BRIGHTS ON,
SO THERE CAN BE NEW SONGS AND A NEW WILDERNESS
TO SING THEM IN
OUR HISTORY HAS GROWN TOP HEAVY
AND WE ARE FALLING INTO THE VOID.
SOMEONE'S BEEN MESSING WITH THE COSMIC CONTROLS,
THERE'S A NEW MAN WORKING THE LIGHT SHOW—
AND WE'LL NEVER BE THE SAME.
DECISIONS ARE STILL BEING MADE THOUGH,
MY TRUE LOVER HAS LOST HER SENSE OF AWE—
DISCARDED IT SOMEWHERE BETWEEN THE ROPE SWING
AND THE NEW BRIDGE:
CONSCIOUSNESS IS ONE AND WHEN I WEEP,
MY BEARD TAKES HOLD OF THE TEARS
HIDES THEM AND WON'T LET THEM GO.
IT TAKES SO LITTLE TO FEEL SO MUCH:
GOD STICKS A SWORD THROUGH THE TOP OF MY SKULL,
RUNS THE BLADE DOWN MY BACKBONE
AND EXITS WITH A CHUCKLE.
LONLINESS IS JUST THE DEVIL, THE CAUSE OF ALL CRIME:
THE TRUE SAINT IS SCHIZOID NEVER ALONE,
NEVER IN NEED OF EVIL.
THERE WERE NIGHTS WHEN THE WALLS BREATHED DEEPLY
WHEN I TAPPED MY HAND ON A ZEBRA SKIN DRUM
AND HEARD THE ECHOES SIX MONTHS LATER.
YOU CAN WALK IN WITH A HEAD FULL OF WORDS
AND END UP WITH A VOICE:
BECOME FASCINATED WITH ECLIPSES AND LIVES OF DISASTER
JESSE JAMES, AND MARQUIS DE SADE,
AND OTHER LEFT HANDED HEROES:
I'D KNOW THOSE EYELIDS ANYWHERE
BRIGHT ORANGE, LIKE THE MOON AND HOVERING
OVER A WORLD OF INSANITY
AMERIKA IS BURNING; DYING MEN ARE SPEAKING
ON THE ISLAND OF OAHU
COOL JAZZ HAS LOST OUT, AND NOW WE GET TO
MOVE:
THOUGHTS AS OLD AS PERSIA FILL THE MIND,
ENLIGHTENMENT COMES TWICE IN OUR LIVING SPACE—
AT BIRTH AND AT DEATH.
MUSIC IS DISORGANIZED SOUND MAKING LOVE TO ITSELF
AND I FINALLY KNOW A SECRET—
TREES ARE NOTHING BUT THE EARTH
KICKING HER LEGS AT
THE SKY
SOLSTICE
WORDS BY JON BUCKLEY

poems by space daisy

THE THING TO DO AT COCKTAIL PARTIES
IS LIE A LOT
SAY YOU HAVE GOT MALARIA
OR CLIFFORD BROWN'S LAST SECRET SESSION ON TAPE
SAY YOU PERSONALLY THINK LSD IS OVERRATED
SAY ANYTHING THAT COMES INTO YOUR HEAD
IT WILL NOT HELP PARTICULARLY
BUT IT IS BETTER THAN NOTHING.

N.Y. VISION ⚬⚬⚬⚬⚬
DRINKS AT THE PIERRE, PAID FOR
ENTIRELY WITH INDIANHEAD PENNIES
CALLING FOR OUR TOWN CAR, BEING DRIVEN
TO BATTERY PARK WHERE WE SIT ON THE GRASS AND
KISS KISS KISS KISS KISS.

L.A. VISION ⚬⚬⚬⚬⚬
STONED, DRIVING DOWN SUNSET WITH
ALL THE SHIRELLES IN THE BACK SEAT
GOING "CHEAT, CHEAT" VERY SOFT
AND I SEE YOU AND YELL ACROSS THE STREET
"WHEN YOU SEE ME IN MISERY, C'MON, BABY, SEE ABOUT ME"
AND YOU SAY "YEAH, YEAH" AND LEAP IN BLAP
WE GOT US A SUNROOF.

the contrariness of the
mad farmer

wendell berry

I AM DONE with apologies. If contrariness is my
inheritance and destiny, so be it. If it is my mission
to go in at exits and come out at entrances, so be it.
I have planted by the stars in defiance of the experts,
and tilled somewhat by incantation and by singing,
and reaped, as I knew, by luck and Heaven's favor,
in spite of the best advice. If I have been caught
so often giggling at funerals, that was because
I knew the dead were already slipping away,
preparing a comeback, and can I help it?
And if at weddings I have gritted and gnashed
my teeth, it was because I knew where the bridegroom
had sunk his manhood, and knew it would not
be resurrected in a piece of cake. "Dance" they told me, .
and I stood still, and then while they stood
quiet in line at the gate of the Kingdom, I danced.
"Pray" they said, and I laughed, covering myself
in the earth's brightnesses, and then stole off gray
into the midst of a revel, and prayed like an orphan.
When they said "I know that my Redeemer liveth,"
I told them "He's dead." And when they told me
"God is dead," I answered "He goes fishing every day
in the Kentucky River. I see Him often."
When they asked me would I like to contribute
I said no, and when they had collected
more than they needed, I gave them as much as I had.
When they asked me to join them I wouldn't,
and then went off by myself and did more
than they would have asked. "Well, then" they said
"go and organize the International Brotherhood
of Contraries," and I said "Did you finish killing

everybody who was against peace?" So be it,
Going against me, I have heard at times a deep harmony
thrumming in the mixture, and when they ask me what
I say I don't know. It is not the only or the easiest
way to come to the truth. It is one way.

henry plummer's grave

tiger thompson

The first gold was washed in Montana
In the year of eighteen-sixty-two
And a wild, hungry swarm came down on Bannack
While the Devil sat waitin' for his due.

It won't take so long from the Big Hole
If you don't mind a hot and dusty ride
'Til you come to the ghost town of Bannack
Where the outlaw sheriff, Henry Plummer, died.

There's nothin' like new gold to start the killin'
Soon Grasshpper Creek was runnin' red,
When a miner struck it lucky at the diggins
He was pannin' out a price upon his head.

The people stood around and talked in whispers,
On every face a troubled frown.
Human life was gettin' cheap in Bannack
When Plummer rode his stallion into town.

He sat so tall and handsome in the saddle,
His words brought new courage to the men,
When he bowed from his stirrups to the ladies
They dropped their eyes and blushed, and smiled on him.

The people chose this man to be their sheriff,
And heard his solemn oath to keep their trust,
But little did they know how Henry Plummer
Would drag the name of Bannack in the dust.

There was gunsmoke on the trail to Salt Lake City
And many a long-line skinner, stout and bold,
Lay dead beside his looted treasure wagon
To satisfy the sheriff's lust for gold.

The vigilantes met in secret council
And judgment was passed by candle flame
As witness after witness named the sheriff
The man behind the bloodshed and the shame.

He made his final plea before his judges
And was told that this day would be his last:
"Well, Gentlemen, if that is your decision,
"Then build your scaffold high and drop me fast."

The night when Henry died upon the gallows,
The town looked up and put aside its fears,
But many a snow-white pillow there in Bannack
Was dampened by a maiden's flowin' tears.

And now they say the ghost of Henry Plummer
Comes riding home each evenin' at sundown
To share the night with rattlesnakes and spiders
—The only livin' things in Bannack town.

Up the Beaverhead the Indian summer's dyin'
Where the tall green wil'ows used to wave
And the dry yellow grass is a-sighin'
In the wind over Henry Plummer's grave.
                              (Postscript)
But the looting never faltered in Montana
And here's a thing that you should know for sure:
That beside the ruling mob called Anaconda,
Poor Henry was a clumsy amateur.

And not abstracted from it, not the Word,
But overlapping like the wet low clouds
The rivering images—their unstopped source,
Its roar unheard from being always heard.

What am
              Though in the river, I abstract
Fence, word, and notion. On the stream at full
A flurry, where the mind rides separate!
But this brief cresting, sharpened and exact,
Is fluid too, is open to the pull
And on the underside twined deep with it.

XVI

IN DREAMS
AND IN REALITY
THE BUFFALO
COMES.

BUFFALO!
BISON ARCHANGEL
FURRY COCK ERUPTING FERTILE
IN THE FURRY CRESCENT
SPURTING SONS AND DAUGHTERS, LAUGHING SO
HARD THE GROUND HUMS.
HIS BLOOD IS BLACK AND IT SLOUCHES THROUGH HIS VEINS
HER BLOOD IS BLACK AND IT SPLATTERS IN THE AFTERBIRTH—
HERDS OF BUFFALO COMING IN THE SUN.
THE MEAT IS WILD AND NOT FOR THE TONGUE—
NO MORE INDIAN-HEAD NICKELS.
THEY'VE ALL STEPPED OFF THE COIN,
ASCENDED INTO SPACE AND TIME.
LOYALTY TO THE ETERNAL CIRCLE
DEMONS IN THE WRITING HAND
BUFFALO-BIRTH REBUILD THE HERDS
HEAR WITHOUT WORDS AND SING WITHOUT VOICES
SHEATHE YOUR FEET IN LEATHER HIDES
AND WATCH ORION WALK HIS WAY AROUND THE SKY
THE BUFFALO COMES
AND WE'RE RIDING
ON HIS
HUMP.

XVII

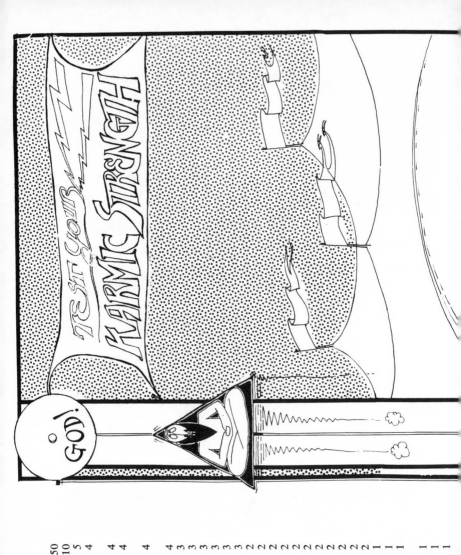

Test your **KARMIC STRENGTH**

GOD!

Find god in India	50
Search for god in India	10
See the White Light	5
Picket the Berkeley *Barb*	4
Beaten by Hell's Angels at a demonstration	4
Ball your mate's lover	4
Make real *music* with an amplified instrument	4
Your commune is busted by a health inspector	4
Peddle the Berkeley *Barb*	3
Watch your mate ball others	3
Bombed by right-wingers	3
Beaten by cops at a demonstration	3
Lead a psychodrama marathon	3
Experience astral projection	3
Original Haight-Ashbury resident	2
Subscribe to Berkeley *Barb*	2
Provoke Roy Kepler to violence	2
Get arrested at a demonstration	2
Attend psychodrama marathon	2
Continue yoga lessons	2
Enjoy meditating daily	2
Eat yogurt	2
Survive a macrobiotic diet	2
Enjoy group sex	2
Turn on, but keep drinking	1
Play an amplified instrument	1
Live in a commune	1
Like eating yoghurt	1
Go to your first feelie with pure motives	1
Read the Berkeley *Barb*	1
Give up writing to make movies	1

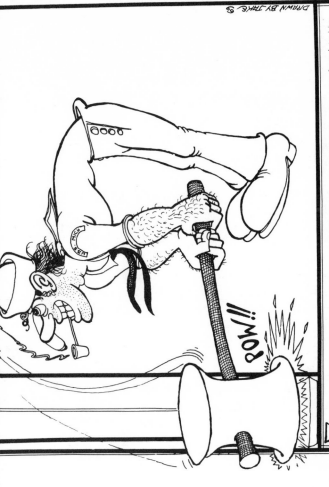

Drop acid — 1
Smoke grass — 1
Go on a macrobiotic diet — 1
Begin yoga lessons — 1
Meditate daily — 1
Participate in group sex — 1
Attend a psychodrama minithon — 1
Attend a demonstration — 1
Cancel subscription to the *New Republic* — 1
Throw away your bra — 1
Turn on, drop booze — 1
Look for love in the Haight-Ashbury — 1
See the *Graduate* more than twice — -1
Be a junkie — -1
Join YAF — -5

You've just been mugged while giving away flowers on Haight Street. You were forced to hire an incredibly hairy rock band for your daughter's debutante party, and the lead singer has just decamped to the potting shed with your wife. The same tired faces you've seen for thirty years on the society pages, drink in hand, looking pasted, are now pictured doing the same thing in see-through blouses and Cassini blazers. Your bridge club is going to have a "mod party" and you're being driven up the wall because you don't know what's in, today, and what's not, and is *that* what's got you by the throat, baby, as you teeter, trembling, on the brink of the Aquarian age?

Be at peace. Through the auspices, courtesy and everlasting patience of the editors of the magazine, you can now rate your own hipness in the relative security of your own home. Free *you*, you can now rate your own hipness in the relative security of your own home. If you score low, don't worry. Trends are circular things and your time may come again, with a sort of awful inevitability.

START HERE!

POW!!!

DRAWN BY JAKE

a kentuckian
at the wallace rally (1967)

gurney norman

I AM BEGINNING these notes at the Cow Palace, writing on the inside front cover of a piece of political literature titled "Wake Up, America," while listening to Sam Smith's American Independent Party Band trying to warm up this gym full of supporters of George Corley Wallace, the Presidential candidate.

I am amazed by this band. There they are, up in front of everybody, Sam Smith and his boys—drummer, trumpet player, a chick named Lisa Taylor among them—tuning up, getting ready to sing what has been billed in the advance publicity as "country music."

Lisa Taylor singing country music?

A combo in which the predominant instruments are a trumpet and a drum, playing *hill*billy?

That's what the signs all said. Country music before the good old country-boy candidate hisself gets up to say his piece.

The first number is that famous old hillbilly song, "Hello, Dolly." Only this time it isn't Hello, Dolly. It isn't even Hello, Lyndon. What Sam Smith and his American Independent Party Band are in all good faith and seriousness, with no sense of irony or tongue-in-cheek, *singing* to us is "Hello, GEORGIE!"

And my mind is truly blown.

For here I have come all the way to the Cow Palace in the expectation of seeing a charismatic Politician From My Native South touch the spleen of ten thousand earthy commoners filling the place with delirium, pandemonium, riots, perhaps even a blood-sacrifice on the stage before our very eyes. Visions of Huey Long and the young Happy Chandler fill my mind, and my ears are made to positively itch by the promise of some true string music from the hill country.

And what do I find at the Cow Palace but Sam Smith and his boys twanging "Hello, GEORGIE!"

Joan Larimore

It's enough to make Pearl Bailey and Carol Channing embrace and share a good old-fashioned integrated female cry.

It's also enough to make me realize that I have misunderstood George Wallace all along.

I've given him more credit than he deserves for being real.

In spite of his madness, I've had a grudging affection for old George ever since he stood in the schoolhouse door. Not that we've ever agreed on much—except, perhaps, that bureaucracy is everybody's enemy. I'm drawn to Wallace simply because he's the most interesting candidate around this year. The bull-pup aspect of him appeals to me. He's tenacious, always pushing at his own frontiers. I like that. Perhaps it could be said that I have come near to forgiving George his villainy simply because he's such an entertainment.

Or was.

Till I finally saw him in person.

Saw the reality of his following.

Heard the reality of his musical band.

Now the most that I can feel about Wallace's whole plastic scene is a sadness so large that my sudden boredom with it is transcended.

Wallace has about as much charisma as the Flying Nun.

If the "anarchists" had stayed home that Sunday, that fact would have been so clear to the world at large that I would be embarrassed to remark upon it now. Some loud and energetic left-wing kids turned out to heckle George, I guess hoping to somehow undermine the man and the shallow points he tries to make. As anyone could have predicted, the effect was precisely the opposite. The anarchists, as George calls them, yelled "Seig heil!" and suddenly the good, decent folk who'd turned out for the speakin' had something to yell about themselves, something to get their own adrenalin to flowing.

But if the kids had not been there, if there had been no bearded ones to contend with, George Wallace's Cow Palace political rally would have been about as arousing, as funky, as down-home as a convention of Jaycees held at a Holiday Inn. It must be stressed, however, that the folk did not *know* their scene was not funky. They truly believed it was. The shouting match with the beards created that possibility—and allowed George Wallace to once again get away with his claim that he's an honest-to-god country boy with red-clay dirt under his fingernails and chicken gravy on his tie.

Sam Smith was allowed to get away with *his* claim that his music is country music, music from the soil, music made by the oppressed, and not the oppressor.

And all the good folk in the audience, them pipe-fitters with the calloused hands, them electricians and truck drivers and off-duty firemen, most of whom have, like myself, moved to California in the last ten years from places like Kentucky and Alabama and Oklahoma, all the good folk in the Cow Palace were allowed to go on with *their* myth that they are still men of the soil who represent America's last chance to redeem her old, lost, rural, Protestant values.

The people at the Wallace rally really believed that image of themselves. And that's why it's all so sad. Sam Smith played "Hello, Dolly," and everybody applauded like it was Hank Williams they were hearing. Sam Smith would invoke the names of people like Hank Thompson and Merle Haggard, and the folks would nod and smile, remembering, and then *go right on nodding* when Smith turned around and offered us "Ode To Billy Joe," a fake country song to begin with, played as an *instrumental* on a *trumpet!* Now and then Sam Smith would manage to say something believable, a few words resonant with leftover authenticity, words like: "Right now we'd like to get Miss Lisa Taylor back out and do another fine song for us. Let's make her welcome," and the people would nod and smile and clap and welcome Miss Lisa like she was Kitty Wells. And go right on clapping even when the song Lisa sang turned out to be "Anytime."

It was enough to make Eddy Arnold walk out of Eddie Fisher's penthouse and take the night train to Memphis, Tennessee.

But, as I think about it, maybe "Anytime" wasn't so inappropriate a song after all: "Anytime you're feeling lonely, Anytime you're feeling blue, Anytime you feel downhearted, That's the time I'll come back home to you."

For obviously that's what most of the Wallace fans are suffering from these days. Plain loneliness. Homesickness. Call it alienation if you have to. Modern jargon does not obscure the ancient fact that you can take a boy out of the country, but you can't take the country out of the boy. George Wallace is singing to all the lonesome, uprooted, transplanted and therefore homeless country boys and hillbillies all over America this year. He's saying "I'll come back home to you, oh lost vision of America," saying it on behalf of all the lonely, downhearted, blue-feeling folks who over the last decade or two have left the last place they understand and taken up in foreign countries like Fresno and Oakland and Detroit and Flint and Indianapolis and Dayton and Cincinnati.

I'm kin to a lot of people like that. In a way, I'm probably one myself. Maybe that's the reason why I can't hate the folks who support George Wallace. Why, finally, I love them a good deal. Old villainous George included.

They're the enemy now, of course. My enemy. And that convolutes the sadness one more time. Any one of them would likely have gone for my throat if he'd had any way of seeing into my mind at the Cow Palace that Sunday, the remains of my Kentucky accent notwithstanding.

I understand all that.

But I also understand how good it is to have somebody you recognize, and especially someone who seems to recognize *you,* come to visit like George does when you're stuck off in some awful foreign land like California or Michigan. For make no mistake about it, the white people from Kentucky and Alabama and Oklahoma who live in Michigan and California now are suffering, hard. It's a psychic suffering as real and as heavy and as loaded as the economic deprivation a lot of their kin folks still live with back in Appalachia, and further south. You can take a boy out of the country but you can't take the country out of the boy. That leaves him in the middle somewhere, split, schizophrenic, wounded, like a bear, furious, and dangerous as hell.

And so the question is, how do you respond when a relative that you love goes for your throat? I wish I knew. It's the thing I'm trying to figure out as I end these notes, hiding inside the headphones listening to Flatt and Scruggs, who have just finished singing "I Wonder How The Old Folks Are At Home," and are now launching into one titled "The Storm Is On The Ocean."

the perry lane papers (II): wayward girls

vic lovell

the original teenybopper

If Perry Lane was the first hippie scene, then Sally was the first teenybopper. She could not live at home, and so she came to live with us. She had violent fights with her father. No matter who she brought home, he didn't like them. She did not work in school. She was preoccupied with how and when she would lose her virginity. When her parents could no longer bear the apprehension and uproar, they gave her their blessing, and she split.

How could they keep them at home after they'd seen Perry Lane? Sally was the first, and the acknowledged leader, of a long line of teenage girls on the lam from straight society. The more adventuresome would live with us for a while, and then move on to other embryonic hippie scenes.

Others lived at home, or were new undergraduates at Stanford, where they would kiss their straight dates chastely good-night, and then come over to the Lane, get high, and ball somebody. They were cute, lively, and except for their sexual availability, which varied unpredictably, utterly useless.

We called them "nymphets," after Vladimir Nabokov's *Lolita,* which was a bestseller at the time. Having rejected their role as status symbols for their parents, they became the same for us: trailing along wherever we went, they were flamboyant proof of our capacity to corrupt the youth, and thus to affect the world from which we were alienated.

Sally was small and slight, with short blond hair and big blue eyes. She usually wore tights with a baggy sweater. She had serious arthritis, so she walked with a limp, like a wounded bird. Her appearance and style were quite different from her contemporary equivalent, who tends to be long-haired, voluptuous, quiet, and dutiful, as well as somewhat vacuous and confused.

Sally was loud, outgoing, lazy, irresponsible, demanding, and at the same time warm, lovable, and committed. She spent most of her time screwing, blowing pot, talking, and reading comic books.

Because she was just a kid, and kids need care, we found we had to change roles. The shift from corrupters of the youth to surrogate parents revealed contradictions in our style of life that have yet to be resolved. We demanded that Sally go to school, study, help with the housework, take precautions against getting pregnant, get a job. She rebelled against us in turn. "You don't understand little kids," she would tell us, and then she would sulk. We would insist that she was not a little kid. Although we were quite industrious—reading, writing, painting, going to graduate school, and creating happenings of various kinds, our claims did not quite ring true, for we could offer no convincing justification for doing anything, and she seemed to sense this.

I would come home, and she would be sitting in the living room. "Hey Uncle Vic," she'd say. "Let's get stoned." She would be surrounded by her nymphet following, plus whatever strange outcasts she had managed to pick up during her daily wanderings. They would already be stoned, so stoned that it would take half an hour to get them out of the house, because by the time the message had gotten through to everybody, half of them would have forgotten it.

"Everybody out, I have to study for my exams." "You never have any fun," she'd say. "I have to study, that's all." "Why?" she would want to know. "Study tomorrow." "Look," I'd tell her, "I have to study now, then later I'll come out and play. You guys have to go now, or I won't get anything done." "We don't have anyplace to go," she would complain. "We don't have anything to do." "Go over to Kesey's." "Ken's trying to write, and Faye's mad at me."

Our relationship became a crazy parody of the traditional teenager-versus-parent dialectic. We tried to restrict her, held back spending money, and disapproved of her boyfriends—who were either uptight, straight and slumming, or utterly degenerate. Our love for her was prevented from getting out of hand by senseless quarrels, which created a safe distance between us.

We'd be getting decked out and stoned in preparation for a peace march or a protest against the House Unamerican Activities Committee. We'd tell her she couldn't go, and there would be a scene. "I want to go demonstrate," she would whine. "You can't go demonstrate," we would tell her, "you have to stay home and study so you know what you are demonstrating against." The trouble was, we did not know ourselves. Our political dissent was intuitive and inarticulate. Sally flunked out of school.

Naturally, since nothing would do but the trip, the whole trip, and nothing but the trip, she got pregnant. There was ideological debate about whether she should have the abortion: naturalists turned against pragmatists, the latter winning out. Money was collected and she was taken to Tijuana. The abortionist asked a few routine questions. Was she taking any medication? She lied, and said no, though she was taking cortisone for her arthritis. Being slight of hip, she had to stay overnight to have her cervix dilated. Cortisone creates a susceptibility to infection. When Sally got back from Tijuana, she was sick, and had to be taken to the hospital.

The incident upset everybody, with the apparent exception of Sally. She never lost her cool. She lived by a maxim that later became one of our slogans: "Everything serves to further."

If the house was a mess, a man had threatened to kill her, the rent was unpaid with no hope in sight, the heat was on and people she knew were getting busted, the icebox and larder empty, it didn't matter, even if everyone else was freaking out.

If you tried to shake her equanimity you got put in your place summarily. Gleefully embracing the chaos, she would say: "Isn't this *bad!* Isn't it *terrible!* You want to smoke some dope?" If you objected, she would tell you that you were a drag and a fink and give you a look of total disgust.

She moved away from the Lane, because she felt stifled by it. We decided that the younger generation was going to the dogs. For want of anything better to do, she got married, and several of the nymphets followed suit. Her husband was a beautiful hypochondriac food freak, who looked like those pictures of muscle builders you see on the walls of men's gymnasiums and acted as gentle and passive as a lamb. They moved into a commune with his friends and got their bread by dealing dope. There were the usual hangups about who was going to whom, but other than that they seemed as happy as clams.

The younger set made sufficient inroads into the local high school scene to attract the attention of the authorities. An Atherton father missed his darling daughter one night and called the police, giving them the license number of the car she had left in.

They found the car parked in front of the house where Sally and her cohorts lived, walked in, and found dope everywhere they looked. They tore apart the stove, the icebox, the mattresses, and the paneling and found more dope. They busted everybody. The thoroughly crazy beatnik who had picked up the missing Atherton girl got beaten to a pulp after the cops took him to the station. They had to teach him once and for all not to mess with the honor of Atherton maidens.

Sally did three months at the county jail in Redwood City. She was unregenerate and defiant, and her morale never faltered. In the jail's psychotherapy group, she announced that some of her best friends were psychotherapists, and proselytized for marijuana as the ultimate medicine to get your head straight.

We visited her every week, no more than three visitors allowed, and fifteen minutes apiece. You had to talk over telephones, with a pane of glass between you, the whole conversation no doubt monitored by the man. We were strangely embarrassed, and felt awkward when we talked.

Released, she was more careful, but otherwise unchanged. We saw less of her, because the people she lived with were possessive, and she wanted to have her own thing. One night someone called us on the telephone to tell us that Sally had been killed in an auto accident.

Your first experience of the death of a loved contemporary has an impact entirely different from the deaths of grandparents, parents, and respected elders. Once in a great while we had asked, "What will become of us?" usually lying in bed after a particularly good screw. We had tried, unsuccessfully, to imagine ourselves greyhaired and feeble, still living together, blowing pot, and playing with our heads. Our speculations were inhibited by the unelaborated and unquestioned doctrine of Here and Now.

Shaggy-though-suited hippies walked with uptight straights past her coffin, wondering at the incomprehensible direction that life had so abruptly taken. We had our own wake, and got supremely stoned. "Sally," Ken Kesey sagely pronounced, "couldn't *possibly* have grown up. Can you imagine her grown up? Can you?" He did not ask how any of us would grow up, nor what an adult would look like, if his style and commitments ruled out a place in straight society.

Having no answer nor vision to deal with this dilemma (which is now even more serious), Sally had faithfully enacted to its tragic end the myth about the fate of wayward girls: the wages of sin are death. Had she not been informed from an early age that freedom meant irresponsibility, laziness, and recklessness? You can try it if you want, because it's that kind of country, but you won't like it. Go ahead. Everybody does, at least for a little while. You'll be back, spirit conveniently broken, ass kicked by entrenched social reality.

But there is, of course, a point of no return. For months, even years afterward, the surviving nymphets had that hobbling gait we knew so well. They limped like wounded birds, ass stuck out behind to balance, as if possessed by Sally's unquiet spirit.

letter from marty

Children complain that their parents just do not remember what it is like to be young. One of the clichés tossed back by the parents is the wistful "We remember too well." And another wall goes up as each generation crawls back into itself: on one hand the future is enticing and on the other the past once was. Today I was thrown back into that past, and it was surprising to discover that it is not at all hard to be fifteen again.

In the morning mail, along with the sale circulars, bills, and invitations to children's birthday parties, was a magazine which I glanced at while drinking coffee with my neighbors. While I talked about babies and school conferences and homework and thumbed through the pages a headline suddenly leaped at me: "The Perry Lane Papers: The Original Teenybopper," by Vic Lovell.

First reaction: Stash it until the neighbors leave. Finally they go. Read it now! Is it the same Vic? Is it me? Fast perusal. I'm not Sally—relief. And then? Nymphet? My God! Well, maybe I was.

I made a fast trip down the hall to a book that had been given me some ten years ago: Jack Kerouac's *On The Road*. With an inscription:

Marty, all my best wishes for your future well being. Like have a ball and all that type of thing. Have been digging this volume myself, I think it has much to say and much to be heard. . . . We miss you around the pad, like you always had us guessing and still do, but anyway be cool, have kicks, and make it back and see us all sometime.
(signed) Vic Lovell

On The Road had been a wedding present and for the ten years that went into a failure of a marriage I carted that book around the world with me.

I met Vic in a coffee shop on University Avenue when I was fifteen. I was just out of the hospital after driving a car off a cliff and got the shakes so bad in Weston's that I could hardly drink my coffee. To calm me down, the man sitting next to me talked some and wound up inviting me to an election-return party. I do not remember turning on the election returns that night, but I do remember getting drunk for the first time in my life.

We were sitting on the floor at Perry Lane and I was drinking rotgut wine and pretending to be unimpressed. There was baroque music and conversation, all of which I found difficult to follow. I do remember insisting that I be home by ten, and Vic got me there. I spent the night throwing up and the morning hearing how I was never to see that person again.

My parents never did see him because he always sent a friend of his to pick me up while he waited in the car with the friend's wife. God knows why he ever bothered to go out with me at all. I was apt to get drunk and pass out or throw up or cry or all at the same time.

I was fifteen and super-impressed at dating a Stanford senior, and I enjoyed cleaning up the place that he lived in. It was a silly little room behind a big house and Vic went to great pains never to let me know that there had been girls other than me staying there. He was a kind man even then. I remember giving him an ashtray I had swiped from a bar in Paris. It was my very favorite thing. When he left the room, he moved into the house with somebody named Dirk, and Perry Lane became "the pad" and the place to go. It was furnished with mattresses from the Salvation Army and I covered them with denim. The next year was spent in telling my parents I was going to the library and then arriving at the pad, where I contributed nothing but boredom. I would take my boyfriend of the moment there and Vic's approval was more important than an okay from any of my friends. He approved of only one, a sailor who eventually became a psychiatrist. My good friends took to making appearances at the pad. It was easier than necking at the Cactus Gardens. And we all had to have some place to go, to be part of the grownup world where we could do what we wanted when we wanted. My convent girlfriends and I would spend hours jabbering about "truth" and "life" and at the pad they would listen. Just as though they had never heard it before or never said it themselves.

We would cut school, change our convent oxfords for white bucks and go to the city where it was easy to meet men. I have since talked about those times with the same girls and we always end up by asking, "how did we survive?" Because we were, as Vic said, hung up on sex. We would neck for hours but anything else was what "bad girls" did. Since we specialized in men and not boys, it is surprising that we came out of it with only bruises.

School was where we went to recover from hangovers; home was where we went to sleep and change clothes; the pad was where we went to live. We all read the *Prophet* and Allen Ginsberg and none of us dared to say we did not understand all the words.

Once in a while someone who did not really belong would find his way to the pad. He expected to find nude dancing girls or she expected panting men. What was more apt to be found was a slightly tacky cottage in the trees with people wandering about having babies and writing papers.

At a party a boy asked me if I was a nympho and I hit him and cried and Vic told me everything was going to be all right.

Another time I said I was going to marry a soldier I had met in Paris. But I never had the nerve to show him to Perry

Lane or let him see the pad. I married him anyway, when I was seventeen, and went back to France—taking *On The Road* with me.

I wrote Perry Lane a few times but it never answered and as babies came and husbands went I rather forgot what it had been like. Then, ten years later, I went back. While driving around the hills and showing my children the places where Mama had been a little girl I found myself near something that seemed familiar. It was Perry Lane but there were no cottages in the trees left. I drove away.

A few weeks later I bumped into a man in a bar. He turned. I apologized and recognized Vic. He didn't have me placed and probably still doesn't. There have probably been lots of me's drifting in and out of pads with ashtrays and hopes. And most of us have gone away, leaving the ashtrays and hopes in the pads. But even though most of us grew up and joined the straight world, we are still what we were then.

Our clichés, "I remember too well," come as easily to us as to those who never knew Perry Lane. But we really have something to remember. I knew nice, kind, and loving people there and I thank them. I hope that when my own children reach the age when they can't tolerate me they will have an equally safe pad to which they can run, and learn, and love. Vic wished me well a long time ago, and I am very well, thank you. I suspect that it is part of his unknown doing.

response to marty

Marty, who wrote us a letter after reading the last installment of the Perry Lane Papers, hung around Perry Lane while she was a teenager during the late nineteen fifties, before the emergence of the life style for which the place later became known. If Sally was the first teenybopper, Marty was the John the Baptist to her Christ. Without the participation of the female of the species, new ways of living cannot be created, and we were hard put to find our feminine counterparts at Stanford University.

We were still undergraduates, and in our way we were as much in awe of her as she of us. She recalled that utterly fascinating bit of blossoming sexual evil who always made it with somebody else when we were in high school. *Gone With the Wind* was still doing that crazy overwhelming thing to the heads and hearts of adolescent girls, with Clark Gable striding rapaciously through their daydreams and nightmares. Meanwhile, the agreed-upon object of their waking game was to turn men on as much as possible while still remaining, at least technically, embattled in virginity until marriage. Such conduct, though thoroughly degrading for all concerned, persists even in these enlightened times. "You wouldn't like me if I gave you what you want," she says, after getting him duly aroused.

In the movie version of Terry Southern's *Candy,* our heroine is indignantly denounced by an angry authority figure: "You," he says, "are a tramp, a tart, a trollop, a . . ." Words momentarily fail him, and then comes the ultimate expletive: "A teenager." The film commemorates the inner odyssey of a generation of girls, caught between the puritanism of yesterday and the awakening sensuality of today, and floundering in the throes of an unrepressed Electra complex.

But twelve years ago, where our story starts, there was no such consciousness, no such identity, and no such commemoration. What did they do before there were teenyboppers? Recall the scenario: Daddy's Little Girl is becoming a Woman. The caterpillar was cute and the chrysalis was dreamy and comfortable, but the butterfly is an affront to his angry impotence, and vice versa. Prince Charming is waiting in the wings, awkward but eager, ready to awaken her with a kiss and steal her away, eventually forever. Father and daughter love each other not wisely but too well, which archaic passion is at once expressed by and concealed behind knock-down-drag-out fights, increasingly violent, jealous, and without apparent rhyme or reason.

She must betray him, or remain a prisoner, but how can she forgive herself for living out his jealous nightmares? One of Marty's friends used to come over, drink one glass of wine, and go into a tirade which went something like this: "Any girl who would do that with a man before she was married is a filthy pig! A pig, do you hear? Something for the gutter." She was young, pretty, and hard. If anyone gave her an argument it only goaded her on to even grosser expressions of disgust. We finally threw her out. We were tolerant of divergent points of view, but what we couldn't stand was knowing that she was going to go right out and do that very thing with some horny stranger, perhaps that same night. He would be old, straight, and anonymous: the first and foremost of the gods, disguised as a bull, a boar, or a swan, so that she would not have to know his true identity.

Marty rather resembled Sally: small blonde, independent, sharp-tongued. She had been to Europe, and spoke French. Sometimes she cleaned up the house, which was always dirty. I seem to remember her drinking homemade absinthe, a vile mixture which sat on a shelf in the kitchen, and had to be shaken every day; it was so bitter that most of us couldn't get it down. We didn't challenge her sophistication. She came across as exotic, precocious, and worldly, and we all took the trip. We sensed that she didn't make out with us because she liked us.

Several times when she came over her body was covered with cuts and bruises. She told me that her father had beaten her. I didn't know what to make of it, or perhaps I didn't want to know. Where I came from, people destroyed each other without getting physical about it. What really baffled me was that she didn't seem to mind too much. She would laugh when she told me about it. For me, it was just another example of the incomprehensible brutality of a world which had somehow wounded us all, and had to be gotten away from at any price.

There was a man somewhere, and he was in love with her, and they planned to get married. She talked about him often. For some reason, I never believed her. Then one day she ran away and got married, and that was that. Her father was an army officer, and she had met the man she married while he had been stationed in France. Her husband was an enlisted man, thus, I suppose, fulfilling both her love and her anger.

Before there were teenyboppers, there were two alternatives: get married early or become a whore.

It's twelve years later now: Christmas 1968. Marty has been divorced for about three years. She lives in the suburbs of Cupertino. Once she sends me a Christmas card; another time I meet her drinking beer in the Alley. People leave here but they usually come back. The wind of karma is no gentle breeze; it's a cyclone, throwing us out in all directions and then drawing us back towards the center.

I read Marty's letter: How much we have lived and how little we can remember. I think anxiously of the mattress covers she made that would never stay on the mattresses. This was all we had for furniture, a decor since become so common as to be tedious. Twelve years of living in circumstances difficult to put in material order. How do you keep the house straight when you are trying to find yourself?

I call, ask if I can come over, she's half asleep, says yes, and gives me directions how to get there. My brains are scrambled from too much Christmas cheer, and nerves frazzled with that undercurrent of holiday loneliness which comes from celebrating relationships past. I get lost among freeways, orchards, shopping centers, and housing projects, squinting through the rain and wipers on the windshield, looking for the one that says This Is It, Next Exit, Only One Half Mile to Go, and then finally, as always, better late than never, I get where I am going.

It's what you might call a bourgeois slum, houses all similar and packed close, but everything new and kept up. The lights in the living rooms are on, trees and shrubbery decked with multi-colored Christmas lights, sounds of people drinking and laughing. A girl runs out onto the street in front of me, and then a man runs out after her, catches her, and carries her back in on his shoulder.

The first thing I notice is that her hair isn't the same color. I wonder if I'm in the right place. It used to be blonde, and now it's red. Mine is longer, and I think I used to have a beard when last seen. So I say I'm Vic, are you Marty, and she says yes, come in, and I do.

She's wearing a long dress, or maybe it's a robe, that reaches all the way to the floor. The house is warm, comfortable, tastefully decorated and I feel good being there right away. I am offered rum in coffee, red wine, and I accept. There's a very small dog that barks a lot, and a quiet, unobtrusive cat. We sit in large, soft chairs.

Does she have any children, or is she one? There are two. They show me things, tell me what's on TV, and then go to bed. They are quite likable, neither bitchy nor wooden. We play a game that we look at each other through a cardboard tube that came inside a roll of paper. I can't stand men that try to get to me by making a big scene with the kids, Marty tells me.

She really likes having children; it's the best thing she ever did. She is going to school at the University of Santa Clara, studying English literature, or something like that. She is not interested in getting married again, at least not right away. She thinks she is happier than she has ever been before.

We try to talk about when we knew each other but we can't remember much; perhaps we don't want to. She tells me about life in the army, and about her marriage, and about what happened to her old friends. I am trying to tell her about all the things that have happened around here in the last twelve years, and speculating about what might have happened to her if she had stayed around. It's difficult to cover that much ground in one night, but we strive for some kind of bringing it all back home.

She is dubious about the movement, the psychedelic thing, the Free University, but she is interested. She thinks people ought to be able to feel alive without working at it so hard. I say yes, but we don't seem to be able to, we have a lot to overcome. We flirt a little.

Once she was having a party, and everybody drank a lot, and there was this enormous Hell's Angel, and he passed out on the couch. In the morning her little boy woke up and went out into the living room and stood staring, rapt in wonder at this gigantic male presence. After a while the man opened one glazed eye, inspected the child, and said: "My name is not Gulliver."

It is getting late. We fall to discussing young girls, yesterday and today, and their strange fates. I am getting drunk, and losing my grip on the whole thing. Suddenly she starts to play opera records, and gives me a running account of who is singing, what they are saying, and where they are in the plot: total loves, betrayals, unforseen disasters, and violent death. I have a feeling of continuity, recognition: we are all romantics at heart these days, and she is very much herself, the same as she was though much grown, and I am very glad of it. I leave, feeling that all is right with the world, because what I'm really worried about is can we grow up, without losing our humanity and our identity.

wayward girls

It is of the essence, in considering the character of our society, to remember that everything is for sale, including the people, their bodies, their souls, and the parts and fragments thereof. Systematic distortions and confusions of identity are fostered in this way. I recall once I was buying a new automobile. I was hesitant, and the salesman, who was new at the business, became momentarily flustered. "They told me," he confessed, "that I should sell myself." "I like you fine," I said, "but I'm not buying you. I'm buying a car."

There was a story they used to tell when I was young and horny. A man picks up a whore, and they go to her apartment. Upon arrival they have a drink, and then it turns out she is somehow mutilated, and has artificial members. She unstraps a wooden leg, detaches a plastic arm, and so forth. Then she asks him what he wants. He says: "You know what I want, take it off and throw it over here." The straight citizen's dirty joke is the hippy's bad acid trip, seen in vistavision and living color, vivid and tangible.

The hottest item on the market is your daughter. The only man who gives you something for nothing, Lenny Bruce used to say, is the guy who knocks her up. This is a commodity with heart, that sometimes looks at you like you were a commodity. If you try to welsh on any deals, violate any contracts, real or imaginary, hell, as they say, hath no fury. Her remedy is simple: if you want to really hurt a man, do something to his property; deliver it cheap, give it away, go over to the competition, or destroy it. Thus she will cut off her nose, or whatever, to spite your face. They've been doing it ever since Juliet fell in love with a Montague, and Helen ran off with a Trojan. If you are a southern aristocrat she will choose a black man, if you are a rightist she'll ball a leftist, if you are an intellectual she will want an outdoor man, and if you lived around here six or eight years ago she was likely to turn up on Perry Lane, there being nowhere else, at that point, to go. Once in bed with the enemy, she continues to fight on two fronts, both on your behalf and yet against you, for her new lover becomes your stand-in. Hers is the face that has launched a thousand cops.

Never underestimate the power of mythology. Since the worst thing she can do to you is get into trouble, trouble becomes a turn-on, and she grooves on catastrophe if it is staged correctly. When Sally got busted, for grass, it was the first time anyone I knew well had been in serious trouble with the law. "What was it like?" I asked her. "You know, man," she replied. "You watch television." I can see it now. The police come bounding in, their heads swiveling this way and that, like turrets on tanks, taking it all in. She and her friends with glazed eyes, watching the tropical fish in the aquarium, like dig that one man, it looks just like my father. They are so stoned they're not entirely sure the police are real. The sergeant announces that they are all under arrest, asks if they have any more dope (besides what is on the dining room table), tells his men to look around, and then asks, or looks as if he would like to ask: "What kind of people are you, anyway?"

Friar Lawrence is dubious about the thing between Romeo and Juliet. He says:

These violent delights have violent ends,
And in their triumph die; like fire and powder
Which as they kiss consume: the sweetest honey
Is loathsome in his own deliciousness,
And in the taste confounds the appetite:
Therefore, love moderately; long love doth so
Too swift arrives as tardy as too slow.

How come we had all those fine chicks around? She is always Juliet, the fairest of the fair, for the virtue she sacrifices is the measure of her revenge. What makes Candy stop running? If every American boy can grow up to be president, it follows that every girl can make first lady. All she has to do is be competent and helpless, beautiful and unobtrusive, ambitious and docile, intelligent and dippy, firm and gentle, sexy and chaste. If she fails they reject her, and if she succeeds they give her a crown and call it love.

The men for whom she is intended are hard and reliable, but without soul or passion, and ultimately a drag. The mirror starts to talk back, accusing her of secret ugliness. She, at least, knows that she is not the fairest in the realm. She puts her fist through the glass, and if her bad luck is over after seven years, she is fortunate. She forgets about sugar and spice and everything nice, turns herself inside out, and undergoes a funky transformation. Where once she was a doll, now she is a slut, a bitch, a female demon who hides her fury behind her meekness, the more so if she was fair. A girl who, still in her teens, had lived with a dozen old men, not to mention several dykes, blown her head off with acid, been twice strung out on smack and kicked it, and covered a good part of continental United States and Europe, said to me: "Good girl? Baby, I was the best girl on the block!"

Reveling in reverie, she dreams of being a slave girl or a whore. She ruminates endlessly over the price that is paid for her: not too much or the buyer will be cheated, not too little or she will despise herself. If she is dutiful, he may come to love her, especially if she passes through enough hands. She is a gambler who places many small bets.

To deny her rage, she strives to please. She will stoop to anything, for degradation combines crime and punishment, leaving no guilt. The past often escapes us, for trivia has not the impact to make endgrams, while anguish is encysted by repression. Hanging somewhere between trivia and anguish, I remember overhearing the following conversation, going on in another room in my house at Perry Lane. Someone said: "You ought to try her, she'll do anything." To which someone replied: "Well, *I* won't." But, of course, we did. They were our people, and we recognized them, for we understood intuitively that liberation meant sometimes making monsters of ourselves.

For reasons which remain a mystery to me, most of the girls who hung around Perry Lane were named Judy. Because of this they were referred to by first name and last initial; in order to distinguish them from each other: Judy A., Judy B., Judy C., and so forth. Judy A. carried a knife or a gun in her purse, because she was always getting raped. She had been raped three times, and she was bound and determined that there would not be another one. If there was, somebody was going to get his you know what shot off. She endeared herself to us by serving as torchbearer for the First Annual Perry Lane Olympics. The torch consisted of a plumber's helper with a burning rag stuffed in the cup, and she held it high, sitting naked on the back of a convertible which was driven around the block before its triumphant arrival. She became involved with one of my neighbors, who was an amateur photographer. He took nude pictures of her at the beach. She was beautiful, and I can still remember the tightness in my belly when he showed a picture of her lying on the sand with the ocean in the background. She became persona non grata when she pulled a knife on him during a quarrel. She disappeared, only to return much later with a nose job and a greatly improved disposition.

Judy B. was the only girl around the Lane who was chaste. She had worked as a call girl and was completely turned off of sex. It was understood that that was her thing and nobody should mess with her. She tried to be cool about it, but she was uptight, mean and defensive. She had come from a wealthy and prominent family, and it was matter of pride with her that she had had class, and not been a common prostitute. You had to follow a code and pass a lot of tests. There was some top pimp who passed on you, and you had to ball him right, and have good manners, and correct grooming. When Judy B. wanted to put a guy down, which was pretty often, she would say, "He's really a *trick!*" It was the ultimate epithet. When she wanted to put a girl down, she would say, "She'd make a lousy whore. She's lazy and doesn't keep herself up." Judy B. was the super-paranoid of the whole scene. At times, especially when she was stoned, the world she experienced seemed to undergo a malevolent alteration. She felt that people were putting her down, and the least little thing would launch her into some imaginary conflict. She suspected any stranger of being an informer or an undercover agent. When a late model car would drive by, she would think it was unmarked police. We became so exasperated with her that when she was around we took to yelling at the cars, "Hey, man. You want some pot?" She was an artist of sorts, and her usual subject was horses. When she was younger, she had spent a lot of time on horseback, riding in the best circles, with jodhpurs, English saddle and the whole bit. Now she painted psychedelic stallions, red, orange, purple, or paisley, rampant in some unearthly realm. As time went on, her visions changed. Having dropped some peyote or LSD, she would see plump, pink, voluptuous Rubens style nudes, in playful or heroic postures, amid swirling draperies. Her hardness gradually melted, and she became sunny and gentle. Finally she started screwing again, got married, had a brief relapse to her former condition, got divorced, married again, and vanished into the East.

Judy C. was the daughter of some prosperous member of the local Greek community. She had been made to feel strongly that there were two kinds of girls, good ones and bad ones. She understood what it was all about, and she determined to have the best of both worlds. This was a familiar syndrome around the Lane. Around the right people, she did everything right, and when nobody was looking, she made the scene. She was, she explained to us, expected to marry another Greek of good family, and to be a virgin at the time. After the wedding night, the bloody sheets would be displayed to the community as evidence of her virtue. Her folks suspected she was up to something, being away so much. One evening she came home stoned and they seized her, removed her panties, spread-eagled her on the bed, and called the family doctor to see if it was still there. She stuck to her guns, and he apparently assured them that it was. After about a year of leading this uneasy double life she married a Greek boy from a good family. She came to the Lane less and less often. One day someone asked her where she was at, and she said, "Ever since I got married I've been losing my imagination. I used to have a really good imagination, and now there's almost nothing left of it."

Judy D. had long, unkempt brown hair. I remember how the sun made her hair shine as she stood washing dishes in the kitchen in the late afternoon, the light blinding in the window without curtains. She usually had a sulky look on her face, and when she smiled it was a smirk. She looked like a corrupt angel, trying to remember where she had left her harp, her halo askew, and the light burnt out. For some reason, non-resident straight types out on the Lane doing a little slumming found her particularly fascinating. When they got pushy she would panic and say, "Get away from me or I'll tell my nigger friend to kick your ass!" Most of the time she had a nigger friend to do it, but I don't recall that it was ever necessary. She was subject to accidentally burning herself with cigarettes, exploding ovens, and bumping into things in the dark. I used to sit, incredulous, holding a lighted cigarette, watching her hand or arm move with apparent autonomous volition towards the burning end, compensating if I would move it out of the way, until the dance would terminate abruptly in a shower of sparks, pain and surprise. One night we were sitting around my living room talking about the sickness of our society, as exemplified by the great popularity of the novels of Mickey Spillane. Someone had a copy of one, which showed on the cover a beautiful girl with bare back hanging by a rope which was tied around her wrists, with a man who looked as if he were going to beat her. Judy D.

suddenly allowed in a flat nervous voice that that sort of thing turned her on more than sex. We tried to reassure her with an academic discussion of polymorphous perversity. I asked her if she could remember anything of her parents. She said she all the time overheard them screwing and when the noises of the act were over, she would hear her mother say, with bored contempt: "Are you done now?" Another time, somewhat later I think, she remarked, with some wonder, "People always want to know what's going on in my head. There's nothing going on in my head. I don't understand why they want to know that."

Judy E. had the body of a woman and the face and mind of a child. She was quiet, subdued, gentle, affectionate, and painfully shy, with a wholesome, natural appearance. She turned out wearing pinafores and bib-top jumpers, white blouse and puritan collar, and saddle oxfords, or blue jeans and too large men's shirts. She liked to read *The Little Prince* by Antoine De Saint-Exupery. She was fond of animals and plants, very old people and small children, and us, and enjoyed hitch-hiking and being out of doors. She projected a powerful aura of innocence. Total strangers would appear smiling, out of nowhere, and present her with food, flowers, money, or simply a kind word, and silently steal away, probably wondering what had moved them so. Being something of a nomad, she wandered all over the country, alone or with a friend, frightened and confused, dippy and dazzled, wondering what was happening. Sometimes she seemed to converse with imaginary companions, or climb trees and pretend that she was a bird. Oddly enough, I remember her sitting on the floor in Ken Kesey's house, playing strip poker, because that was the game that night, and being amazed at the fullness of her breasts and the roundness of her thighs. Though she was quite cooperative, the one who loved her most could not get it up when she was ready.

I was greatly fond of Judy F., who was passionate and understanding, and a little older than these others. We dropped psylocibin together once, and at the top of her high she announced to me that she was, in reality, a witch. I scoffed at this, making out that I thought her superstitious or neurotic, but I think that even then I knew that I was trying to engage and dispel a persistent demon which would not let me be. I forced myself to stare into her eyes. The room was suddenly filled with the hissing and crackling of fire. She laughed hysterically. Her face dissolved into the twisted visage of an old hag, and then the empty sockets and fixed grin of death.

Such girls are beloved of young men who felt unloved or betrayed by their fathers, and therefore identify and empathize. They are fond of bohemians, revolutionaries, artists, criminals, and saints, and of older men, and of men who are boyish and immature. They are myth, both timeless and contemporary. As the Buddha sits, awaiting illumination, he is tempted by the sexy daughters of Kama-Mara, the god of love and death and illusion, subjected, as it were, to a kind of cosmic strip-tease. He looks at them without flinching, and he sees that they are all his mothers from his previous lifetimes, and as he does so they turn to skeletons and vanish.

As Romeo, come to break the news to Friar Lawrence, says:

> I have been feasting with mine enemy;
> Where on a sudden one hath wounded me,
> That's by me wounded.

on carrying a torch

paul marienthal

RRing   RRRing   Ring   RRing*
"this marathanxmerniszmer yah"
"Hello Paul, this is Connie, did you leave a note last night?
Well, you burnt our door down. Bye"
"yah"

(It's a little candle fetish I have. I sever the little tip off a
candle and stick it to a little note. Then I leave them for young
romantic things.) Satisfied that I'd made an impression on the
wench, I went canoeing about the lake. In fact, I was so pleased
with myself that I composed an entire notebook of candle-notes
to leave about and profess my heat for the world. One goes,
"Constance my love, your warmth could not be compressed into
a mere stick of wax." Another goes, "this burning wick sucking
up the redhot liquid does not compare to your bubbling eyeballs." Pretty poetic, huh, sure to melt her heart.

It was late afternoon, 2:30 or 4:00, that I wandered back up
to my room, slipped into my gigantic monk's habit (that looks

* the "Rings" are uneven cause the little old lady at the switchboard has
epilepsy in the mornings at 7:30.

like a psychedelic Ku Klux Klan suit) and slumped to the bed satisfied.

RRing RRRing Ring RRing**

"Hi Paul, this is Alvin Barder, down in the lobby."

This fellow seemed to be fishing for a response, so I said, "Hello Alvin, I hope you're enjoying it down there. Have you looked in the guest book—my mom did a wonderful nude study of a Stanford Squaw, class of 69."

"Ummmmmmmm Mister Marienthal, this is Alvin B. Barder, Deputy Santa Clara County Fire Inspector, First In Charge. Can we chat a while?"

CLICK

It takes, in my estimation, 30–31 seconds to get from the lobby to my room—so let me quickly describe the next 30–31 seconds:

fire inspector?   my god   Fire
    I burned down the door
    Candles!

                        Jesus my room
Sidhu Caramanis Kamal Marshal Lezak Pal (an Indian not a dog) frisbee in the hall "hey assholes get in here grab all the candles throw em in Malinowski's room"
              bodies in out in out in in out out
                candles in a pile
Barder Coming   Shit one more armload   Got It

(STOP: I'm holding the action in midair for half a second. This is where we are. Two guys are throwing the frisbee up and down the hall, it is now half way between the hand of Pal the Indian and the light bulb directly between Melvyn Malinowski's room and mine across the hall. Sidhu, Caramanis, Kamal and me in the tent are flying back and forth grabbing and heaving candles —making pretty good time too. Alvin Barder, First In Charge

    ** the old coot has a relapse at 4:32—mighty cool for telling time.

(as we will call him) is coming up the stairs. I have the last armload of candles. I am turning around, just ready for flight across the hallway to Mel's room. At this point let's interject one additional fact: My estimation was fucked up. Apparently it takes only 27–29 seconds to get to my room. Sadly, let the action begin!)

Turn   fly   the door
          My   God   Barder
                  WHAMMO
FLASH   GLASS   LAUGHTER

At this point tragedy has simply overwhelmed the scene; and in a noble gesture to myself I'm going to end it. It is gruesomely clear what has happened. In the next few minutes, Alvin, First In Charge unhooked himself from me, stumbled to his feet, shaking off wax and glass, and looked fatly at the turbaned bodies contorted in shrieks of ecstasy about the hall. His face really didn't react till he weaved into Melvyn's room and saw the pile of candles. (2nd additional fact: To say "pile" isn't quite fair—it contained nearly 400 candles). Standing still, his jaw kinda twitching uncontrollably, he fumbled into his pocket, yanked out a plastic card that I figured was a credit card for sending people to jail. Then he sorta pushed the thing into his face. His face didn't see it for a while. Finally the credit card must have appeared to him, and his mouth began to twitch and quiver and finally he splut out "wa wa wana if you wan to a lalawyer if ya want." Then he repeated a little better, "you wanta you can get the lawyer." Slowly his muscles got together and he read off all the rest of my rights put together. I must tell you that I didn't see any of this, I was tangled in my hood. When I finally got free, Barder was in my room enjoying the atmosphere (like the punching bag I made from a cast of my sister's left tit). He said in a lovely crisco tone, "Marienthal, you know why I'm here, I know the whole story, suppose you tell me exactly what happened." Looked like I was caught by the short ones. (I was not helped by Sidhu who was still heaving in hysterics on Malinowski's floor.) Sorta stunned, I spit out the whole thing. I like candles cause my mom thinks she's a gypsy and she always had em so I have a lot and I left this note and I feel terrible about burning down her door and I'm not such a really bad guy and I'd be glad to cooperate—good judgment I thought. Alvin, First In Charge kept smiling with warm understanding, so I made a nice little tape recording for him, and he smiled and winked, so I did too. In fact, it all turned out pretty convivially in the end. We were just like buddies—the fire inspector and me. We talked about police, and probation officers, and he assured me, yes he assured me that my great cooperation would be a factor in his report. And also, I would learn from this whole thing that the police and everyone over there were really on my side. I might even understand the True Goodness of the System. Jesus, ya know, if he had stayed five minutes more I was gonna enlist in the marines. As he left, he shook warmly, said he'd have a chat with the DA, have it all cleared up in a week. He also suggested with a grin that I go and help Sidhu who was dying of convulsions on Malinowski's floor. "Bye, Mr. Barder" "Bye, Marienthal, soon." Groovy groovy cat. A Far-out Man. Wondered why he—oh well, he's just doin his own thing. Sock it to 'em, Al.

new chapter

Just like Alvin had warned, I got some correspondence from his office something that read like: "Date, March 27, 1969; Time, 10 A.M.; Judge, Hon. Sydney Feinberg; Viol., 13001 HSC; Case, #14." Alvin, First In Charge warned me I might have to appear. He said the County probably would charge me with double X screw over dash minus 4Q good Pi of the State Code of Ethics and Good Sportsmanship or something. He explained the reasoning this way: "If I had asked for a fire permit and been given one, I could have burnt down Connie's door. Therefore I would probably be charged with burning without a permit." A minor charge.

March 27 arrives—this is by the way in the middle of spring "vacation." The morning sun streams luscious bananas into my fruity fucking mess. I awoke to the RRing RRRing Ring. It is Gina Lolabrigida calling to say good luck. (Later I find out it really wasn't Gina Lolabrigida at all.) I attire my body in striped dapper shirt. Knot up the black tie borrowed from Raphael Diaz. Pick out two luscious caressing socks. And debate between the old brown cords and the good gray ones that were worn last in November '67. (3rd additional fact: The snap on the gray ones comes undone every time I stand up. So I wasn't sure if I wanted to come forward in court and have my pants fall down. But I finally decided on the gray ones. If my springing fly bugged the Judge, that was his thing, not mine.) Off I sped on my red Schwinn Flyer. Zipped up to the County Court House, slipped into Room B, Hon. Sydney Feinberg presiding (hoo ha, a nice Jewish boy). 9:30, early, great. Alvin, First In Charge was there—waved and winked. Ah, Justice. The beautiful System. The Navy. The Air Force. The Marines. I would probably love them all. Maybe I'll be a career policeman, helping folks to help themselves.

I am running amuk like some fucking hero in the rice paddies when I'm awakened by the swish of rising bodies:

"The Honorable Sydney Feinberg"

I quickly leap to my feet into the hush, my snap flies open and down goes my zipper, Grizzippp----------

"Be Seated."

It's all very informative I tell myself:

Ah, Case Number One, the teenage drunk driver. Doing 95 in a 25 zone. Officer didn't know there was a girl in the car till he pulled over and they separated—not so good I thought for this guy. A student at S.F. State. Also not so good for this guy. $300 fine. Not good at all for this guy.

Case Number Seven: Ah, great, little old lady goin too slow on the freeway. 22 in the left lane. Says the officer made her nervous with all those lights and sirens, pulled her foot off the gas to slow down. Right. Feinberg smiles. $70 fine. Not so good for the little old lady.

Case Number Twelve: Middle aged man, second offense, defacing public property (I was later informed that this fellow had written "Feinberg is a Jew" in red paint on the side of the County Court House.) Not so good for this guy. $200 fine.

So far my reactions are mixed. Hon. Sydney Feinberg seems to be helping out the budget alright, but people seem to have not done such good things.

Case Number Thirteen. I am Next: "MANSLAUGHTER." I am stunned. I do not hear much of the rest. A guy all bandaged up is led in from the side. "Night of January." Was arrested, and a couple of other Perry Mason things. Apparently the Hon. Sydney Feinberg suggested to "Manslaughter" that he get a lawyer pretty quick. Not good for him at all.

Case Number Fourteen. Paul Richard Marienthal: I leap to my feet, my snap went spring and my zipper went grizzipp (the lady next to me chuckled). I strode forward. "Charges." (Wait a second here. These are the words we expect to hear, right: "double X screw over Dash minus 4Q good Pi of the State Code of Ethics and Good Sportsmanship"). Okay, lets go on. "Charges" Attempted Arson"

Omy Fucking God

The Hon. Sydney Feinberg made a suggestion, "Go get a lawyer." Not so good for me either.

new chapter

I figured the Hon. Sydney Feinberg probably had something good goin on inside his head being a nice Jewish boy and all, so I went and got a lawyer. A very nice man, I like him a lot. He says I'm a little naive about things—and that I should stay that way. We talked about police and things. He explained about how the lady DA, a lady named Mrs. Kangaroo, wasn't such a nice lady at all, and that not so many students like Alvin, First In Charge real well either. As I was leaving he recalled something Mrs. Kangaroo once said to him in court. She once said to him in court, quote: "A conviction is good for a young man."

new chapter

O Goody Goody Gum Drops; I am in court again waiting to
meet Mrs. Kangaroo. We are all going to have a talk with the
Hon. Sydney Feinberg. Certainly Mrs. Kangaroo will like to
do that. "Case Number Fourteen. Paul Richard Marienthal:"
Spring Snap griizzippp. My lawyer and me step forward, but
where is Mrs. Kangaroo.   "creeek"   In the back of the room
the big oak doors creek open; and then in kinda waddles the
ugliest, the ugliest, the ugliest thing I've ever looked at. My
stomach starts churning and bubbling. "Not in court, it doesn't
look good," whispers my lawyer. Jesus, she looked like a fucking
koala bear that hadn't been humped in 23 years—pathetic. Like
a mashed up carrot in brown tweed with black glasses and a
nose—Christ it was a hook, bent sideways like some big rhino
had been butting heads with and lost. Ugly Ugly hair. Orange
and gray with green splotches like birds had been shitting in it.
And a mouth. Her lips musta been run through a reaper or raper
or masher; flimsy like pickled watermelon rind and green like
that. Just an ugly ugly woman. She splotched up to the front,
undid the clasp on a portfolio that had Marienthal in red letters
an inch high on it, and then fucked herself. Hell, no, she smiled
sideways kinda. She squeeked. The lady had no voice, all she
did was squeek. First thing she squeeks is "I request a private
meeting with counsel and Your Honor for a moment." She was
verbally pissing in my ear. So there I stood, trying to look not
there with my fly opened, as the three "conversed." It all seemed
to be just jolly as all hell up there, humming and squeeking, until my lawyer turns around and his eyes look like they were just
trampled by a rogue red ant. And then Mrs. Kangaroo inches
her bodice around, her lips were quivering green and pusy and
her foaming eyes were the color of bright flaming shit. Her hook
sucked up the dust. The Hon. Sydney Feinberg announces, "The
DA has requested and is granted more time to prepare her case
against Mr. Marienthal."

(I imagine pissing in *her* ear.)

Later my lawyer briefly related the "conversation:" "Your Honor, Alvin says that deviate has 5000 candles. He's a pervert. He goes up in the early morning hours to all the rooms of girls who shun him away. He goes up in some sheet or something but strips it right off and burns the candles and dances in a frenzy around the flames naked getting all his sex running naked around the flames watching them and dancing like a pervert. This is a sick child, and needs a psychiatrist and a conviction— I must have more time you must send him to one right away." That was the "conversation." My lawyer and the Hon. Sydney Feinberg were a little stunned; agreed I'd go and chat with some people—the County Probation Officer, and the County Psychiatrist—if it makes Mrs. Kangaroo happy—off we go—weeeeeeeeeee.

new chapter

The Hon. Sydney Feinberg was very kind, gave me whole bunches of weeks to think up good stuff for my chats with the Shrink and the Probation Officer. (Let us for convenience and a few other things, call him simply the Probeoff—sounds curiously like jackoff doesn't it). Let me add that by now my balls weren't hangin so low. The penalty for attempted arson is 6 months in the dirty hole and/or a $500 fine—either of which would raise some serious doubts about my summer vacation. My Dad dropped me a little note of greeting too, written on a match cover from Moms. (All nice Jewish boys know that you should never eat at a place called Moms—it's traditional.) It said, "My son, what will you do if they find out you really are a pyromania-crazed sexual deviate? Love, Your Dad."

So I fly up to the County Building, and stride right into Mental Health. I lean up against the counter, wait for the lady to finish doing the charts on her horoscope—it gives me confidence alright. "Hey Stud" (to a bearded long haired cat in levis next to me). "Hey Stud," I say, "what's your perversion?" He says, "The name is Michael Cohen." This fellow seemed to be fishing for a response, so I say, "Oh, a nice Jewish boy—" "No," he says, "the

County Psychiatrist. Marienthal? Come This Way." Well, it turns out Michael Cohen is a nice Jewish boy alright, cause we end up talking about lox and cream cheese and water bagels how they stale in the ice box, and that he thought *his* mom made the worst matzo balls in the world—it is a tradition to think *your* mom makes the worst matzo balls in the world. I even guessed at where I didn't think I was really a sexual deviate at all (though by this time I was really having my doubts). We parted reluctantly, "Shalom" "Shalom"—lovely man. Now, On To Probation. The air was a little thicker in the Probation Dept. So I slumped into a couch and grabbed a *McCalls*. Just as I was getting to the good girdle ads in the back, I feel this tug on my shoulder. Guess who; well you're right, it was the Probeoff. "Come this way." (Not too original, the nice Jewish boy downstairs and the Probeoff must have gone to the same charm school.) For some fucking reason this guy's got his chamber about three hundred yards down the hall, and he's in an awful hurry to get there. Bastard ran heavy as my mom's matzo balls —kalomp kalomp he kalomps into a door 20 yards in front of me. When I straggled in, the phone was dangling in his flabby fingers—he crammed into one of the red buttons and screamed, "Has the mileage gone out yet; it better not have." SLAM. Grabbed a pile of papers, starts ripping through them, scratching stuff onto the top one. Oh my, he speaks! "Brothers?" "two, 16 and 8" "Sisters?" "two, 22 and 7 months" "Same parents?" "yes" "Hmmmmmmmmmmmmm, yes I see." That was all our conversation for the forty minutes of our chat. He did ask one more question, but my jaw was jammed so he answered it himself, "Married or any of that shit?" Then he stroked a giant black X over a whole sheet of paper. Since my end of the conversation was somewhat limited let me just relate some of the Probeoff's revelations: Quote: No Marienthal. I don't really care what happens to you. You haven't even been convicted yet. Or: You know, there's a lot of fuzzy area in cases like this one. It's not all black and white. There's a lot of gray. You may get 3 months, you may get all 6. You never know how the judge will feel that morning. And stirringly: "You know the DA wants to put you in the pen. Thinks you're nuts. How 'bout it Marienthal?"

As I leave, I read the cartoon on his door. A rich old father guzzling martinis on the veranda is saying to his little boy, "Well son, how's your childhood going?"

Both of the generous thoughts of these two prophets went right into the report, which I suspected was getting fairly chubby. The Probeoff enthused: "many many many sisters and brothers. No recommendation." Michael Cohen, in a true show of solidarity speculated: "Marienthal definitely knows the difference between right and wrong." In California this is the definition for sanity.

climax

Has Mrs. Kangaroo fucked herself this time? It seems Sydney Feinberg was due to retire last Wednesday, but Mrs. Kangaroo wanted more time to prepare her case against the dangerous deviate. This I am thinking doesn't make Syd too happy. Seems he was going to Tahiti with my lawyer, who also isn't too happy. She also requested a 9:00 o'clock hearing, seems she has an appointment to bounce around on some eight-year-old at 9:30. (I think he left a card on her windshield, signed by every kid on her block saying, "Mrs. Kangaroo is a Dirty Old Man." Maybe she's sueing for defamation of character. She'll lose, I don't think they'll find any.) Syd made a face when she asked for this time—but said he probably could make it if he missed his breakfast. I think his mom, Mrs. Feinberg, will be very angry with Mrs. Kangaroo for making her Syd miss breakfast. That is a real shame, cause here it is 8:55 and I am wandering around thinking of my bulging tummy, which is just brimming full of a great big breakfast. I am wandering around in the lobby of the courthouse thinking of all these goodies, and sneaking a peek down the long hallway every once in a while, catching a glimpse of Syd in his robes flying around like a witch back in his little chamber.

So I'm lurking about, thinking, when who do you think comes in—well, you're right, it was Alvin Barder, First In Charge. He was wearing this baggy maroon zoot suit, but the most amazing thing of all were his shoes. My God, they were like little armored tanks. Wing tippers ten inches wide and bottoms. Jesus Christ the goddamned things were eight inches thick, looked like solid steel. Maybe they had motors and were mounted with hidden cannons. How he lifted his leg got me. He steered his shoes over, periscoped his arm, "Hello Marienthal," then he drove back toward the witch's chamber. Maybe he's gonna flatten Syd with his shoes. Then the Probeoff flies by, weird I think, "Hi Kid"—just like Johnny Unitas and the greasy hair ad. Then he zooms back into the chamber. Then my lawyer, he pauses for a second, says, "Take this quick, it'll keep your stomach down, I just saw Mrs. Kangaroo, you'll need it." He accelerates away, down the hall to Syd's place like someone was just about to wipe his ass. I suck down this giant green capsule—feel great. But then. Oh Fucking Mother of Jesus. My breakfast. Now I know why he took off in such a fucking hurry. I was trapped. My God. The Kangaroo. Yes, Mrs. Kangaroo in bright yellow stockings and a long long spongy black wig. And if you think you've seen some ugly women in your life, oh Jesus, my goddamned belly (apparently the orange stuff with the bird shit in it is a wig too. My lawyer says she's got one in a platinum pageboy, speculates that she's bald—ha ha). She waddles toward me but I spin just in time and stare at the horizon or I wouldn't make it, so I only guessed she went on down to Syd's place. Just wait till they get a look at her down there. Maybe Alvin, First In Charge will open fire with his shoes and end the case right here. No shots—but I do hear a muffled belch—I hope it's Syd. I hear some footsteps, I hope it isn't you-know-what (even thinking its name made my tummy bubble). Phew, it was only an ugly ugly secretary. "Marienthal, your trial will be heard in chambers. The court-room isn't open for business until 10:00."

Business? I immediately thought of the credit card Alvin, First In Charge has, and how I needed it right now to put what's-its-name in the clink, cause for sure the next time I see her I'm gonna barf all over. In chambers, pretty snazzy. Right in the scrotum of the system. Down Down Down the hallway.

I'm careful to start rubbing my eyes as I stroll into the chamber for fear of barfing on sight. I turn to where I hope Syd is gonna be and open "EEE," I spin just in time to keep the volcano from erupting out the top of my throat—a close call. Syd is reading, so he doesn't hear; and I guess everyone else is reading too, but it's obvious I better not look around to find out. He is on about page ten of a two hundred page novel (I must let you know that my lawyer has not shirked his duty. He has met privately with Syd eight or nine times, brought in some character witnesses, not so easy to find, and Mary, Satisfied Mother of Jesus, have mercy on his soul, met alone with Mrs. Kangaroo.) It is about forty minutes later, everyone is madly flipping pages, and I'm getting to feel like a giant red erection cause I can't move my neck for fear of my belly. Finally, oh finally, Syd slams his portfolio shut "Vwabang." "Vwabang" "Vwabang" "Vwabang" "Vwabang-squeek." I was right, they were all reading. There's silence except for a little squeeking, then Syd says, "I understand, Mr. Marienthal, that 6 months in jail would alter your summer plans." There is a pause. "Counsel, do you have anything to add to this report." After that little introduction I am hoping my lawyer will sing a little song, or soft shoe a little dance or challenge Alvin, First In Charge to a foot race, but he says, "No Your Honor." "Mrs. Kangaroo, do you have any more juicy little tidbits to throw into the campfire, hmmmmmm?" I like his tone of voice very much. There was a long long pause. Then there was a squeek, a little itsy tiny squeek. Then a bigger squeek, a little bit higher pitched. More and more squeeks, higher and louder, squeeks and more squeeks. Then there was a funny sound like convulsed sobbing and then a lot more squeeking and convulsing. It got louder and louder and louder and then all of a sudden Mrs. Kangaroo in her highest ear-ripping squeek of all began squeeking

"In the interests of Justice"
"In the interests of Justice"
"In the interests of Justice"

She squeeked on and louder and louder sobbing and squeeking and convulsing until Sydney yelled, "Enough." Then he pointed out, in a delightful tone of voice, that he didn't really think this was new evidence he could use to convict me of attempted arson. Then he swiveled about and groaned, "Marienthal. This Is Bizarre. No More Candles. Swim to Hellespont. And In The Interests of Justice, I DISMISS THIS CASE."

W e e p   S o b   C o n v u l s e   S q u e e k
I saluted, began rubbing my eyes again, and skipped down the hall crying,

> Up into the air Junior Birdmen
> Up into the air Upside Down
> When you see those Wings of Silver
> When you see those Wings of Tin
> You'll know that the Junior Birdmen
> Have been sending their Boxtops In

I paused in the lobby. The Probeoff zoomed by, "S'long Kid." I knew he was proud of my greaseless hairs. Alvin Barder, First In Charge steers over, clutches into neutral, periscopes his baggy arm and drives away. Then my lawyer. We smile. I give him a groovy little purple pill I've got hidden in my fluffy sock. He drops it and floats across the long lobby and out. And then . . . and then, MY HOLY CHRIST OF MOTHER SCREWING GOD. NO. IT CAN'T. IT WON'T. IT SHOULDN'T. IT COMES . . . NEARER AND NEARER AND squeek squeek squeek squeek squeek squeek squeek TRAPPED. squeek squeek "marienthal" . . . I t—u—r—n —ulp— I caught the first bubble, "marienthal, after all this" hurry Kangaroo hurry my breakfast is "I'd just like" oooh "to" look out "meet you." "Hel-hel-lloo." I grabbed her greasy fingers and wobbled them a little and she waddled around and started moving for the doors—oh please, hurry hurry ohh, volcano bursting bubbling, Mrs. Kanga, oh, you're gonna get, Oh Christ she couldn't open the door, she pushed and pulled and pushed and pulled and finally got a nasty crack to open up and she slid her body o o o out. And then . . . even the horizon didn't help.

to a siberian woodsman

wendell berry

1.

YOU LEAN at ease in your warm house at night after supper,
listening to your daughter play the accordion. You smile
with the pleasure of a man confident in his hands, resting
after a day of long labor in the forest, the cry of the saw
in your head, and the vision of coming home to rest.
Your daughter's face is clear in the joy of hearing
her own music. Her fingers live on the keys
like people familiar with the land they were born in.

You sit at the dinner table late into the night with your
      son,
tying the bright flies that will lead you along the forest
      streams.
Over you, as your hands work, is the dream of the still pools.
      Over you is the dream
of your silence while the east brightens, birds waking close
      by you in the trees.

2.

I have thought of you stepping out of your doorway at dawn,
    your son in your tracks.
You go in under the overarching green branches of the forest
whose ways, strange to me, are well known to you as the
    sound of your own voice
or the silence that lies around you now that you have ceased
    to speak,
and soon the voice of the stream rises ahead of you, and you
    take the path beside it.
I have thought of the sun breaking pale through the mists
    over you
as you come to the pool where you will fish, and of the mist
    drifting
over the water, and of the cast fly resting light on the face
    of the pool.

3.

And I am here in Kentucky in the place I have made myself
in the world. I sit on my porch above the river that flows
    muddy
and slow along the feet of the trees. I hear the voices of the
    wren
and the yellow-throated warbler whose songs pass near the
    windows
and over the roof. In my house my daughter learns the
    womanhood
of her mother. My son is at play, pretending to be
the man he believes I am. I am the outbreathing of this
    ground.
My words are its words as the wren's song is its song.

4.

Who has invented our enmity? Who has prescribed us
hatred of each other? Who has armed us against each other
with the death of the world? Who has appointed me such
     anger
that I should desire the burning of your house or the
     destruction of your children?
Who has appointed such anger to you? Who has set loose
     the thought
that we should oppose each other with the ruin of forests
     and rivers, and the silence of birds?
Who has said to us that the voices of my land shall be strange
to you, and the voices of your land strange to me?

Who has imagined that I would destroy myself in order to
     destroy you,
or that I could improve myself by destroying you? Who has
     imagined
that your death could be negligible to me now that I have
     seen these pictures of your face?
Who has imagined that I would not speak familiarly with
     you,
or laugh with you, or visit in your house and go to work with
     you in the forest?
And now one of the ideas of my place will be that you would
     gladly talk and visit and work with me.

5.

I sit in the shade of the trees of the land I was born in.
As they are native I am native, and I hold to this place as
     carefully as they hold to it.
I do not see the national flag flying from the staff of the
     sycamore,
or any decree of the government written on the leaves of the
     walnut,

nor has the elm bowed before monuments or sworn the oath
of allegiance.

They have not declared to whom they stand in welcome.

6.

In the thought of you I imagine myself free of the weapons
and the official hates that I have borne on my back
like a hump,

and in the thought of myself I imagine you free of weapons
and official hates,

so that if we should meet we would not go by each other
looking at the ground like slaves sullen under their
burdens,

but would stand clear in the gaze of each other.

7.

There is no government so worthy as your son who fishes with
you in silence beside the forest pool.

There is no national glory so comely as your daughter whose
hands have learned a music and go their own way on
the keys.

There is no national glory so comely as my daughter who
dances and sings and is the brightness of my house.

There is no government so worthy as my son who laughs, as
he comes up the path from the river in the evening,
for joy.

book review:
reflections on the last days of the late, great state of california

judith rascoe

No RED-BLOODED Californian could read this book without falling all over the floor in an orgasm of self-love. Perhaps this is a metaphor to pursue. Imagine California as an adolescent boy who's just had his first lady; two weeks go by; she says she's pregnant. He goes home, and for one long aching evening he revels in his own sense of enormous size, potency, power and prospects. But she's trying to get him to settle down. How can he, a superman like that? She stomps off and has the baby in a Florence Crittenden home. Or she aborts the baby. Our hero falls down in self-pity; nobody realizes or cares that he's the father. Lives have been changed, but he's been forgotten . . .

Thus, California. Curt Gentry has suggested, now, the ultimate adolescent daydream: "I'll die and then you'll be sorry!" And then he kills off California with a supercolossal earthquake that levels all the highrises and finally drops everything west of Truckee into the rolling waves. Bye-bye, Mother America, see how lonely your old age is now! I'll tell how much you'll miss me: you'll miss me to the tune of

38 congressmen
2 senators
Transamerica, Del Monte, IBM, Rexall, Safeway,
Kaiser Steel, Southern Pacific, etcetcetc
lottsa movies
most t.v.
11% of the US oil supply
100% of the US supplies of almonds, artichokes, Crenshaw melons, garlic and—well, 99.8%—nectarines
10 million automobiles, give or take a VW

ah-ah-*ah* . . . Before you start jumping up and down on the ground to make this fable a reality, remember that a world without Ronald Reagan, the Los Angeles freeway system, Crenshaw melons and RAND would also be a world of unemployed automobile workers, radio soap operas, *very* expensive salad stuff and apple-pie morality. It would be a trip not by memory lane but by US 101 to the wonderful world of Depression, 1934 . . .

But are you important, California
(They say that you're a painted, tainted girl,
da-da-dum-da-da)?

I don't know, even after I've read Mr. Gentry's book. I gaze on the possibility of lost artichokes, of the Huntington Library and San Juan Capistrano and the studio that makes "The Name of the Game"—all under water—and I wonder . . . But then, Mr. Gentry's book is a partisan book. He obviously loves the California of incomparable landscapes, sour dough bread, superscientists hotly pursuing cancer cures, social experiment—

"The truth is, we never really understood California. We didn't understand because we never really tried."

California has become the metamorphosis of James Dean! And you know what James Dean would have thought of a bunch of creeps like Ronnie Reagan and George Murphy. You know what James Dean would have thought of a bunch of creeps sitting around in singles-bars in San Francisco, leering at typists. And what James Dean would have thought of somebody who went around cutting down redwoods just to make a little lousy cash.

Yes, Mr. Publisher, your book is as "remarkable, informative . . . as the fabulous state it depicts" as you say on the blurb page. Honestly. This book will tell you all about Delano, Brown-versus-Reagan, weird cults, by-the-hour motels,* the Watts riot, the UC FreeSpeech whatsis, Knotts Berry Farm, YAF, etc.

Get lots and lots of copies of this book and mail them to relatives Back East, friends Back East, and Californians-in-exile. (The latter will cry a lot when they read the book.)

This book also contains a very careful description of a whopping big earthquake and its possible effects. Last chapter, "Paradise Lost" is worth anybody's 95 cents alone. Sci-fi fans note (last year I read an awful sci-fi book about a Big California Quake. Ground opened up and squeezed people's feet in crevices. Tall buildings leapt in a single bound. Lottsa screams) and also earthquake buffs.

But before I let this go, with my blessing (and, I should add that Mr. Gentry wrote a painless history of San Francisco called *The Madams of San Francisco* and *The Dolphin Guide to San Francisco and the Bay Area.* Both in print, in paper. Why not start a library?) . . . anyway, I would like to wonder aloud, again, about my sneaking suspicion that California may not be quite so important as we'd (you'd, me'd, them'd) like to believe. Everybody in California liked Barry Goldwater and he lost. Everybody in California liked Ronald Reagan and he didn't get anywhere. Everybody in California

---

* Dear readers. I have asked in vain among SoCalif friends if it's true, as Mr. Gentry says, that there are hostelries called the No Tell Motel or Tonite's the Nite Motel in the Southland where one pays by the hour and where the intercom softly but firmly counts down ("twenty minutes . . . ten minutes . . .") Do you know?

knew Richard Nixon couldn't make governor, much less President. And he won. Stravinsky is Russian. The Huntington Library is full of books written in England. Richard Burton is a Welshman. Mike Nichols lives in New York. If Alioto speaks true, the Mafia ignores us. Pot grows wild, but in Kansas—whoever smoked a California poppy? A California poppy is a sham. Harmless, inscrutable. There's a mystery here. "San Francisco," said a friend, "is full of first-rate people doing second-rate work." Is this true? there is a mystery here, which even Mr. Gentry cannot express. But Otis Redding could . . .

> I left my home in Georgia
> Headed for the Frisco Bay
> . . .

A lot of folks, including Mr. Gentry and Mr. Gentry's publisher (who says in the blurb that the book is also "rambunctiously unbelievable"), keep using the word
UNBELIEVABLE!
to talk about California. It is possible to suffer, here, from a bad case of the galloping incredibles—note my note about the motel: it represents a moment of vertigo as I imagined and tried to plant in sandy reality the notion of a motel called the NoTell where offstage voices count down the hour. But, patriots! our motto is Eureka! I have found it! . . . not *incredible!* Persons who feel the incredibility gap are apt to do bad things because they don't believe their surroundings exist. Consider all those axe-murderers: "It all seemed unreal, officer. It was like I was in a dream." Eastern businessmen say, "Incredible" just before they buy incredible parcels of landscape and cover them with credible crappy cottages just like they used to see back in Indiana. Indiana is credible because it looks so dopey. I am not convinced that California exists because it has topless waitresses. Go-go ergo sum. There is a real and lovable California. Just as there is within the swollen, histrionic adolescent, a real, lovable human being. Before you drop that popsicle wrapper, smoldering roach or sugar-cube, remember that California is real, in spite of all the superlatives. Whenever somebody tells me about "incredible" California, I know he's talking about Indiana in drag.

dark by four-thirty and blowing from the west

karl burton

DECEMBER in Minnesota, and I am home for Christmas, which was yesterday, and so today is the 26th, a Thursday, and I have gone back out to the lake with Jeff to work on a vast hairy engine he is building up in the basement.

It is maybe 4:30, for as I go over to answer the telephone I see deep blue out the window, and even through the walls the cold is growing palpable. I answer the phone. It is my mother, calling from town. She tells me quickly that her sister Dagny has been found dead today, having hanged herself in the basement of her home in Barret, Minnesota. The funeral is to be Monday, and my mother asks if I can extend my vacation through New Year's so that I can go to the funeral. This is easily done, I assure her, and I say I will deal with it, and I am coming back into town tomorrow afternoon, since we will go up to the farm Saturday morning.

I drive my mother, my sister, and myself up to the farm Saturday morning. It is cold in the Cities when we leave, five below or so, and just slightly overcast, but by the time we get to the farm 180 miles away, it is somewhat colder and grayer and the wind is coming in nasty gusts from the west, scattering little fans of hard dry snow along the tops of the drifts and the surface of the road. The weathered white paint of the house matches the landscape perfectly in color, so that only the hard angularity of the house separates it at all from the land itself.

My uncle Karl has had the man from the county bring his road grader up the driveway, so that the path is clear, scraped harshly into the frozen gravel; but already where the drifts are highest on either side the snow is beginning again to encroach. It will not be clear in the morning.

As we go in the house, Mathilda, another sister, meets us, and embraces my mother, saying "Oh, Evangeline, so good to see you, but isn't it terrible, at a time like this," and my mother mutters and pats Mathilda on the back and then Mathilda, wiping her hands on her apron, leads us into the dining room, where are two sixtyish women that I have seen before somewhere, obviously relatives, but mother knows them and it is "Why hello, Rosa, I haven't seen you for so long." "Why Vangie, it's good to see you." "And you, Beatrice, too," and so on, and my sister and I fade out as all four of them move into the kitchen to work on the dinner that is in preparation. Through the rest of the afternoon they continue coming: Olga, a sister from Minneapolis with her husband, Hank, and their children (my contemporaries); Gretchen and David; and Maria and Ronney, also from Minneapolis; and Borghild, the eldest sister, who comes down from Fergus Falls ten miles away; and then Karl comes in, having been down to Barret helping John, Dagny's husband with funeral arrangements. Then Clarence, Borghild's son-in-law, and Evelyn, her daughter, with Charles, their son (and again my contemporary) and his fiancee Janice.

And we all sit in the big living room and talk, in strange little groups, two or three people getting on some irrelevant subject common to them and talking about it for four or five minutes, and then lapsing into silence, as two or three others begin on something else, totally unrelated; then long silence where no one says anything, but perhaps someone picks up a magazine and looks through it desultorily and puts it down again. Eventually Clarence and Evelyn leave, since they have cows to milk at their place and it is getting on six and dark now outside. Shortly the rest of us all eat dinner in the big dining room, by numbers alone enough to remind me of being up there for a harvest as a kid, with nine or ten of us sitting around the old table, but there were less city relatives then, and mainly men: we would devour piece after piece of roast beef, and pitchers of water and milk, so that Mathilda would be continually going to the kitchen for more, while the huge bowl of steaming boiled potatoes slowly diminished, and at last, then, we would finish, and sit for a few minutes, and then go back out into the fields. The same now, but the food diminishing less rapidly, with a strange silence resting on the table, a conscious avoidance of conversation. Karl is the first to leave the table, comes back in his one blue suit that he has worn since the first time I can imagine or remember him having occasion to wear one, that being my grandfather's funeral in 1958, my Uncle Karl not being normally a church-going man, having little truck with authority in any form, whether governmental or godly. Karl is back, with his long thinning hair combed slickly back over his scalp, looking irritated at the rest of us, but especially the women, that we are not yet ready. They assure him that there is not any great hurry, and the rest of us go to change.

I come back downstairs, now in my suit also, and find myself to be the next one ready. Karl is pacing up and down in the dining room.

"Women? hunh? They'll have us all late again. Goddamn seems like the least they could do is be ready to go see Dagny on time, for Chrissake. Past seven-thirty already and we're to be there at eight-thirty: with the weather like it is we should leave plenty time to get to Elbow." I mutter something equivocal about its not being all that late; yet. "Goddamn we weren't hardly on time for Richard's funeral even, and I had said to Mathilda hurry up over and over again."

By this time my mother and sister and the Minneapolis relatives are all back and ready to go, but Mathilda and Borghild are yet upstairs. Karl is muttering, against the protestations of my mother and Olga, but they avail nothing, and he finally says "Well I'm going to go now; I'm not going to be late again on the account of some fool woman." Olga says, "Oh Karl, there's no point you getting so anxious about it. There's still plenty time yet, and there's no point you going off by yourself when there's so many of us." "No, Olga, I'm going now." "Well, why don't David and Gretchen and Hank and I all go in my car now and take you with us; we can leave now and you'll get there in plenty time." Karl eventually agrees with this, and the five of them leave.

By this time I am getting a little anxious myself, but everyone appears in time after all. By now it is incredibly cold, and blowing maybe thirty to thirty-five out of the west. The snow is blowing across the road in the wind, in feathery white streaks through which, normally, the edge of the road can barely be seen. Any time a car approaches us from ahead, however, its headlights reflect off the snow, all of which is a foot or less above the road, so that it looks like nothing so much as the top surface of a cloud as seen from an airplane. Which would not be so bad if there were any landmarks with which to locate the road, as opposed to the surrounding countryside, but snow has drifted the ditches in level with the road, so that ahead appears the top of a cloud, a hundred feet wide, and dead level, with thirty of those feet devoted to pavement and the rest terra incognita and indubitably not where I want to be. The effect in the end is that one steers slightly to the right of the oncoming car, and hopes foolishly that *he* knows where *he* is.

We reach Elbow, driving in on Highway 59, with the snow banks six feet high on either side of the street, the entire world white with the neon signs of downtown diffracted in sparkling flecks of blue and pink by the blowing snow. No one moves down the sidewalks now, and as we go around into the residential area where the funeral home is, we see the yellow lights of the set-back houses gleaming defiantly through the cross-hatching bare trees in the yards.

The funeral home is unusually discreet for these days, an ordinary one-story house converted, and we go in into what was once someone's living room, where now are set six or eight rows of folding gray metal chairs. An unctious man in a dark suit relieves us of our coats, his voice as smooth and glistening oily as his hair, murmuring mild condolences, leads us all in among the chairs, where at the front is a fancy modern coffin with Dagny in it. We file around the chairs and pass by the coffin in a line, each looking down in their way at the unnaturally rosy face; Borghild with her head cocked to one side and her body facing more towards the feet, so that she looks as if suddenly arrested in passage and frozen: beginning to cry now behind her veil. Someone comforts her; they move with an oddly weary half-stumble back to the chairs, like infantrymen in films helping each other back from the front. We all sit down again. Clarence and Evelyn's group have arrived before us, and so most all of us required are there when John and his two sons and two daughters come in; Peter and Joan bringing their wife and husband respectively as well. John is a great massive man, with a huge chest and shoulders that somehow give him the feel of an upside-down pyramid, surmounted by a long large head that is only barely distinguishable from his neck. Joan is holding his left arm, and Peter hovering near his right. His whole frame is warped forwards, so that he is looking downwards, but not due to any deflection of his neck, but rather his entire torso, again the same stiff walk that seems to be totally for the purpose of avoiding staggering. Like birds in front of snakes we all watch him go around to the coffin, all horribly fascinated, embarrassed for him and yet unable to turn away and give him his privacy. He stands for a minute or so looking at the body of his wife, and then turns and is led back to a seat by his son and daughter. It is eight-forty by this time, and still the minister hasn't showed up to do some sort of memorial service, and the funeral home operators—one of whom is the unctious fellow of the doorway, the other of whom looks like a golem created from clay as a clumsy image of the first—are standing in the doorway, their heads together, worrying about it. Their fears do not come true, however, for five minutes later the minister arrives.

The minister is a big, jovial man of 55 or so, with gold-rimmed glasses, who delivers a short oration that is similar in effect on me to a high-school football pep talk, equally full of platitudes and unrealities, but furthermore specially designed, or so it seems, to make us all gloss over the central fact and reality of death, and somehow steer us quickly past that vicious shoal, eyes and minds averted, onwards into the snug harbor of God's eternal life. The minister quickly wraps it all up with an air of long practice, shakes John's hand in a fatherly manner, and quickly departs: in my fantasy, at least, to his next funeral, to which he is already late, being on a tight schedule.

We all gird ourselves for the weather again, and go out to our cars and drive to Barret and John's house for some sort of gathering, the exact purpose of which is never made clear, except that the implication to me anyway is that it is to keep John occupied and keep his mind at rest at least until it is too late for everyone else and he must go to bed and face his loss in the dark and loneliness as best he can, hopefully so tired he will fall asleep quickly.

We pack ourselves into the little house and drink coffee and beer and talk, most of the younger relatives in the kitchen by themselves, repeating the farm living room performance of the afternoon, speaking in short unconnected paragraphs to each other. My cousin Peter, Dagny and John's son, has been in the Los Angeles area now for two years working as an assistant art director for ABC, and he and I start to talk, having the California experience in common, so that both he and I have gained a mythical sort of quality, being "Californians," considered to be initiates into the life of the Promised Land; but at the same time, as initiates, we alone are aware of the hollowness of that particular dream. We have a shared knowledge that throws us together because no one else is inclined to believe it. Moreover, I have been working in the tech theater and he is at least in that vicinity, working with sets for television. So I start asking him questions about the tech aspects of television production and the design problems, and he answers, and while it is a subject that normally I would probably not be likely to talk with him about, it comes in bits and flurries, so that I am from time to time drifting out in the living room to see what the rest of them are about; the older ones, the brothers and sisters. They are sitting down, in chairs and on the floor, and talking about nothing when, just as I come in, John suddenly hauls himself erect from the couch and starts to plod off through the front door onto the porch. Someone says "Kathy go with him, will you?" and Kathy gets up and follows him and someone tells him it is cold out there, he doesn't really want to go out there; but they both disappear, and reappear a bit later, John holding quivering in his big hands a very nice antique china bowl and an old cut-glass vase. He explains, very slowly, each word dragging the next out at long length, how these he had bought at an auction and was to give Dagny for Christmas. And he tells about each, and of their value and scarcity, which is simultaneously appreciated by the city relatives, for whom such pieces would in fact be both difficult to find and ridiculously expensive, and yet with some odd sort of loathing at the implications of the speech: "These are beautiful pieces and Dagny would have loved them had I given them to her, we all knew her well enough to have known that, but I never gave them to her, because I went down into the basement where I had them hidden two days ago and found her dead, hanging by her neck from a rafter. But she is dead now by her own hand because she couldn't stand something anymore, or what?"

And John makes it worse with each trip, coming next with an old earthenware water jug and a small gilt 1870's picture frame: the next time a cobalt blue glass vase and a pewter teapot; and finally with a full armload in a single object, a wood and mechanical gas-filled cigar lighter of 1910, with a heavy old fashioned battery to provide an ignition spark when a lever is pulled and all manner of complicated mechanisms move about on top, uncovering eventually a flame. Each object is passed around the room slowly, finally to be stacked on the mantle.

Each time, he moves with the same slow heavy motions, like a man trying to walk in the gravity of Jupiter, and I wonder who else is thinking what I am, that he is going down those long stairs into the basement and bringing this stuff up, does he remember explicitly two days ago when he went down there? Does he pass now in such a way that he can see where he found her then; does he remember her as she looked tonight after the tender ministrations of the morticians and remember how she looked down there that day in the dim light when he found her?

And each time he comes up he moves more slowly, and is more haggard, so that when he stands explaining about each object, he slowly weaves back and forth on his feet as if drunk, and the people sitting nearest him cannot get up but must sit alert, ready to leap and steady him should he start to fall, which seems to be imminent.

Sunday morning by ten or so the line has diminished to nothing outside the bathroom and everyone is dressed and eating breakfast, and I have to get out, so I take the car and go out for a couple hours and take pictures, coming back around 12:30 in time for dinner. Afterwards those who need to change clothes, do, and we set off again, this time for Barret, where the funeral is to be, in one of the local churches.

The weather is supposedly much better now than last night; that is to say because the illumination comes from the sun and not from headlights; the blowing snow doesn't reflect so badly, so that it isn't bad going at all. David is right about the area by Ten-mile, for it has an inch of glare ice underneath the snow, and in places is drifted over two feet deep but for one lane.

We get to Barret, and park behind the church, where the long high gray shapes of the limousine and hearse are already waiting, incongruously clean after all the other sand and slush-spattered cars, white salt stains all over their sides. We go inside and down into the church basement, where we have been told to wait. The basement is light green, with enclosed beams in the ceiling to support the church floor, standing on round steel pipe supports, the floor dark brown institutional asphalt tile, with long folding tables set up and dozens of folding chairs, bringing back immediately the church dinners with the great white paper table-cloths and everyone standing in line for his plate of meatballs and mashed potatoes; with speeches afterward, or perhaps Luther League nights, with thirty or forty teenagers playing absurd games and being instructed, the boys at least there mainly on the odd chance they may be able to pick up some nice piece, but, my own experience being any guide, an odd chance indeed. But the atmosphere is different now, and within twenty minutes or so there are sixty or eighty people down there, most of whom I have never seen before. There is a vast silence. On my right and ahead of me sits a woman of maybe 58, with tightly curled hair and a long brown coat and rhinestone-trimmed glasses, staring straight ahead in a sightless parody of grief, occasionally turning her head to her companion of similar vintage and visage and mumbling something and shaking her head slowly from side to side. John and his children and their husbands and wives are sitting on the left of me, seven of them in all, all alone along a long table with space and chairs for twenty, but no one will sit there. Rather they sit everywhere else, and wait, and watch, and shift their minds into some void I cannot penetrate.

At last the call comes for us to go upstairs, filing up the stairs at the back in the proper order, surviving immediate family first, followed by other family, followed by other family, followed by everyone else. The church is unfortunate, in that it began as a simple and straightforward country church, plain and austere, yet with its own special graciousness; yet it has lost this graciousness in a badly-planned trade for "modernity," with a new electric organ and concessions to fanciness, which only become somehow vulgar, destroying one quality without replacing it with another. The minister turns out to be the same one as at the funeral home the night before, which is also unfortunate, from my point of view, anyway, since I will have to sit through even more of the same drivel, which proves indeed to be the case, but everyone else seems to be by and large perfectly satisfied with it, so I cannot really complain. He eventually finishes, and the service is over, and we lug the surprisingly heavy coffin out-

side and slide it into the hearse, and then go back to our cars.
The burial itself is to be at Parkdale Church, where all the
Sageng family end up, which is between Dalton and Fergus,
which puts it some thirty-five miles away. So we set off, one car
after another, following the gray hearse into the swirling snow
and the silver gray of the afternoon sky.

We pass the Ten-mile Lake cutoff from Highway 59, and as
we pass it I notice the now-deserted Ten Mile School, where my
grandfather taught in the early nineties, standing now gaunt and
gray on a hilltop. To the left the sun has passed the meridian,
and I see sundogs for the first time, four brightly luminous fake
suns arranged in a circle around the true sun: reminding me of
Richard's funeral, which was in March some years ago and the
first time I ever saw Northern lights.

Parkdale church is nearly the epitome of the "country
church," standing on the top of one of the multitude of low,
steep glacial hills that make up southeastern Ottertail County.
Shaded by now-bare black oaks, surrounded by an old cemetery,
it would make an ideal Christmas card picture, except that now
in the dead of winter is a bit too cold and savage, even to the
eye, for the sensibilities of suburbanites.

We pull off the highway into the parking area, and from the
angle from which we now see the church, it suddenly reminds
me of some time when I was quite young, for my grandfather
was still alive, and some woman was writing a book and talking
to him about the old days in the county, and he dug out old pictures; the one I remember of him and his father-in-law, Knud
Brandvold, standing in the somber black coats of the times in
front of the church on the Fourth of July, 1897, on the occasion
of the second annual church picnic, the picture showing those
two men and a hundred or so others with miscellaneous wives
all standing in a great crowd before the church: horses gently
cropping the grass in the background in the area by now all
filled with graves. Parkdale luckily has so far avoided the fate of
its sister church in Barret, being really impressive inside in the
plain manner of its building. The family plot is on the left side
of the church, and shaking and jarring there now in the wind

that comes sweeping across the hills all the way from Saskatche-
wan and Montana, is a ludicrous green canvas awning contrap-
tion, built upwind to shelter the graveside. As I get up to the
grave, silly as the thing looks, I cannot help but have some
gratitude for it, for within the space of one small minute the
wind and the cold have gone through my heavy Mackinaw coat,
a suit coat, a sweater, a shirt, and an undershirt to chill me right
through to the center. My face and ears, at least, no longer hurt,
while my feet will approach numbness in the next minute or so.

But we all stand there shaking around the grave, while the
minister goes through his hurried litany. "Ash to ashes, dust to
dust, from thence thou came, and thence thou shall return"
making the sign of the cross on the head of the casket with a
sprinkling of sand from some special shaker designed for the
purpose: the wind grasping the sand and whipping it away into
the snow instantly. As soon as he is through we all run back to
the cars and drive back to the farm for more food and gathering
while I am remembering that were it not for modern technology
(the tractor-mounted hydraulic backhoe) there would be no in-
terment until spring and the ground thawed out enough to permit
digging. And Gretchen, who is with us, says, in a strange levity,
"It's no wonder Minnesota was settled by Norwegians—nobody
else would have been crazy enough to put up with this weather."

When we get back to the farm I check the thermometer,
which is on the lee side of the house, and find that it is, at three
in the afternoon, twenty-six below. We all wander about between
the living room and dining room holding plates with sandwiches
and cookies and salad and drinking coffee for a while. It strikes
me now most forcibly that in all this time, no one has ever
speculated, at least publicly, about why Dagny killed herself.
Everyone knows that she had been depressed often, and that
she had been in and out of the state hospital a couple of times,
but it is still clear too that no one thinks of her as "crazy." The
whole question is avoided in silence. Finally, my mother and
sister and I decide to leave so that we can make most of the
drive back to St. Paul in daylight, so we move about expressing
the proper sentiments and saying goodby.

By nine we are back in St. Paul, and unpacked, and having sat around for a while for appearances, I call up Jeff at home and say "Hey man, I been to the funeral and I'm back and I have no mind left," and he says "Right, I'll be over in twenty minutes," and fifteen minutes later I hear the 'Stang pull into the driveway, and I go out and we drive in the cold of the city to the Triangle Bar in Minneapolis, where we sit down at the bar and listen to the blues, and I sit leaning forward over the bar, holding a bottle of Bud between my two hands and drinking from it: so that after a while of silence I only say "Shit man": and I am back all the way.

the perry lane papers (III): how it was

vic lovell

I AM thirty-four years old now, older than Jesus when he was crucified, having lived out what was, so I am told, during the Dark ages a man's life expectancy, and still trying, as they say, to find an authentic voice. There was a time when literate men wrote constantly, and if you want to find out what was happening then, you have an endless supply of journals, essays, chronicles, histories, letters, poems, plays, and novels, which you may pore through. Scholars of the future will have the mass media, official documents, and artifacts galore, but I suspect they may be short on personal statements.

I would like to think that this state of affairs is shortlived. The prospect, more and more often advanced these days, that the written word and the printed page are about to lose the kind of importance that they have had for so long in civilized communication depresses me. I would prefer to believe that what we have today is merely a hiatus, or even that when it is all over it will be found that the statements were made after all, and that they had merely to be discovered and understood, like any other time.

Even so, there is a problem. The people I know who write seem all to be susceptible to a kind of doubtfulness and fumbling which I believe to be new in our times, or at the very least, of greater degree. They wonder if writing is really where it's at anymore. They do not have that transcendental faith in the validity of what they are doing which you feel when you read even the most insignificant written material from previous centuries. Some persist, some experiment with new forms, some dabble in other media, and many wind up doing nothing. In the circles I have traveled, this lack of faith has at times extended even to the spoken word. Having had the realization that most of what people say is nonsense, and rather tedious and dishonest nonsense at that, the hippest people around often sit together in silence, glancing uneasily at each other, fearing that anything they say will only make things worse. It is difficult to get very far into any really serious conversation without someone mentioning that whatever is really important cannot be put into words, and that talk about the matter at hand is probably a substitute for feeling or action.

Myself, I freak out every single time I sit down at the typewriter, and my anxiety and confusion have nothing much to do with what I am supposedly there for, but rather with the commitment and the time which it takes to set something down on paper. It seems that there is virtually nothing of any consequence which I have not changed my mind about many times over, nothing which has happened to me which I really understood at the time when it happened, and nothing which I could say or write at this point or could have said or written at any other point which was or is or ever could be nearly as important as my getting up and going out and being deeply and intimately involved in whatever is going down right now.

Ever since I can remember, I have felt the urgency of keeping up with things. Every day the roll is called, every day the word is given, every day events outrun my expectations, and every day I feel like crying out with all the anguish and joy of a new-born child, anguish on some days and joy on others. At this moment, only a short distance away, students from Stanford University are trying to shut down Stanford Research Institute, an event which I have dreamed of for years. They are fighting the police in the streets, and while I am writing my next door neighbor comes home from the fray, exhausted, full of wild tales, and still trying to get the tear gas out of her eyes.

Last night my next door neighbor on the other side comes home from Berkeley in the same condition, having apparently been shot at by the National Guard. Today the action is heavier there, and someone who calls me on the telephone says that people have been killed by police bullets. At a time like this I am sitting at home, having made up my mind that now is the time to try to write down something about how me and mine got to where we are now. I am wondering if I am being prudent or chickenshit, which alternatives I am often examining myself in terms of.

The trouble is, life without continuity is disorienting. Maybe I am finally beginning to become old-fashioned, but I really want some coherent sense of where I have been and where I am going, and so I have to start somewhere, and it might as well be now, which means staying home and indulging in memory and reflection. I have already forgotten too much. I used to think that if I accumulated enough experiences understanding would come of its own accord, in some final form, but now I know better.

I am a citizen of the San Francisco Bay area, and I live in what is called the Midpeninsula, which centers around Palo Alto, Menlo Park, and Stanford University. I came to Stanford in nineteen fifty-three, as a Freshman, and went to school here for a total of nine years, earning three degrees, ending with a Ph.D. in psychology. I also went to the University of California at Berkeley for a couple of years and worked a few years at Stanford at the Counseling and Testing Center, where the students may go when they become upset or confused, and worked a year at the Counseling Center at San Francisco State College. After this I dropped out of academia, except to join in the struggle against it.

All of this accounts for my formal education, my profession, my income, my being here, and for a great deal of my time, but says nothing really about what my life is all about. When it becomes necessary for me to prepare a vita or a resume or fill out an application detailing education, training, jobs, putting my one and only signature to cover letters, affirmations, oaths, and so forth, I want to scream over the lie in which I participate, because what mattered all that time was to create another kind of career entirely, and it seems terribly tragic and wasteful that so much of myself went into relating and adjusting with a society in which I could not really believe.

In the beginning I tended to assume that my life would be as an outsider. I think I had some vague romantic notions of being an intellectual, or bohemian, or simply a failure and an outcast, and that would be it. But fairly early in the game I saw that there was such a thing as history, and that it was going on around me, and that things would change, perhaps in my favor, so that I could participate without withdrawing. I thought, I will begin now and try to find another way to live, and not let everybody else make me feel bad about it. Without in the least knowing where to begin, I began anyway, and many others began, each in their own way, and after a while we had something going for ourselves, though for a long time none of us could say anything articulate about what. We experienced what Timothy Leary used to call the numbers game: if there is one of you, you are insane; if there are two, you have a relationship; a few more and you have a cult; still more and you have a movement, and so forth.

While many of us despair, I become more and more optimistic, for it seems to me that beginning something is the most difficult thing of all, and that the birth of a dissident minority is far slower and more painful than the later emergence of some kind of consensus that society must change. Everyday what were once remote and outlandish fantasies, excursions into ironic humor, casual speculation, and anxious whimsy, just such stuff as this comes to be what reality is made of. When they finally come to get us, we used to tell each other, we would turn them on. This prospect, together with the implausible flights of imagination which accompanied it, used to send us into gales of hysterical laughter. And yet, this very week the National Guard invaded Berkeley and were met, among other things, by innocent appearing girls who offered them fruit and pastry laced with marijuana and LSD. It didn't work nearly as well as we used to think it would, but then all tactics take time to perfect.

There is cause for optimism, even for joy, but not for complacency or frivolity. It was some fourteen years ago that Allen Ginsberg wrote that he had seen the best minds of his generation driven mad, but the madness which he had seen was only a drop in the bucket to the madness that was to come. Four years ago I attended a meeting of the student movement at Berkeley. The movement had won control of the student body government in the wake of the Free Speech Movement, and the response of the administration had been to attempt to abolish the student body government as a compulsory organization. One student spoke and he said that the time would come when the movement would have to occupy space and say to the authorities that, "if you want us out of here you will have to kill us." The student felt that if someone died, it might settle something. Though the idea was immediately rejected, he was applauded sympathetically. Now someone has died in Berkeley, and still nothing is settled, nor seems about to be.

These spectacular confrontations become ever more frequent and more critical. They come as a surprise to those who control and administrate the established institutions, and often enough to those involved. They are like icebergs, with nine-tenths of their mass below the surface of the water in which they float. What lies beneath that which is visible is an incredibly complex accumulation of small but significant changes in the daily lives and patterns of thought of large numbers of ordinary people who eventually find themselves doing extraordinary things.

My own life in the American underground began about twelve years ago at Perry Lane. Just as every dog has fleas, so every college and university had such places near it then, where those who were in but not of the campus lived. Nowadays, of course, much larger areas are liberated, and low cost housing is a political issue, exacerbated by the foolishness of the campus administrators, city planners, and local power structures who hope that the no accounts and troublemakers will go away if there is no place for them to live.

Behind the Stanford University Campus are the grassy meadows and rolling hills of Portola Valley, and then the Santa Cruz Mountains, and then the Pacific Coast. Every year there are new housing developments, shopping centers are built, and roads are widened. The land behind the campus gradually loses its woodsy character, but twelve years ago Perry Lane was not inaccurately classified as a rural slum.

The cottages in which we lived were old and small and rented cheaply. They nestled among ancient valley oaks, pepper trees, acacias, and eucalyptus. On the ground there was wild grass, planted grass, or flowering myrtle. Much of the area was covered with dense shrubbery. At one end of the block, in front of the house where I lived, there was a huge oak tree growing right out of the middle of the street, growing right out of the pavement. The tree was shaped like a wish bone with the apex pointing down and the two ribs stretching upwards. At twilight, silhouetted against the sky, it looked like a giant with arms upraised, as if on guard. The Stanford Golf Course was one block away, and along its edge ran San Francisquito Creek. Normally, the water ran a foot or two deep. In the heat of the summer it was often reduced to stagnant pools, and in the winter it ran fast and deep and threatened to overflow its banks. Old timers remembered that once you could catch crawdads and steelhead trout. The banks of the creek rose up from ten to forty feet, and there were bridges across it at various points in the golf course. If you crossed the bridge and walked towards the campus you walked by the riding stables and then found yourself on the edge of Lake Lagunita, Stanford's part-time lake. The lake was filled with water from the Searsville Reservoir. Sometimes it was there and sometimes it was dry and you could walk across it. Around the lake was the western edge of the Stanford University Campus, about a twenty minute walk from Perry Lane.

Most of this still remains, but the topography is gradually altering. I first saw Perry Lane in my undergraduate years at Stanford, moved there in 1957, and left six years later in 1963, when a large portion of the land was sold and cleared. The developers built six large, expensive, tract type houses. Although most of the old homes remained, along with the oak tree in the middle of the road, the essential character of the place was destroyed. Four key living units were gone, together with most of the trees, shrubs, and open space. Many similar residential situations in the same general area met the same fate in the next few years, the rent tended to go up in those that remained, and that was pretty much the end of it. Succeeding generations of dissidents have lived in East Palo Alto with the blacks, or in older, more run down housing in Palo Alto proper. These events marked the end of a tradition over half a century old, during which Perry Lane and the area around it constituted Stanford's proper bohemia. Throughout that time it had been the home of generations of unconventional students and professors, radical intellectuals, artists, and writers. While I lived there The Lane and the area immediately surrounding it were known as "Sin Hollow," a name which it had had for more than thirty years.

Thorstein Veblen, author of *The Theory of the Leisure Class,* and one of the great radical critics of American society, lived there in 1907 in a house called Cedro Cottage, with a menagerie of hens, cats, cows, horses, and students. Veblen, an eccentric scholar who wrote in the areas of economics, politics, sociology, and anthropology, was a socialist and had a reputation for being involved in improper sexual adventures. Among the projects at which he apparently worked at the time was a book called *The Higher Learning in America,* first published in 1918, in which one may find the broad outlines of the view of higher education in the United States which is currently proclaimed by the New Left. He found the academic community dominated by business interests which subverted its proper goals and values, and concluded his book by saying that ". . . from the point of view of the higher learning, the academic executive and all his works are anathema, and should be discontinued by the simple expedient of wiping him off the slate; and that the governing board, in so far as it presumes to exercise any other than vacantly perfunctory duties, has the same value and should with advantage be lost in the same shuffle."

Veblen left Stanford the following year, but he returned to Cedro to die some twenty years later, and we imagined that his shade was still with us when I lived there, although the site where Cedro had stood was by then a school yard. Mrs. Ann Sims, his stepdaughter, lived and still lives around the corner at one end of Perry. In the house there is a small bronze relief of her step-father, done by her late husband Ralph, who was a metal sculptor. Mrs. Sims has been active in the Peace Movement for over ten years, and seldom misses a demonstration. A reporter called once to ask about the bohemians. She told him she did not understand the word.

Among the more eminent former residents of The Lane are Louis M. Terman, psychologist who studied and measured human intelligence and carried out one of the first survey studies of sexual behavior and marital adjustment, Felix Bloch, physicist and Nobel Laureate, and Lincoln Moses, presently Executive Head of the Statistics Department and Associate Dean of Humanities and Sciences at Stanford University.

In my day The Lane attracted a variety of people who, for one reason or another, were on the lam from straight society. Some of the best known of these are Ken Kesey, author of *One Flew Over the Cuckoo's Nest* and the subject of Tom Wolfe's best-selling biography *The Electric Kool-Aid Acid Test*, Richard Alpert, psychologist who, together with Timothy Leary and Ralph Metzner, were thrown out of Harvard as a result of their work with LSD, and who then authored *The Psychedelic*

Experience and became the national gurus of the psychedelic mystic, Robb Crist, who later became Executive Director of the Midpeninsula Free University, James Wolpman, now principal lawyer for The Movement in the Midpeninsula area, Chloe Scott, who has taught creative dance movement locally for over twelve years, and George Ralph, who was elected student body president of Stanford University in 1956 on the basis of his proposal to eliminate student body government on the grounds that it had no important function, five years before SDS. Three blocks away, in a oversized crash pad called The Chateau, there lived for a while a rather unorthodox rock band called *The Warlocks,* which was later renamed *The Grateful Dead.*

Though it is only six years later, much of what we did would not now shock a local high school student. What started at The Lane, and at other places like it, now grown to a mass movement and having various organized and socially active manifestations, does indeed baffle, enrage, and terrify the parents, but you can often detect a mellowing and gradual acceptance even there. The mass media now inform the older generation of the changes that are going down, and their educative tone seems to indicate that the reader is expected to adjust his sensibilities. The most restless of our youth seem already impatient with the new life styles, and may be ready to go on to something else, perhaps even more mind blowing.

Be this as it may, it all seemed pretty wild at the time, and the visions we had, the questions we asked, and the problems we encountered are more than ever with us now. As for myself, the Perry Lane experience provided the foundation of my identity, and most of what I have done since has consisted either in constructing the rest of the building or altering this foundation where I have found it wanting. Some people I know want to stay high all the time, but I have come to feel that it's best to go up and come down, leaving plenty of time and space to get oneself together in between psychic explosions. There's a lot of spiritual indigestion around these days, and in the long run the outcome is often the refusal of further nourishment by the perforated soul. I write in hopes of consolidating my experience, so that I can better assimilate the next revelation. There is a long distance still to be traveled. A subculture is not a culture, and a life style is not a way of life. The best, and the worst, are yet to come.

Seated behind my desk, in the capacity of college counselor or private psychotherapist, I have had ample opportunity to view the dislocation and alienation which have characterized the past decade. In the short run, the sudden and rapid advance of new visions, new values, and new alternatives have often served only to compound the confusion, but I believe that we must not hesitate to move on. The critical points in historical transition are always the most painful for those involved. We must recognize this pain, celebrate it, and pause to understand it and minister to it, but we cannot stop or go back.

This imperative, and the perils and urgencies it implies, have been the subject of the principles and slogans of the day. In the human potential movement the talk is of Risk and Trust and Going With It and Breaking Through. The black liberators cry Revolution In Our Time. The psychedelic gurus say The Way In Is The Way Out. The tacticians of the New Left explain that When You are Threatened or Isolated You Should Take The Offensive. The sign on Ken Kesey's bus simply said Further.

I know we have to keep going, but I really do want to know where. Maybe I am getting old. Maybe there isn't even time to ask. Among turned on people and social activists, one of the heaviest put downs going is to say that someone is trying to figure out what to do next. Given that one is trying to figure that out, thinking about the past and the future is not considered the method of choice, since this distracts from the here and now, which is where the action is.

Here I am, doing it anyway, I hope my friends will forgive me, not tell me how straight I'm getting. It seems to me that the most important of the assumptions which underlies the current insurgencies is the Enlightenment belief that we can be much better than we are. This is nothing new, but what seems to be new is the faith that we can do it now and the conviction that we must, and the fact that this conviction and this faith are informed by concrete experiences which we have had. In our own lives, we have been touched by salvation, and by the possibility of complete damnation.

It was on Perry Lane, and from the karma that I acquired there, that I had these concrete experiences. It was there that I first felt love, sensuality, creativity, spontaneity, and the sense of human community, and it was also there and thereafter that I first felt the possibility that total disaster could overtake mankind if something were not done, by each in his own way, if only to drop out. When I get disoriented, I try to remember how it felt.

2 a.m. in oakland

ann thrift

THE CITY has no roots, no past—only the present, the moving, shifting, restless change. Solid it seems, built of rock to stand forever, and none born of it can ever leave—its ugliness, despair, the lonely searching currents, the pain lives in their blood like a parasite. They can never be free. Sad and weary, blues and jazz were born there, music of paradox, of pleasure and pain, the music of escape, and yet expressive of the things they all flee. The city has no roots, no strength binding us to the earth below, the earth lying suffocated and hidden from life and the light. The city has no soul, and it kills the souls of those who are drawn back, again and again, to this ancient prostitute, so tired of life that she is beyond pain, beyond birth and death and sorrow, with the mindlessness of an inanimate object, the paradox of a bloodless being which yet has life drawn from her children. And although most eventually become mindless, soulless, heartless, they search for love and warmth and joy, sadly and painfully groping for each other in the dark rooms, without privacy and yet always alone—Noise, confusion, glaring lights and sweet agonizing music—there is no peace in the city, no quiet, no rest—always tense and half-awake, like animals in a jungle pacing the streets, but misplaced—they are men living like beasts, not knowing what their pain is, for it is too close, too united to their beings. To cut off the city is to cut off an arm or an eye or a heart. And so, when the beautiful love, the fragile peace, the tender joy is born, it is more poignant, perhaps seemingly more intense.

I would like to share some beauty with you, I want to know you and get inside your life. Baby I wanna love you. I want to make you laugh, I want to see your eyes look at me with all of you coming through. Maybe some other time. . . .

It's late and smoky, but I can't sleep—I'll keep staring into the long night, wondering what you're doing, out in that prowling city, that damn jungle—Baby it's killing you: it's war, it's real it's got me by the guts, it's right here and I can't run away—I hate you City, and you laugh mockingly at me as I sit here and the tears fall. I hate you to the core of your being. You slap us in the face, you kick us in the balls, and when we turn around spitting like cats to fight, there is no one but each other, and so we destroy the only ones who can save us from you, the monster we created, not knowing it would betray us and bleed us to death.

And so you breed us, your children, for war and hatred.

The old whore has life in her yet—she is still beautiful somehow, the cruel bitch. So beautiful I can love her knowing as I do the evil she makes, and hating her at the same time.

Someday I'm gonna see you lying dead and bleeding on the street, and something inside me is gonna scream "Murder" soundlessly. And I won't cry, not for a long time, because I know that out there somewhere your death is waiting, like a crouching animal waiting for you. And it could be any time, even right now. I lie in bed awake with the smell of gas and the cockroaches, the ash-trays and the coffee-cups, waiting for you, my street-fighting man, but also waiting for your death, so that when it comes something inside me can die too, and I'll stop hoping for something better, I'll be mindless like the rest. And when I do cry, honey, I'll be saying goodbye for the last time, and it'll hurt like hell—but hell is where I live. I'll get over it. And you don't even know.

Come home soon, honey—I'm blue and lonely. I feel hopeless, futile as I stare out the window to the streets you walk every day, to the life that is yours, that I know; but I can't save you from it, baby, it's too big. Let's shuck and jive, have some wine and soul music, and forget for a little while what's outside. Let's smile at each other and laugh with our friends, so we don't end up crying all the time. Let's make a little love and hope the real thing comes along someday.

all about our vasectomies: a stitch in time saves nine

robert cullenbine and ivan

Population control is the issue now, in recognition of the fact that Nature, in an errant moment, endowed man with a built-in, paradoxical capacity to breed himself literally out of existence; we're pouring out babies at an alarming geometric rate, a circumstance long known to working-class mothers and recently seized upon by holders of large capital resources. Popular contraceptive techniques have been stopgap and, in light of the consequences, remarkably slipshod—Honey, did you remember your pill? You *what?*

Permanent contraception—sterilization—has been virtually taboo among even better-educated, sophisticated circles, but with increasing concern over side effects of the Pill, the popularity of the "population" issue and the growing inability of even upper-income families to reproduce indefinitely, sterilization is becoming a more palatable alternative.

The vasectomy is a simple form of male sterilization, legal in all fifty states, and 75,000 men were vasectomized last year in

the United States alone. The enthusiasm of these people is caus-
ing the barriers of fear and superstition to fall even more rapidly.
The operation itself, performed in the doctor's office, is the sim-
ple cutting of the two sperm ducts—the vas deferens—*that go from*
the scrotum up into the penis. Bob Cullenbine and Ivan are two
members of the Free University who have had vasectomies.
They're satisfied, and their voices haven't risen, at least at the time
of this interview:

(why)

Cullenbine: Ivan is like the first guy who ever took LSD. Now
that he's gotten his tubes snipped, he's an evangelist for vasectomies.

Ivan: I was a population nut long before I was a vasectomy
nut. I was a parlor bore about the expanding population clear
back into the Forties. I had mine in November, 1968. The
psychological effects are the normal anxieties any man gets
when someone's fiddling around down there with a knife. The
only noticeable physical effect, other than sterility, is about 10%
less ejaculation fluid.

Cullenbine: It hurts less than a dentist giving a shot of Novocaine.

Ivan: There aren't any aftereffects; every so often I think
about it and sort of smile to myself and say, "Boy, that's the
best thing I ever did." It's about 40% reversible.

Cullenbine: I did it because Carole gets freaky behind the
pill, and because our third child was conceived while she was
on the pill. We've now got three children, it's a big thing to take
care of them. I don't think people should have more than two
children, and I've already got three.

If you get this idea on your own, and don't have experienced
friends to help, where do you turn for advice?

Ivan: Call your physician and don't ask him where's the
best place to get a vasectomy, ask where the *doctors* get their
vasectomies.

This one urologist puts in a double knot, and then loops the needle through the tube itself, so a plug is formed, and he thinks the plug itself is the real thing that holds the sperm back.

(shaving)

Ivan: I agonized over it. I tried my electric razor and it started to pinch a little bit, so one day at work I decided, all right, I'm gonna do it. So I got this pair of scissors, a brand new pair, from the stationer, sharp as hell, and went into the men's room and started cutting away. It's really surprising how well you can do with just a pair of scissors. It made me feel a hell of a lot better. That night I tried using my electric razor again and did it successfully, with only minimal pinching.

Cullenbine: I did it in our bathtub, on my knees. I used my razor with the edgetrimmer for sideburns. It was slow, gentle but didn't hurt at all. Then I used a brand-new platinum blade to touch up the remainder. Didn't cut myself once. I took a hot bath afterward. No aftershave.

Ivan: The only change in my self-awareness was just a generalized, cold anxiety syndrome.

Cullenbine: I felt freaky. I felt like I had a newborn baby rat extending down there.

(*Carole Cullenbine adds: he was nasty, irritable, feisty and unpleasant.*) I had a real urge to expose myself to everyone around me, to let them see the sacrifice I was going through for the good of my family and humanity. It's growing back, now, it's reached the length—the hair, that is—of about an eighth of an inch. I'm starting from scratch, sorta.

(preoperative frights)

Cullenbine: I woke up once before the operation having dreamed that I was looking down at a tombstone sticking out of my pubic area, with *Rest In Peace, 1970* chiseled on it. I fantasized painting my balls and penis red, white and blue, stripes and all, with little messages to the doctor, like *a stitch in time saves nine* and *go easy, brother, you're fooling with my destiny.* I saw myself wearing one of those buttons saying, *I quit.*

Ivan: I don't recall having one noticeable dream about it. I had apprehensions, general worry, and went into it like I go into any operation. I chickened out three times before going through with the interview. All sorts of elaborate excuses.

Cullenbine: Yeah, about eighty-seven times during the two days before the operation, I said, fuck it, man, it's just not *natural,* I'm not gonna do it, I'm gonna have all the kids I want.

Ivan: It's done in the doctor's office, under local anesthetic. First he mainlines some demoral . . .

Cullenbine: My first fix.

Ivan: Earlier in the day you generally take a tranquilizer. Then he gives you the demoral, and you talk. We talked about Esalen.

Cullenbine: I gave him some Free University literature.

Ivan: Then he rubs some cocaine on the injection area . . . cocaine has a topical anesthetic effect, a surface effect. When he sticks the needle in, you don't feel a thing, because most of the nerves are on the surface. You feel nothing, don't even imagine it.

Cullenbine: I'd have reached down there and gotten some for my nose if I'd known it was cocaine.

Ivan: Freud was the person who found out that cocaine could anesthetize the surface of the skin.

Cullenbine: I was scared shitless when I went in there, and I told him so. I told him that I have a very low tolerance for pain.

Ivan: The minute he puts the demoral in you feel a sudden rush.

Cullenbine: I didn't feel a rush for about ten minutes, I was so scared. He said, "Breathe heavily," and I felt the rush. The fact that he mainlines it indicates that he knows how freaked out most guys are. I felt for a while that it's unnatural, there he is going into the system, snipping stuff that was meant to be there. But then, the pill is unnatural, and we still don't know what it does to women.

Ivan: The sperm sort of back up, swim into your bloodstream and are metabolized.

Vern Gates suggested the other day that you just have the tube shunted through to come out your back. . . .

Cullenbine: Yeah, or out your ear. That would be interesting.

Right when he was putting in the Novocaine, I was thinking that we could *never* live in a society where this sort of thing becomes required. When this becomes involuntary, it's not worth living. I was thinking this while he was doing it. This is something a man has to choose himself, personally, voluntarily. Forced, it could be one of the most brutal, savage things that could ever be done to a person.

Ivan: But physically, it's quite comparable to circumcision. It took only 20 minutes. This doctor's done 2000 and has never had a failure. (*Ivan's wife Sheila adds: When he was first talking about it, I didn't like it, because I was thinking of having another baby. But now, as a means of birth control, I think it's absolutely great.*)

(*Carole Cullenbine: I was afraid Culley wouldn't do it. I was all for it, all the way through. His mood changed only about four days before, and a couple of days following. He was freaked, frightened. I don't blame him. I would have been, too.*)

Cullenbine: Afterward, we drove home, I got into bed, issued instructions that I wasn't to be disturbed by anyone, and the doctor had already told Carole that her greatest responsibility was to keep the kids from jumping up and down on my middle. I went to bed, had about nine dollars worth of magazines, and it was pretty good.

Ivan: I wasn't really incapacitated. You should stay flat for two days, and that's it. Use an ice bag: sometimes there's swelling. The pain I noticed after was a small amount of sharp pain from the incision, but that was just minor. The incision is right on top of the balls. He only uses a compress bandage, no adhesive. The initial pain lasted only a couple of hours. It was supplanted by a kind of dull ache, like you'd been playing softball and the ball hit you.

Cullenbine: I felt like I'd been hit in the crotch with a board.

Ivan: The ache lasts about two days, aspirin helps keep it down. I've never had a recurrence.

Cullenbine: On the third day I went down to the Free U and painted all day. It hurt then, but on the fifth day I finally got a supporter, which I should have done in the first place, and there's no pain at all.

Ivan: You should take a long, hot bath every night right after the operation. I'm doing a book on this. There are *no* worthwhile books in the field right now. It's going to be a small, A-to-Z compendium with a couple of case histories.

(afterthoughts)

Ivan: If you have any sexual problems relating to contraceptives, vasectomies are the answer.

Cullenbine: The doctor said that a lot of people's sex lives have gotten *better,* because the woman had been afraid of getting pregnant. When she gets over that fear, she really gets with it. (*Carole: Let's face it. One labor pain would wipe you guys out.*)

Ivan: One interesting negative effect was noted some time ago by a British medical journal, which reported that a number of child-laden laboring class men got vasectomies, and for the first few months, it was a real honeymoon . . . both the husbands and wives were no longer afraid, and were really able to screw up a storm. But it had increasingly bad effects on the women, because the wife wasn't able to use the normal weapon of refusal. And guys with impotency problems should think twice about this operation.

Cullenbine: The doctor says the only psychological problems come from guys who were sick before the operation. The operation isn't a copout; having problems afterward means there were problems all along.

Ivan: The doctor is sharp enough to decide whether a person is suitable for the operation by interviewing beforehand. Grounds for unsuitability are known impotency problems, or being brought in involuntarily for the operation. They always make sure the wife is 100% behind the whole thing.

Cullenbine: But it's something between a man and a doctor, like an abortion should be solely between a woman and a competent doctor, it's none of a man's business.

Would either one of you have any reservations about doing this again?

Ivan: Unhesitatingly, no.

Cullenbine: I'd do it again in six months, if this doesn't take. I'll know in a few weeks, when they take this sperm count. They're going to stare down into their microscopes and see this little intercellular shipwreck.

Ivan: If the operation is done right, the success level is virtually one hundred per cent. And most of this guy's patients are doctors. (*Sheila: Women's tube-tying is much less reliable than a vasectomy, and a harder and more painful operation. Doctors don't make any guarantees.*)

Cullenbine: After the operation, there's still a few inches of tube full of sperm. If anyone wants to have a Cullenbine baby, I'm still good for another month or so. I passed the word at a Free University meeting the other night, but there weren't any takers. Sort of a clearance sale.

organic gardening for suburbanites

gurney norman

MANY SUBURBANITES are unhappy with their lifestyle and entertain notions of "getting back to the land" some day. Gardening on a small scale begins to make that an actual possibility, at the same time that it brightens the suburban context itself. A family with even a small amount of land can be close to the earth if it will take that land seriously *as land,* and not just "space" to park a car in, or set up swings for children. I know of four vegetable gardens in Menlo Park and Palo Alto, and undoubtedly there are more. One couple virtually subsists, as vegetarians, from a backyard garden in Menlo Park. To me they are into the most radical activity going, and as far as I know they aren't "political" at all. Their activity assaults *directly* the premises of industrialism, and specialization. A million people who know how to raise food like they do seem to me a greater threat to "the system" than a million people with guns, in an infinitely more creative way. And the raising of food is a learned thing.

part one: work

Last fall I spread a layer of mulch over the spot I intended to till this spring, stable bedding and horse manure five or six inches deep. By February, after two months of rain, the under-layers of the mulch had already rotted into the earth, so that when I began to dig in preparation for the spring planting, it was easy to thrust the spade to its hilt in the sodden mulch and saturated ground beneath. Throughout February I dug eight or ten hours a week, lifting spade-size bites, turning them, going on, till finally the entire patch was dug to a depth of about a foot.

In March the ground dried enough to sift and break down more finely. I was working with a fork by now, inch by inch, foot by foot, over and over again, breaking up the clods and clumps of grass, tilling in the mulch until it disappeared. I lost count of how many times I went over the plot with spade and fork. I remember estimating at one point that I'd dug more than 50 hours. A rototiller could have done the same job in an hour or two, but when I'd finished I was glad I'd resisted the temptation to use one. My relationship to the place I live is abstract enough as it is, imagined, for the most part, through the windshield of my car as I drive along Willow Road, the Alameda, El Camino, University Avenue. There was already enough machinery be-tween me and the world to volunteer for more in the garden. It felt good to be intimate with a portion of Menlo Park's earth. Digging into it, I dug this place as never before and that was the first reward of this year's experiment in organic gardening.

In late March I laid off the rows, six of them, plus beds out to the side for lettuce, radishes and carrots. The carrot bed was a special experiment. I'm interested in gardening inside the context of the typical suburban home, where space is limited and the soil is usually dead and hardpan. So I built a frame five feet square, small enough for the smallest back yard, covered the bottom with screen to make it gopher-proof, and in it began to manufacture soil.

The process was similar to making compost. I put in a layer of sawdust, a layer of horse manure, a thin layer of dirt, some kitchen garbage, wood ashes, old hay and leaves, then additional layers of all those things until the box was full, nine inches deep in organic materials soon to become rich humus.

That was in February. After a two-month soaking in California rain I planted carrots. I planted them too thickly, the first of several mistakes I made from inattention and excessive zeal. But after some thinning the remainder flourished. We began eating them in late May when they were about two inches long. Chloe and I have had carrots every day for over two months now, and I've given a lot away. The one box, five feet square, produced over 200 sweet carrots of middle size from one 29 cent packet of seed.

Two rows of beans, a row of cucumbers, the beds of radishes and lettuce were equally successful, and now as we move into August on the downhill side of summer it appears there's going to be a bumper crop of tomatoes. I have 7 plants laden with about 20 tomatoes each, just now ripening. We've had at least 50 large cucumbers from the one row, and they continue to sprout. The two rows of beans provided about 20 substantial messes. I gave some away, and have two messes drying in the attic. There was so much lettuce it began to get tough before we could eat it all. A couple of zucchini plants have contributed to three or four meals, and we had some new potatoes from the experimental plantings I made in sawdust. I calculate roughly that the garden produced enough food for at least thirty abundant vegetarian meals for two people, and that does not count the tomatoes.

Or the failures. My worst failure was the pepper plants, which all summer suffered from some strange blight or bug I could find no organic solution for. One plant is finally producing a few peppers, but it's crippled. Two other plants died. Gophers destroyed two tomato plants and four bean vines. (If anybody knows a sure-fire solution to gophers, I'd be pleased to hear about it.) I was a poor planter when I was making the cucumber row. In my enthusiasm I planted the seeds too deeply and they never sprouted. A planting of celery in the empty radish bed never came up. Too little water, I figured, but I'm not sure.

Even in death, however, the lost plants and failed rows provided a harvest of experience. I learned from the mistakes, and don't expect to make them again.

With two exceptions, I was faithful to the organic principle throughout. I even covered the balk between rows with a layer of straw mulch, which prevented weeds and helped enormously in keeping the ground cool and moist. I fertilized entirely with organic materials, mainly manure and compost from a pile I made last fall. I purchased small bags of commercial organic fertilizer—bone meal, blood meal, composted steer manure and a product called Milorganite, made from Milwaukee sewage—to familiarize myself with organic products available in stores. I ordered a thousand earthworms through *Organic Gardening* magazine and added them, plus about a zillion ladybugs my friends Kathleen and Leta gave me. I also grew some sunflowers to attract certain birds that feed on certain destructive bugs, though the flowers were so late in maturing I doubt they helped much. They're beautiful, though, and weren't any trouble beyond watering occasionally.

I cheated twice. I might as well admit it and get it over with. Once, early in the season when an army of slugs and snails threatened, I panicked and put out some poison snail bait. I felt so guilty I went out next day and removed it. Later, just as the potatoes were about to flower, some bug or blight caused them to wither and (mea culpa), I dusted them lightly with an insecticide. Dismayingly enough, it seemed to work. The potatoes stopped deteriorating, I almost wished they hadn't. No wonder people resort to insecticides too casually. It's such an easy way out of a present dilemma that even an idealist such as I had to work at it to keep in mind the fact that the price of chemical life in my garden, now, is chemical death, later, for other plants down the ecological stream from me. It was discouraging to see how paltry my ideals were, once my gardener's back was against the wall. I hope I'm skilled enough next time to avoid the insecticide temptation at the first crisis.

part two: reward

From the outset I was determined to avoid relating to the garden abstractly, in terms of "poetry," or "ideas." My usual tendency is to reduce my experience to metaphors, then render the metaphors in words, and I wanted to beat that rap this time. Food, chewed up and swallowed, was what the garden was all about, and nothing less than that was going to satisfy. I wanted the experience to come alive outside my head, in the concrete world, and achieving that of course was the prime reward.

But the thing I'm pleased to discover, now that the garden is a fact, is that I'm not as nervous as I was about abstractions. Abstractions built out of other abstractions can lead to actual sickness, I believe. But abstraction derived from the concrete is like the other side of the coin, yin and yang. It feels good to talk about gardening, now that the work is done. Feels the best in a long time, in fact. Like dessert, after a good meal. It's amazing what a little honest, sweat-producing work can do for a nervous head.

So stuff has been occurring to me: talk, for instance. The difference in the quality of talk that grows out of true experience, against talk that grows only out of other talk. Talk among people who never do anything but talk, vs. words between people who have other things to do with themselves. Drawing room conversation dependent on other drawing rooms, against conversation among people who've just come in from the world. Political opinions based on other people's political opinions, against a politics growing from the life you've personally lived. It's all like the difference between a wax apple, and one just dropped off a tree.

And this: rules. How we've all gone around crazy the past

few years in revolution against rules because they are rules; discovering some rules that are bad, deciding all rules must be bad, so what the world needs is anarchy. Head filled with such cheap crap, then coming up against something like a garden, entering into the work of it as if: this is *my* scene; *I* decide the processes of this garden because I'm a free man and I'm going to do my thing. So your thing is to spray water around. "Express" yourself in water. It's so . . . *esthetic*. The curve of the spray is so . . . *poetic*. It's a veritable art form, no less, the avant-garde of agriculture. Jackson Pollock with a green thumb. Spray here, spray there, spray all over God's whole creation cause I'm going to do my thing.

Well, do tell. Because what's happening, the reason all those beans and tomatoes and carrots are, like, *drooping* a little is that you've damned near drowned the things. And so you learn: the gardener doesn't make up the terms of his relationship to the garden. He doesn't invent them out of his precious head, change them around according to his petty whim. The terms exist before he gets there and they'll still exist long after he has gone. It's like the plants are saying: "Give us none of your hip esoteric shit; we want water, and we want it in precise amounts, according to the varying root systems of each plant. We want fertilizer, and if you don't know how much, find out. Find out about nitrogen, about phosphorus, about potash. For if you expect anything from this garden, you must know what the garden expects of you. There's a reality among these rows, stuff is going on bigger than all of us, so dig it. You are only a part of what is happening here. Fit yourself into the scheme. Abide by the law, and maybe you'll be pleased that you did."

Then this: pick up a radical newspaper, see a picture of the entrance to an Army post. Fort Dix, probably. And above the gate and the M.P.'s helmets is a sign that reads: "Obedience to the law is freedom." It's one of the philosophical highlights of the gardening season to read those words in political terms, and shudder; then read them again in terms of the natural world and think: how true, how true.

part three: how to go about it

A dozen gardeners will tell you a dozen ways to start gardening, and probably they'd all be right. This is one way:

1. Buy a book called *How To Raise Fruits And Vegetables By The Organic Method*. Subscribe to a magazine called *Organic Gardening*. The magazine's address is Rodale Press, 33 East Minor Street, Emmaus, Pa. One year, $5.85. You can order the book from the same address or buy it locally at the Whole Earth Truck Store.

2. Begin a compost pile. Here's how:

Compost

Every suburban household produces enough organic materials to make compost. There are several different recipes in the gardening book. One will be suitable for your scene. The main thing is to begin thinking of all organic materials as VALUABLE. Stop burning leaves and throwing away kitchen garbage. Begin saving it all: grass clippings, leaves, wood ashes, kitchen garbage. (Yes, it is possible to compost kitchen stuff without odor or flies). You will need to import some sort of nitrogenous activating agent such as manure. You may have to buy it. Ask at the garden supply center. When you've assembled the materials, layer them together according to the recipe you have chosen.

Earthworms

Worms are a groove. Order some. 1,000 for $4.00. (see classifieds in *Organic Gardening*.) They loosen the soil, and fertilize it, and speed the composting process. They multiply and work for you full-time, year around.

3. Begin preparing your soil for next spring. A corner of your yard. A large box. Along the margins of your driveway. Using the book as a guide, spade it up, work in available organic materials, mulch it with straw or leaves for the winter.

4. From your book learn which vegetables are best for your area, and your soil. Learn all you can about the eccentricities of each vegetable you intend to plant as soon as the season begins. In California, a lot of stuff can be planted in February.

5. Buy a small soil-test kit. From $2.00 up. You don't have to have one, but they are fun, instructive, and add to one's sense of intimacy with the soil.

the great mazatlan shakedown

jon buckley

PART I

This is one of those stories that deserves a book to properly tell it—a massive volume recounting in detail the lives and times of those wild enough to live them. But for now it's enough to call it Mexico and let it stand at that.

It's a place in space and time where the stars must shine through check-out stations, the kind of place where soldiers hang out in every railroad depot, and even the peanut vendor is a part-time cop. But there are many compensations: rock-heavy beaches with shale set close as paving stones; endless rows of dancing cacti; and as always there are Jack-in-the-Box taco stands with weird characters from the north fumbling with pesos and other unknown factors ". . . I'd like some hot fudge on my tacos please . . ." . . . (long pause) . . . "well, how 'bout some mayonnaise?" And late at night when I was feeling righteous, I'd laugh myself into a hammock on the sand, tilt backwards to gaze at the moon, and in the quick silence, the dark close kiss of heaven and earth made my head sing.

If you looked close enough, you could spot the local gypsies—tented down in camper-busses, or hugging the warm bare ground,

or rollin' into Mazatlan; three of the drunk tired clock in the
morning, 36 hours with a bus driver who learned his trade at
Hollywood destruction derbies (". . . pulled into Nazareth, was
feelin' half past dead . . ."). the screaming babies—cackling
breast-beater—chickens and fishwives Express is home free.
(". . . just wanted to find a place where I could lay my
head . . .") With me and my brothers strolling right into the
local police station (cleverly disguised as incognito anarchists)
like lamb chops cooked, prepared, and seasoned for the mouth
of the Beast, (". . . hey mister can you tell me . . .") asking
in our simple way for directions to a campground (". . . where
a man might find a bed? He just sighed, shook his head—
No was all he said.")

Well, I don't have to tell what kind of place it was.

It was just a *Bad Place*.

There's this smell that evil locations carry with them; it hangs
around draft boards, jails, and military installations of all kinds—
I'm sure you'd know it if you got a whiff of it. It's an odd mixture of bad karma, bad cigars, bad breath, and lots of cheap dis-
infectant. And right there in that building, walking among us
like a living being, was that very odor. It mixed itself in with
garlic and bacardi: fumes, forced itself up your nose like some
kind of olfactory rape, and surrounded the three young surfers
frisked up against the wall—and it didn't make them very happy.

By that time neither were we. Awareness suddenly dawns
that there are all these Mexican dudes done up in uniforms,
pencil-thin mustaches, and heavy vibes, all toolin' around and
just what are three clean-living boys from Palo Alto gonna do
when Someone-In-Authority over the whole shebang walks over,
flaps his arms, pulls his pants up past his navel and clips out
in starched military English:

"We don' like longhairs—we cutdemoff!"

The thing one must appreciate is the directness of it all. Such
efficiency! Here in this foul hole at 3:30 in the morning is this
living cartoon yelling about shaving our asses, all the while
hitching and tugging at his trousers to keep them up around his
solar plexus. It makes the heart grow warm to know that a truly

accomplished asshole transcends all national, ethnic, and cultural barriers . . . they're all around us, and their numbers are uncountable.

We did, however, beat a somewhat hasty retreat, assuring the gentleman that we were simply three harmless fanatics on our way to visit our great shrine at Big Fallas, Ariz., the spot where muscatel was first brewed in these United States, a tale which didn't leave a big impression.

"Take your religions elsewhere!" he called after us, manfully yanking at his zipper.

But after a cheap night in a cheap hotel we were on our way—to that mythical place where the sun can warm your head with streaks of reddish-brown, to a place where the air is alternately heavy with the smell of sweet smoke and clear with the ocean breeze, to a place of refuge where you can take your sandals off, curl your toes in the sand, and rest your eyes in the shade of some friendly tree. Or so it was we told ourselves as we gawked and bought, drank some tequila, gawked and bought more ("Diamond Jim" Pierre taking his usual impressive haul), till straining at the gunwhales of our rucksacks we walked the dusty road from town to the beach and waited patiently on a corner for that One Last Bus—Waited patiently for the clattering beast to come eat us, digest us, and spit us out on some fine stretch of country where the mind can flow at ease and the taste of good rum becomes familiar.

Instead we got Hernando and The Weasel. Enter stage left, pulling up to our bus stop in their late model Ford with the Texas license plates, looking all down home and friendly in their straw cowboy hats and stay-prest everythings, asking in their broken wet-back tongue if we wanted a lift, and we (being full of trust for our fellowman as well as tequila) take them at their word and pile in the backseat. All three of us. Plus beards, canteens, watchcaps, shopping bags, a softball I swiped in San Diego, dirty underwear, exotic aromas . . .

And we're rolling down this seawall road in Mazatlan, happy as high quality sardines in a tin can, looking at the scenery, jabbering away about how the Turista Bureau was right all along—Mexicans are friendly if you give them half a chance and—

"Wha's yor nems?" our driver inquires smoothly.

So we tell him. Our first names. And Jake reaches across the seat to shake hands . . . and there's nothing there . . . and we begin to get just the tiniest bit nervous.

"What's *your* name?" I try to sound smooth and fail miserably. He remains silent. The car is picking up speed. They're rattling on in Spanish in the front seat and a few key words start to filter in. The backhairs of my neck are standing straight up and there's 20 pounds of adrenalin careening around my system and sure enough—

there's that smell again.

We watch the Inevitable as it unfolds before us: Hernando edges to the roadside, two badges are flipped open in our faces, and our new friends quickly dissolve into cops.

PART II

"Out."

They liked that word.

They liked it so much that they said it over and over for about three straight minutes—three minutes while Jake looked at Mark and Mark looked at me and I looked towards heaven; minutes while we silently inquired about our collective sanity for leaving home and loved ones 1100 miles behind, traveling through mountain and desert just to join the swelling ranks of those poor unfortunates who have been busted (and shaved) by the Mexican pigs.

Both Hernando (I finally got his name—off his Policia I.D.) and The Weasel (a first class rodent for sure) kept a close eye on us as they stripped our packs and pawed through our wallets. The Scene is familiar. Some people seem to have cop-magnets built into them that attract the fuzz from miles around, and ours were functioning at topspeed that day.

Our amigos seem to be in no hurry, and now I guess neither are we. "Our time is their time," I call forlornly after our Bus as it passes us by in the mid-day heat. The whole comedy is truly frightening: the largest sucking hand guns I've ever seen are draped casually across their buttocks like some form of cancerous growth—and I'm not about to be on the receiving end.

By now they've finished strewing most of our gear around and are mumbling something about loco gringos. They eye Mark's camera suspiciously and clumsily fumble lenses from hand to hand till he positively fidgets over to them and rescues his babies from their clutches.

So far, so good. The carefully concealed stashes have stayed stashed.

But now they're into nooks and crannies—poking and ferreting out our secrets: pouches, medical kits (but it's a *sterile* bandage senor! Rip) exploring and probing until— until—

"Hah!"

Knives.

Two fine hunting knives and a stiletto, old friends to their owners, are mercilessly kidnapped, but our interrogators are getting bored and besides it's about that time of day when all good Mexican lawmen knock off for a few cervezas—

but they're not *quite* finished.

Jacket pockets reveal key rings, note books, assorted pesos, my pill case ("no comprende," and my thanks to the patron saint of smugglers soar skyward); the action by now is mere formality, just a few more spots to hit: Jake's grab-bag of essential traveling tools, things no self-respecting artist would be without—red pens, guitar picks, old Free U membership card, rapidographs, a few mouth harps, a pack of zig-zags . . .

zig-zags.

Oh, they're hot now. Rolling papers! The universal incrimination! The Weasel is getting frantic in his pokings and pryings. He juggles and shakes things and turns things inside out and from one of the harps in the palm of his hand is falling a few flakes of . . . of . . . of . . .

Oh No!

The Weasel's nose actually begins to twitch.

"Ahhh. Mary Juana."

He hovers over the greenery and croons the words as if some long lost lady friend has just re-entered his life.

The words snap both men back into action; their hands are everywhere, patting our levis, checking leather pouches—

They are rewarded. A carelessly placed stash sets both of them to jabbering about police stations; my bowels are doing back-flips, the mind slips into double-clutch, and my mouth opens of its own accord in the most torrential stream of offerings, promises, prayers, solicitations, and plain agony that those two had ever seen.

Paranoic-panoramic visions of Mexican jails with shit all over the wet concrete floor and poor Jon locked away till the eyes rust out from rot—

AIEE!!!

O no senor in nom de dios be merciful o in nom de *Jesu* senor o no imprisonade o no por favor, por favor!

They are unmoved.

"There ees nomore maryjuana en Mexico," says Hernando with a straight face while he fondles the illegal tobacco pouch in his hands. Mark's eyes bug out of his head and my mind boggles trying to remember all the beautiful blossoming green plants that we'd counted growing wild by the roadside on the journey south.

No more grass in Mexico? You are out of your stay-prest mind, amigo. But that doesn't help too much 'cause here are these two goons leaning casually up against their late-model-Ford-with-the-Texas-plates eyeing the gyrations and incantations of these three madmen with a puzzled expression of half-amusement-half-suspicion stamped on their faces.

And in spite of my frenzied attempts to tell the world in both English and Spanish how It's All A Lie and that the weed doesn't belong to us at all but was slipped into our baggage by some malicious surfer in Tijuana—

Hernando is still making noises sounding something like: "You . . . are . . . heepees . . . we go station de policia, pronto, vamanos!"

AIEE!! (again)

Down on my knees in a performance that would have done credit to any Academy Award Holder, the barrage continues unchecked, flowering off my stuttering tongue in a vast river of bullshit. I cast quick sideglances at the two of them, my thinking processes ride out of suspended animation and the Great Realization finally hits—

They're cops, like any other cops, in any other part of the world, and sure enough they've been giving us the old shakedown shuffle as nicely as any vaudeville routine you've ever seen.

Soooo—

Hernando starts insisting vehemently, making vague gestures back towards town; The Weasel suddenly becomes *very* sympathetic and somewhere along the line of conversation the magic word is dumped into the picture like a delicately placed bulldozer—

Dinero?

But of course! From our sad supply of funds we empty pockets, pouches, wallets, and envelopes—we throw greenbacks like confetti;

pour pesos on the carseat like tickertape

in a wall street parade—

it looks like a lot.

It is.

It's all we have.

We wait breathlessly for the verdict; Hernando examines his fingernails, The Weasel is counting it up quickly, too quickly . . .

"Too leetle, too leetle."

They stagger back under another explosion of prayers and exhortations, they are tiring of the show, and I'm watching for the Critical Moment.

As they begin to count our money one last time, my last five dollar bill flutters down to nest among the other pieces of currency like a pigeon coming home to roost.

The agreement is sealed: $88, 3 knives, and a stash of high quality grass in exchange for Freedom.

Pretty cheap when measured against two years in a Mexican jail.

And they hem and haw and dicker and we lay it on a little thicker—

O no senor o yes we are leaving your beautiful country o gracias you mutherfucking swine . . .

And they're gone.

And we're gone; packed up, packed off, and trundled away to a safe spot under the seawall.

There is silence. Then a bit of grumbling. Then
there's this giggle and
the giggle turns into a snort
and the snort into a roar and
it rips out from my belly and climbs up
my throat to echo out of my mouth
in a hysterical hyena belch.

Yes, it's a fact of life that because of the way that I live, my sense of the Absurd must be kept in razor-sharp condition, and it often leads to a kind of psychic flash that isn't really a vision or a prophecy, but rather a sort of "glimpse"—

And I'd glimpsed Hernando and The Weasel sitting back in their late-model-Ford-with-the-Texas-plates, rolling a fat one, toking up at our expense, counting out our spare change and laughing. Laughing! Laughing while Jake and I laughed and counted out our carefully concealed traveler's checks, figured our losses, and planned wild plans.

Some of our bread bought us time in Sabalo—time enough to get cooked by the sun and blessed by the moon at night.

Some of it bought treasure of a greenish gold hue that now lies ingested in our brains or hidden in an old light tower; and some of it even paid for part of the long way home.

So we shouldered our worldly goods and walked down the length of the beach and thought deep thoughts about how The Road is like grease for the soul; how it fills in the cracks, takes off the tarnish, and burns away the rust that too much city living can leave in a man. It's full of unmentionable disasters, delightful surprises; it's funky and it's hard—
but it's *real* and it's there waiting for any man with balls enough to reach for it.

And somehow that's all connected to the great shakedown in Mazatlan, which is not something that you can really think about with your head; it's got to be felt with blistered feet and a keen sense of the Ridiculous. But now you know *that* part of the story, and *I* sure know it, and somehow I can even work up a little sympathy for the Hernandos and The Weasels of this world, 'cause they'll *never* know it—

and sometimes that makes me just a bit sad.

how to weave a tangled web

ed mc clanahan

"Responsibility . . . the ability to respond." ROBERT DUNCAN

Some while back, during one of my more-or-less-annual pilgrimages to my Kentucky birthplace, I came uncomfortably close to having my ass handed to me in a local tavern by three surly, burly young bucks (well, Emory and Cecil were burly; Jimmy-O wasn't all that threatening) who took exception to my longish hair and Abner Doubleday mustache and pointy California frootboots and tinted granny glasses. Those who recall my description of that encounter may also understand that because I am by trade a teacher, and because with a lot of luck and every last modicum of sangfroid I could muster, I managed to turn their hostility into something roughly approximating communication, I think of that evening in the Pennington Club tavern as one of the signal occasions of my life. I was—still am, by god—rather proud of my performance as a teacher that night: *You guys ought not to be so quick to judge people,* I had reproached my assailant-designates from the pedagogical summit when they inquired why one of my obvious eminence chose to go about in public all got up like some kind of androgynous weird-o. To my delight—and my relief—they seemed receptive to the lesson, and I went home satisfied they wouldn't be quite so eager to coldcock the next fine-feathered freak who comes tripping down the pike.

At the time I little suspected that I would shortly thereafter be confronted with a situation which mirrored that one almost perfectly; except of course in a mirror image everything is reversed, so that this time the very same discretely dandyish adornments that had very nearly done me in that night in the Pennington Club, this time they afforded me perfect *immunity* from harm! Hoist by my own petard! Fornicated by the fickle finger of fate! Caught by the short hairs (as it were) in the grinding metaphysical machinery of history repeating itself!

Here's the way it went this time around:

I have to begin by explaining that I do my writing in what might charitably be called my "office" in downtown Palo Alto, a rather grim little dust-hole* upstairs above Palo Alto's version of the Pennington Club, a scruffy, low-rent rock-'n'-roll-'n'-fish-'n'-chips establishment known (until recently, when it underwent a whole series of overnight metamorphoses of name and decor) as the Poppycock, a kind of hip honkytonk. And to that I must append the observation that anyone who professes to know Palo Alto but hasn't checked out the Poppycock corner simply do not know whereof he speaketh. Because if anything at all has happened around here lately, the odds are it happened somewhere within the general vicinity of the Poppycock. On warm-weather weekends that corner jumps forty-eight hours a day: There are junior high dropouts and strange, strung-out old spades, adolescent acidheads and swiftly aging speedsters, motorcycle madmen and wilted flower children, sparechangers and affluent rock musicians and plainclothesmen and *nouveaux riche* dealers, all in all probably the freakiest, far-outest scene from Sunset Strip to the Haight. It's grimy and gaudy and ugly as sin, and sometimes more than just a little scary; but it grooves, it's alive, I

---

* Actually, it's nowhere near as squalid as I've made it out to be. But I've always been enamored of the artist-in-his-garret trip.

love it. True, there's despair aplenty on that corner; but there's also more raw upfront ecstasy going down right there on the street every Saturday night than there is in Burlingame in a month of Sundays.

All the same, I must confess that along about Christmas, when with the chilly weather the street people began to invade the upstairs of the building, swarming through these dim scabrous hallways like vermin in the hide of some mangy old mutt, holding court in the unoccupied offices, performing their weird rituals in the toilets, along about then even I began to get a little edgy. My place had already been broken into once (for some strange reason the marauder had ignored all my meager fixtures except an obsolete edition of Roget's Thesaurus and two ancient packets of Heavenly Blue morning glory seeds, to which he was entirely welcome), and we'd also had a recent and rather serious burglary at home, and the prospect of getting scored on yet another time was not a happy one.

Which is why, late one evening during the Christmas holidays, as I was heading home from a party, I went out of my way to drive past the Poppycock and check my office; the weather had turned decidedly nippy during the last few days, and as a consequence the traffic in the halls had been especially heavy: a couple of times that afternoon someone had actually tried my door while I was inside working.

Anyhow, the atmosphere that night must have been just right for conducting adverse vibes, because sure enough, someone had smashed the lock on my office door and made off with my nice new Hermes portable typewriter, along with a malfunctioning, relatively worthless set of sleazy hi-fi radio components and a few odds and ends, a notebook and a pocket mirror and a couple of coffee spoons. But it was the loss of the typewriter that really distressed me—that plus the fact that the knave(s) had strewn my manuscripts and papers around the room in a manner brazenly bespeaking a profound disrespect for Art. Well, I decided indignantly, puffing myself up like Colonel Blimp, naturally we can't have such barbarous hooligans running about loose, flaunting their contempt for the Finer Things before the world, indeed not, why they'll poison the public sensibility!

Thus fuming and muttering, I flounced off to the PAPD station and reported the burglary, and four policemen came to the office and were thorough and efficient and courteous (though I did spot one of them somewhat speculatively eyeing my mustache), and went away saying there was hardly any chance at all I'd ever get my goods back. (*Mea culpa,* by the way: while I was waiting for the police to arrive, I'd poked about the room in search of clues, smudging fingerprints wherever I touched, like an inept rookie in the Crimestopper's Textbook.) So, finally, deep into the middle of the night, I grumbled my way home to bed, where I dreamed grumpy dreams till late the next morning, when I was awakened . . .

. . . by the voracious racket of a local land developer's bulldozer crunching away at my neighbor's house, the same gluttonous godamned bulldozer that will be gnawing on my own house any day now. Then I remember the dreary events of last night, and those cartoon dreams in which my Hermes sprouts little wings and flies away, and I groan into my pillow. Two things to be mightily pissed off about before I've even got my eyes open. Somehow this does not look like my day.

Sunk to my earlobes in the blackest kind of mood, I sit till nearly noon at the kitchen table, slouched over a cup of lukewarm coffee, churlishly bemoaning my ill fortune to my writer friend Jim Hall, who's visiting from back East, and mourning the loss of my typewriter and the destruction of my neighborhood and the end of all that's good and true and holy in the land. And then the phone rings.

"Ed?" a dimly familiar voice asks, somewhat querulously. "This is Gabby."

"Who?"

"You know. Gabby? That used to be in your class?"

"Um, um, oh yeah, sure. Gabby. Right." And slowly a face emerges out of the recent past and attaches itself to the voice: Gabby, a Texan, politically radical, long-haired, a grad student from another department who was working on a pretty good novel in my fiction-writing class a year or so back. A nice guy, Gabby; he was a little older, a little more mature than most of my students, and we'd been occasional coffee-drinking buddies ever since I'd known him. But I haven't run into him for the longest time, didn't even know he was still around, how come he's calling me, probably wants me to write him a recommendation or something, o shit that's all I need on this gloomiest of all possible mornings.

"Right. Hello, Gabby. How you making it? What's happening?" But I ask it warily, thinking If he wants me to write a godamned letter for him I'll tell him some sonofabitch boosted my typewriter, that's what I'll tell him.

"Hey, listen, man, have you still got your office at the Poppycock?"

What have we here? "Yeah, sure. Why?"

"Well, look, let me ask you something, and if the answer's no then just forget I called. Okay?"

Uh oh. Sounds like a recommendation request, all right. But sure, I tell him, go ahead.

"Well, then," he says, "tell me, did you get robbed last night?"

"*What?*" All of a sudden my ear has socked itself like a suction cup to the receiver. "Yeah, damn right I did!"

"A typewriter? And some hi-fi stuff?"

"Yeah, right! Right!"

"Well, if you can come over to my place right away I think you can get it back. The guys that took it, see, are friends of this girl that lives with me, and one of them's here now. He came to see if I was interested in buying a typewriter, and when he told me they ripped it off of an office over the Poppycock, I kind of thought it might be yours. You better hurry, though. I can't guarantee how long I can keep him here."

Incredible! A freaking *miracle,* by god! I nearly garrotte myself on the phone cord laying hands on a pencil and paper to write down Gabby's address and his directions for getting to it, and within a couple of minutes Jim and I are in the car and on our way, Jim going along for moral support, and for the adventure.

And all the way across town to Gabby's address I chatter exuberantly about how I am after all a generous, large-spirited sort, who'll probably let bygones be bygones as long as I get my goods back, blah-blah-blah—it never once occurring to me, of course that the one truly generous act performed so far in this curious little melodrama is Gabby's phone call, he having done me the undeserved kindness of assuming that I am, when all is said and done, a generous, large-spirited sort who'll let bygones be bygones.

So, unburdened by such over-nice considerations, only minutes after Gabby's phone call we pull up in front of a shabby old gray stucco house bearing the number he has given me. Its window blinds have all been pulled, so that it looks out upon the world with a blank, noncommittal stare. Standing like one of those miniature plaster-of-paris jockeys in the blighted, thumbnail-sized lawn is a middle-aged gentleman of color, regarding us with baleful, bloodshot eye from beneath the bill of an improbably spiffy-looking golf cap. Could *this* be our man? For the first time it occurs to me that just possibly I am dealing with the Genuine Article here, that maybe I'm about to confront not some wretched, stoned-out little street-creep supplicating my forgiveness, but a band of cold-eyed, hard-nosed professionals, real honest-to-god Criminals. A disquieting thought, that; tends to put things in something of a new light. Suppose they make me buy back my own typewriter? *Then* where'll all my high-minded magnanimity be, just when I need it most?

"Y'all huntin ole Gabby?" the man asks as Jim and I, circling him warily, edge across the yard toward the front door. "Me too, I was jis goin seem too, at ole long-hair Gabby, he my ole buddy ole Gabby he is, y'all come wimme, we go see ole Gabby, he right there inna house, I ain seem sence three or two days ago, mean him's ole buddies, ole neighbor buddies, at Gabby's a good ole boy ainny, sheeeee-it you better bleeve he is, he my ole buddy . . ."

And so on . . . and on . . . and on. It is the first wash of a floodtide of words that seems to flow from him ceaselessly and effortlessly, an aimless torrent that begins nowhere and goes nowhere and ends nowhere, as if his tongue has somehow come unfastened at both ends and sputters on of its own free will and accord, cut loose of its last flimsy moorings to his mind. Right away I flash *speedfreak! speedfreak!* But as he joins us I immediately detect the breath of Sweet Lucy on the air, and I understand this here is no doped-up desperado, no cat burglar, no bloody thievin' wog, as we used to call 'em down on the ole plantation. This here is the neighborhood lush, is who this is.

We are on the stoop now, and he is already rapping briskly at the door. ". . . so ole Gabby he say Albert you all right by god, he say he like to git aholt of some of them nice tomaters I got in my garden, I gone *givem* some by god, I jis come by to fine out how many does he *want* . . ."

The door opens and Gabby is standing in the hall, looking pretty much the same as when last I saw him, way back in the early autumn: he's got a little more hair, I suppose, but then for that matter so do I; who in fact does not?

"Hey, come on in," he says amiably. "Where'd you find old Albert?"

He does not wait for an answer, thereby giving us to understand that we might have found Albert nearly anywhere. As we enter I see that Gabby is smiling, which reassures me, yet at the same time he looks a bit preoccupied, distracted, which unnerves me. (Later I am to discover that his uneasiness grows out of some utterly unrelated negotiations he has going with yet another set of people, who haven't even arrived yet. Naturally I would not presume to speculate here upon the nature of his deliberations with them, especially since it turns out to have nothing whatever to do with me and my Hermes. But of course as we are entering the house I've no way in the world of discovering what's making Gabby jumpy, so I immediately take it for granted that our arrival has brought it on, which makes *me* jumpy.) As Gabby leads us down the dark hall toward the kitchen I feel as jittery as an over-wound wind-up top, as if at any moment I might disintegrate in a small explosion of tiny springs and cogwheels.

". . . got them tomaters over there *this* big, I say to the ole

woman I jis gone take some to old Gabby, yes by god, that Gabby
he a good ole boy by god, I take him and little Miss Mercy some
of these here tomaters, what I say was . . ."

Now we are in the kitchen, and there, sitting at a table piled
high with dirty dishes, pots and pans, old newspapers, books,
manuscripts—in short the kind of kitchen table no self-respecting
graduate student would be without—sitting there at one end of
the table is a very pretty girl—Miss Mercy? was that what Albert
called her?—with a blond baby on her lap, and across from
her sits what has to be the world's scruffiest hippy. I recognize
him right off, he's a Poppycock regular, just a kid, maybe seventeen or eighteen, a barefoot psychedelic waif with a pale, pinched,
meager little face beneath a wild snarl of dark matted hair
that reaches halfway down his back, and a wispy little boy
goatee, and an unbelievably dirty old plaid flannel shirt with
the sleeves half rotted away, and about a dozen greasy leather
pouches, stuffed with who-knows-what weird substances, dangling from the beltloops of his crusty jeans. As we enter the
kitchen Gabby says to him, "This is Ed," and through the hanging veil of hair he looks up at me, me and my fashionably longish
coif and my Polack-mod fifty-dollar hippy specs, looks up at
me with the sweetest, saddest, shyest, most incredibly winning
smile I've ever seen, an impossibly beautiful *gift* of a smile,
and holds out his hand for me to shake, and says, softly and
with perfect ingenuousness:

"Hey, man, meet the cat that ripped off your typewriter!"

"That's Scrounge," Gabby says. "I already told him you were
coming."

And then we, Scrounge and I, are shaking hands and giggling
like a pair of perfect fools, and I am charmed beyond measure,
and utterly won over.

". . . I jis might give ole Scrounge some tomaters too, don't
he look to y'all like he need some, little ole skinny thing, I never
see the like . . ."

I am beginning to realize that Albert's gibberish is to social
intercourse what the tamboura is to Indian music, a kind of
liquid atonal drone that rushes along just beneath the surface of

the conversation, bubbling up like a wellspring wherever there's the smallest silence.

"Listen, man," Scrounge is saying, "I mean I got to tell you, man, like, we wouldn't *never* of ripped off your shit if we'd known you was a hip dude!"

Me? A hip dude? Me, this aging Peter Pan in pointy boots? Surely he can't mean it, surely he's setting me up for some awful put-down. But his voice and hang-dog expression are so heavily freighted with earnest apology that finally I'm unable to harbor even the slightest doubt of his sincerity. It is perhaps the grandest compliment I've ever been paid in my whole life . . . so grand that it completely crowds out of my consciousness the fact that, however much it distresses him to have to confess to having inadvertently ripped off a hip dude's shit, Scrounge is not the least bit abashed at admitting he's a thief.

"Well," I hear myself saying, "I don't really care about the hi-fi stuff. In fact, you can keep that if you want it. I would kind of like to have the typewriter back, though, if you could manage it."

Now for Chrissake *I'm* apologizing. And why the billy hell am I offering up my hi-fi gear as ransom before anybody even asks for it? This whole business is putting me through just about the maximum number of changes I can handle in one sitting.

"No, no!" Scrounge assures me. "We'll get it *all* back, man! Only the thing is, I ain't got it here with me right now. Who's got it right now is Brainwave and The Beast."

Brainwave? The Beast? *Zut alors!* What next?

". . . so I say to the ole woman I reckon I gone give ole Gabby some of that good squarsh too . . ."

"Yeah, Brainwave and The Beast took it all with them. But I'll go find them, man, and get it back for you! Hey, man, I'll go right now, yeah, hey!" In a sudden burst of energy he leaps up from the table, and I see all over again how pitifully frail he is. A rag, a bone, a hank of hair, that's Scrounge. "Why don't *everybody* come, shit yeah, let's go find this dude's shit for him!"

But for all his fragility he evidently packs around a lot of personal magnetism, because almost at once he has the whole roomful of people—remember now, there's Gabby and the girl and the baby and Albert (". . . I got tomaters *and* squarsh I gone givem by god . . .") and Jim and me and, oh yes, Scrounge's big black dog, who as I recall was under the table until Scrounge stood up and brought the dog up with him like some kind of strangely malformed shadow—all of us suddenly swirling about this cramped little kitchen in the wake of Scrounge's enthusiasm, which is already propelling Scrounge himself out of the kitchen and down the hall. And now somehow the entire mass has packed itself like a school of compliant sardines into a space about one-third as large as the kitchen we've just escaped, and Albert is babbling and Scrounge is inviting us to go with him and we are declining and the baby is babbling hardly less coherently than Albert, and the dog—whose neck, it turns out, is bound by a seven- or eight-foot length of twine to Scounge's wrist—is barking gaily, and then there is a knock on the door and Gabby opens it and admits two guys who are obviously the ones he has been expecting, two long-haired, shifty-eyed, anarchosyndicalist dope-dealer types with their collars turned up and their hands jammed in their coat pockets, and Gabby coughs nervously and asks them if they've come to look at the room, heh heh, and they cough nervously and say Oh yeh, that's right, the room, heh heh, and Gabby shuffles his feet anxiously, making ready to lead them off, but before he can get them mobilized Scrounge parts the assembled multitudes by leaping to the little peephole window in the door, and he peers out and giggles and announces, "Uh oh, this is about to get interestin'! Here comes Brainwave and The Beast!"

Flash: *o shit they're gonna be as big and mean as Huns and they're not gonna know he's given me back the typewriter, and as soon as they find out what I've come for they're gonna take my own Hermes and pound my poor ass right into the floor with it and then this mob will panic and trample me to death right here in this very hallway!*

The door swings open and somebody yells Hey, Brainwave! and in bops a Chaplinesque little bundle of rags and bones and hair who could be Scrounge's double and is in fact (someone tells me later) his brother. The two of them fling themselves into each other's arms, embracing and crying out each other's names—"Scrounge, baby!" "Brainwave!"—as joyously as if they haven't crossed paths for years and years; and I relax a little, thinking if this is the biggest size they come in, I guess I'll be all right.

Until the door swings open one more time and into the melee strides a great slab-shouldered, scowling ogre wearing Levi's and a Levi jacket and cycle boots and a thick chain for a belt and the most remarkable head of hair I've ever seen, a dense yellow shock the exact shape and color and texture of a haystack, except for the short, ropy queue that swings loose from the crown of his skull; and within this strange hummock of hair are these pale, cold, blue eyes glowering, darting furiously from face to face in the sullen half-light of the hallway, a griffin with a lion's mane and the fierce eyes of an eagle, a Caliban. Behold, The Beast!

And the dog is yipping and Albert is yapping and the baby is yowling and Scrounge and Brainwave are whooping and Gabby and his colleagues are mumbling conspiratorially behind their hands, and we are all milling around treading all over each other's feet . . . all of us, that is, except The Beast, who stands motionless and silent in the midst of all this clamor, savagely glaring straight at me, and I am thinking, exactly as I did that time in the Pennington Club last summer, *This ain't no kind of place for a respectable thirty-six-(no; thirty-seven-)year-old-college-English-teacher-father-of-three to be hanging out in!*

But before I can give any more than passing consideration to Jim's and my chances if we were to bolt for the door, Scrounge wraps one arm around Brainwave's shoulders and the other around The Beast's waist and draws them through the burgeoning assemblage to where I'm standing and cries above the din:

"Hey, you guys, meet the cat that we ripped the typewriter off of!"

". . . the ole woman say I ort to give some of them tomaters to them folks down the street too, but I say hell no, and she say . . ."

The Beast is squinting into the gloom, his ice-blue eyes just inches from my own, his small mouth working slowly, as if he savors the taste of the rage that's rising in his gorge. Our eyes stay locked that way until, after the longest possible time, he reaches out, and grabs my hand and pumps it vigorously, saying:

"Aw, no shit, man, was that your place? Hey listen, man, we wouldn't never of ripped you off if we'd of known you was a hip dude!"

"Right, man!" Brainwave says, pumping my other hand and breaking into an ecstatic little dance of mock-dismay. "Right! We wouldn't *never* rip off a hip dude!"

"We got to get this dude's shit, man!" Scrounge cries. "Where's it at, man?"

"The typewriter's over at the other place, man," Brainwave offers.

"Yeah," The Beast says, turning back to me, "we can get the typewriter right now. It's over at this place where we slept at last night. But listen, man, I ain't so sure about your hi-fi stuff. Because the thing is, see, The Spirit's got that."

The Spirit? The *Spirit?*

". . . biggest tomaters ever I seen . . ."

"Right!" Scrounge says. "Let's go get his typewriter, before The Spirit gets it! This here's a good dude, man, let's get his shit for him!"

"Yeah!" says Brainwave, and "Shit yes!" hollers The Beast, and the dog yelps something that sounds suspiciously like "Fucking-A!" and Scrounge flings open the door and believe it or not the four of them split, vanish, evaporate before my eyes!

Watching the door swing slowly shut behind them, I am numb, speechless, baffled: I can make no more sense of their leave taking than I had been able to make of them when they were still here in the flesh. Will I ever lay eyes on them again? Will I ever really catch up to my lovely little Hermes, with its wings as fleet as those that grace the heels of the deity from whom it took its name? Alas, I can only confess that once again I am beset by doubts. But I bite my tongue and bide my time.

Meanwhile, the congestion in the hall is easing as suddenly as it had set in. Gabby waves me an indifferent farewell, and he and his misanthropic associates, still growling amongst themselves out of the corners of their mouths, slouch off toward the rear of the house (that will be the last you'll see of them, by the way; none of them reappeared while we were there), and the baby toddles through a doorway off the hall, and Albert lurches after him (". . . you wait up there, liddle buddy, ole Albert gone git you some good squarsh . . ."), and the girl follows them and Jim follows her and I follow Jim; and now we are all in the living room, which is pretty thoroughly littered with the baby's toys but otherwise rather barren. I seem to recall a couple of worn overstuffed chairs and, I think, a rump-sprung couch . . . in any case, a generally undistinguished room.

"Don't worry, man," the girl tells me, reading my glum expression as she gathers up the baby and settles on the couch, "they'll be back."

Albert has somehow finally managed to get his mind off his vegetables; his attention is now fixed inexorably on Jim's bald head: ". . . how come you head ain got no *hair* on it if you one of these hippies like ole Gabby, how come ole Gabby he got *plenty* hair but you ain got no more then a, uh, *tomater,* or a *squarsh* . . . ?" And Jim is mumbling, "Well, uh . . . well, uh . . ." seeking a cranny in which to wedge his answer. But Albert isn't leaving any openings: ". . . well how come you got that liddle ole bit of hair on the edges and ain got none on *top,* I never see no hippy didn't have no *hair* before, how come you so *ball,* man, hee hee hee . . ."

I slump wearily into a chair. "Sure," I am half-heartedly declaring to the girl, "I know they will."

She too hears the way my voice sags beneath the weight of skepticism. "*Truly* they will, man," she assures me serenely. "They're beautiful dudes!"

I try to say, "They *are!*" But despite my best efforts it comes out, "They *are?*" Guiltily I cover it with another question: "Is your name . . . ?"

"Mercy," she says. "I, you know, go by that. I started using it last year when I was dancing topless. Miss Mercy, they called me."

"How long have you known Scrounge and Brainwave and The Beast?"

"Oh, a long time, two or three months, I guess. They used to come in this place where I was a waitress. The Beast is from around here, I think. He's, like, a dropout. Scrounge and Brainwave are runaways from back east somewheres. Virginia or somewheres."

Virginia. Rednecks in drag. The mind boggles.

"The thing is, they're really *pennystricken,* see." She pauses to let that sink in. "They live on just what people give them, and sleep just, you know, wherever they happen to feel like it, with a chick sometimes, or in The Beast's car. So like whenever I run into them I bring them home with me and feed them. I really *love* those three dudes, man, *truly* I do. I mean, they wouldn't of done anything like, you know, ripping off your shit or anything like that, if they hadn't of been, you know, drunk."

"Drunk?" I am flabbergasted. "You mean they *drink?* They aren't dopers?"

"Oh, I guess they, you know, get stoned now and then, just like everybody else. But what they're really *into* is wine. They're juiceheads, mostly."

Despite my astonishment, I have to concede after reflecting on it that this is actually one of the more cogent facts I've managed to glean about them. As something of a tippler myself, I too have harkened upon occasion to the call of the wild grape. But I've been sort of reluctantly assuming, of recent years, that us juiceheads are a dying breed; and the shock of learning that we've merely been underground, just waiting to be rediscovered by the avant garde, is almost too much for me. At last! a cultural revolution I can lay my body on the line for!

"How about The Spirit?" I ask Miss Mercy. "Who's he?"

"I don't know too much about him," she says vaguely. "I

think he's, you know, a spade or something, maybe." She leans back and peers around the edge of the window shade and says, "Hey, there they are, they're back!"

Before I can even begin to get myself collected again, the door crashes open out in the hall and in the blinking of an eye they materialize before me, Scrounge and Brainwave and The Beast and the dog, all four of them grinning broadly and the dog wagging his tail besides, and dangling from The Beast's big right hand, which he is holding out to me, is my Hermes portable typewriter!

"Far *out!* Hey listen, thanks, I . . ."

"We ain't too sure about the hi-fi, though, man," Brainwave says, shaking his head sorrowfully. "Because The Spirit's got that, see."

And I am clearly given to understand, from the sonorous fatalism of his tone, that he is Trying to Tell Me Something: The Spirit, that tone is saying, ain't got quite as much respect for hip dudes as we do, so don't sit up nights waiting for him to bring your hi-fi home. But so delighted am I to have made the grade as a hip dude, to have actually won admission to the august company of these splendid fellows, that at this point I couldn't possibly care less about the wretched hi-fi. What's one hi-fi more or less amongst us hip dudes? To *hell* with the hi-fi! Let The Spirit take it and go with it wherever the spirit moves him!

(He evidently did exactly that, by the way: just the other day Scrounge was telling me, for what had to be the hundredth time, that The Spirit was due to show up any minute with my hi-fi. I have yet to lay eyes on either.)

"Tell me, how'd you all break my door lock?" I ask them, chuckling as merrily as if it had been the Bank of America's place they'd busted into, instead of my own.

"Damn if I can remember," The Beast admits, scratching his head. "We were drunk as shit, man."

"You *kicked* it off, you dumb fuck!" Brainwave chortles. "You were so drunk you kicked the fucker right off, and can't even remember you did it!"

"Oh yeah, that's right, I did," The Beast muses, blushing modestly at the gargantuan proportions of his drunk.

"Hey listen, man," Scrounge tells me, "we really got to get shakin', see. Because we got to get to this chick's house that said she'd ball us if we get there before her old man comes home from work. So we better split. We're sorry about the hi-fi, though, man, we really are!"

". . . I reckon you just about the first ball head hippy ever I run into . . ."

We are all on our feet now, and The Beast is shaking my hand again and Brainwave and Scrounge are sort of plucking at my sleeves and imploring me one last time to forgive them for ripping off such a hip dude. And I, of course, am doing so with all my heart, trailing them halfway down the front hall to bestow upon them the blessing of my infinite mercy, grandly dispensing absolution and all the while feeling guilty as sin for stealing the very bread—or, if you will, the wine—from their mouths. For want of something better to offer them in recompense, I mention that I just might try to write about them sometime.

"Good fucking deal, man," The Beast says heartily. "You can say anything you want to about me. Because I can't read anyhow."

"Hey, Mercy," Scrounge calls back from the front door, "thanks a lot for the breakfast, man!"

"Sure," she says as the door slams after them. "Later, man."

I go back into the living room to gather up my typewriter and rescue Jim from Albert (". . . I jis wisht you'd looky here how *shiny* this ole boy's head is . . ."). I am just thanking Miss Mercy for her hospitality and asking her to thank Gabby for being such a good guy, and Jim is just about to maneuver himself into position to make a break for it, when we hear the front door open again, and suddenly The Beast is framed once more in the hall doorway.

"Hey listen, man," he says to me, "you ain't got any spare change you could loan us, have you?"

I come up with thirty-five or forty cents, which I'm half

ashamed to offer him; I can't help feeling that it's mighty piss-poor wages for all they've done for me. But The Beast seems perfectly content with it.

"Thanks, man," he says cheerfully. "Later."

". . . hey you ole Beasty, if y'all gone git some wine you won't forgit ole Albert would you now goodbuddy, you member how ole Albert give y'all some Lucy the other day, you member that don't you buddy . . ."

For once someone has said something which Albert deems worthy of a direct response. But he's too late, for The Beast is long gone once again. And this time Jim and I are close behind him.

"Bye, bye," Miss Mercy calls sweetly as we slip out the door. "You dudes hurry back, now."

". . . shore y'all come back I git you some of them tomaters too, my ole woman she like to see a ole ball head hippy, I take y'all home with . . ."

Jim and I reach the stoop just in time to see an old Ford ragtop pull away in a great cloud of blue exhaust. The dog is hanging half out of the gaping hole that used to be the rear window, barking his head off, and The Beast and Scrounge are waving good-by out the far side of the car, above the tattered top, and Brainwave is leaning out the window on the near side, his hair flying, his hands cupped to his mouth to make himself heard above the roar of the engine.

"Hey," he yells, "do you cats realize how *weird* all this stuff is?"

Indeed I do, friend Brainwave, I think contentedly as the old car, listing and yawing, careens around the next corner and out of sight. Indeed I do.

And on that happy note this story ought to end, for it now has all the elements of a pretty fair saga—pathos, humor, mystery, suspense, a nice upbeat ending, even a moral of sorts: There's no fool like an old fool, I think it goes. But there's one more thing to deal with, and no way in the world to get around it.

I refer, of course, to the as-yet-unresolved matter of the Palo Alto Police Department. And the only way I can tie up that particular loose end is to trace the tale through yet another tortured convolution:

Obviously (or so it seemed), I couldn't simply turn my back on the whole affair and leave the entire Palo Alto constabulary hotly pursuing phantoms. I mean, suppose that by some wildly improbable stroke of luck they actually *caught* my three felons? Even worse, suppose, for godsake, they caught *me* with the loot, suppose they charged me with receiving stolen property, or fencing my own typewriter? (Bear in mind, if you will, that this had been a particularly trying day, and that in the course of it my paranoia had been turned on and off a dozen times, and somehow all these possibilities seemed very real at the moment.) So, I decided, why sweat it, I'll just drop by the station and clear the whole matter up once and for all, I'll simply tell them that by the craziest kind of coincidence the thieves attempted to sell my goods to an old friend of mine (no, wait, a *former student,* that covers a multitude of peccadilloes, such as my association with persons who consort with known criminals, for instance), and that he happened to recognize the Hermes and informed the culprits that their victim was a good guy who didn't deserve to be so foully used, and so persuasive were his arguments that they instantly saw the error of their ways and agreed to give me back my goods, and to go forth and sin no more!

That much of it sounded only mildly implausible, and it would be an easy story to tell, since it had the added virtue of being entirely true. But from there on the going got a good deal stickier.

For one thing, the police would certainly inquire as to whether I had personally encountered said suspects in the flesh in the course of these deliberations. Well, nossir (I'd tell my interrogators), you see they made my former student promise not to get them into any trouble before they'd give him back my stuff. Hmmm, we see; and mightn't we just have this, uh, "former student's" name? Just for our records you understand, purely routine procedure. Well, nossir, you see my former student made *me* promise not to get *him* into any trouble before *he'd* give *me* back my stuff. So I guess the case is, heh heh, closed, right, officer? But I do want to thank the Department for its invaluable assistance in this little matter, please deliver my personal compliments to the Chief, there's a good fellow.

Well, I did it, I actually brought it off. I sauntered into the police station that afternoon and offered up this concoction of half-truths to a gravely non-committal young patrolman, who dutifully wrote it all down in his casebook and thanked me for dropping by, and I walked out feeling that, all things considered, I'd done the right thing.

And it never seriously occurred to me to question that conviction until very late that same night, when I was sitting in the kitchen recounting the day's adventures to a friend, and the phone rang, and it was Lieutenant Somebody of the Detective Division or whatever they call it, and he wanted to know What means this business in this report, and wouldn't I like to clear up the record, and didn't I understand that after all a felony had been committed, a *felony* Mr. McClanahan, and I'm sure you understand that you can't just walk in here and halt an investigation of a felony, sir, just because you personally happened to be fortunate enough to get your property back, don't you realize that there have been other burglaries of a similar nature in that neighborhood, and do you think it's fair, Mr. McClanahan, that you should get your property back whereas other persons do not get theirs back, don't you realize that the burglaries will continue until these people are apprehended, it's too bad you don't feel you can co-operate with us, it's irresponsible citizens like you who make police work difficult, click.

I was so thoroughly unnerved by the intensity of this dressing-down and so disarmed by the iron logic of his argument that I never even thought to ask him why the billy hell he'd found it necessary to deliver his godamned lecture to me at one-god-damned-thirty in the morning. My end of the conversation went something like Well, yessir but . . . Yes that's so but . . . I can understand that but . . . Right but . . . Yes but . . . Yes but . . . Yes but . . . By the time he hung up I was positively reeling.

He's right! I told my friend after I'd recounted Detective Somebody's diatribe. He's dead right, why *should* I be immune from harm when my neighbors were getting ripped off, what kind of world was it where the very same stupid mustache and hair and stuff that got me into trouble with Emory and Cecil and Jimmy-O saved the day for me with Scrounge and Brainwave and The Beast? Wasn't that just one more manifestation of the one-eyed, short-sighted, bigoted bullshit I was always ranting about?

Well, yes, as a matter of fact it is, said my friend, smiling wryly. So why don't you just call the cop back and turn in your new buddies?

What? Turn them in? Turn those beautiful dudes over to the cops after they trusted me enough to admit their guilt to me? That's *insane!* And anyhow, I feel just the way Miss Mercy does about those guys: "I really *love* those three dudes, man," she said, "*truly* I do." Well, by god, I feel the same way. You think for one minute I'm going to sacrifice people I love on the altar of some miserable godamned abstraction? That's ridiculous!

Well then, said my friend, his smile broadening, you could always look them up and give your typewriter back to them. Or if you want to save yourself the trouble of running them down, you might just take an ax to the typewriter, and get shut of it once and for all.

And then at last I got the point. Which is simply that as long as there's a need to choose between love and duty, there will be those who agonize that they cannot fully commit themselves to either. And their agony shall become, in the end, itself a kind of commitment. And they shall be called—among other things— writers.

And that made me feel at least a little better about the whole thing . . . if only because it told me what I was supposed to do.

a letter to ed mc clanahan
and gurney norman
in california

wendell berry

That was a lovely time we had out there,
those months of talk and laughter, correcting us.
Our words took on a generosity of time, passing
in the free equality of men who knew each other
as boys. We escaped all deadly official boundaries
into the natural brotherhood of countrymen,
Kentucky speaking in us, mountain and river and ridge,
before a California hearth-fire, half the night.

*

Now back in Kentucky, far from you again,
I often think of those days and nights, and long
for their music and their mirth. And then
I remind myself: The past is gone. Remember it.

*

Returning, I always put on a new body,
waking in wet dawn and going to work.
Weary at nightfall, I learn again
the trusting departure into sleep, so deeply
here I might as well be gone. Already
a new garden has fallen from my hands
into the ground. Having trusted seed
to the world, how should I not be a new man?

*

The cities have forgot the earth,
and they will rot at heart
till they remember it again.
In the streets, abstraction
contends with outcry,
hungering for men's flesh.
In the city I measured time
by the life of no living thing,
but by the running down
of engines. I grew a skin
that did not know the sun. Now
once more I have shrugged
in my city skin and sloughed it off
and emerged, new waked.

*

The streets of the broken city
nurture the vogue of the revolutionary
—another kind of politician, another
slogan-sayer, ready to level the world
with a little truth. Those who wait
to change until a crowd agrees
with their opinions will never change.

*

But the man of the earth abides in the flow.
The ground moves beneath him, and he knows
it moves. His house is his vessel, afloat
only for a while. He moves, willing
through a thousand phases of the sun,
changing as the day changes, and the year.
His mind is like the dirt, lightened
by bloom, weighted by rain.

*

The fragment of the earth
that is now me is only on its way
through me. It is on its way
from having been a tree,
a school of fish, a terrapin,
a flock of birds. It will pass
through all those forms again.

*

(*for Chloe, this one*)

I come into the community of the creatures:
lily and fern, sycamore and thrush,
they turn to the light, and to the earth again.
Light and leaf, man and wife,
bird and tree—each one
a blind dancer, whose partner sees.

*

And friend and friend,
together though only in thought,
our bond is speech
grown out of native ground
and laughter grown out of speech,
surpassing all ends.

*

In spring I always return
to a blue flower of the woods,
rising out of the dead
leaves whose life it is. As I look
it wears my face's shadow.
A man always overshadows
what he sees, his presence
becoming part of its mystery.
So all his ideas fall short.
Unless his speech humbles him,
keeping him steadfast in love
beyond his understanding,
he goes blind to the season.
Speech can never fathom
this flower's silence. Enough
to honor it, and to live
in my place beside it. I know
it holds in its throat a sweet
brief moisture of welcome.

Early May, 1969

notes on contributors

WENDELL BERRY is a farmer/teacher/novelist/poet/essayist who makes his home in Port Royal, Kentucky. Among his recent books are *A Place on Earth* (novel), *Farming: A Manual* (poetry), and *The Long-legged House* (essays), all published by Harcourt Brace Jovanovich. Those who are familiar with his work consider him one of the most important young writers in America.

RICHARD BRAUTIGAN is *that* Richard Brautigan.

KARL BURTON attended Stanford in a program combining English and computer science. He was recently sentenced in Minnesota to a year and a day in Federal prison on two draft-resistance counts.

MAX CRAWFORD is a Texan, a former Wallace E. Stegner Fellow in Stanford's creative writing program, and a former editor of *Redneck Review*. "The Abysmal Baptismal" is excerpted from his unpublished novel *The Backslider*.

GERALDINE DAESCH, who lives in Redwood City, California, has a Ph.D. in microbiology from Purdue. She has published many papers in scientific journals.

L. J. DAVIS is a young novelist (*Whence All but He had Fled*, *Cowboys Don't Cry*, *A Meaningful Life*,) who served as the titular head of the *Free You*'s New York Bureau. He occasionally writes on politics for *New York* Magazine. We got his better stuff.

MATT DEWELING is a Stanford graduate from Los Angeles, currently working as a house painter in Palo Alto.

PATTY FOGEL now lives in Berkeley, where she operates a restaurant called The Beggar's Banquet.

THOM GUNN's "At the Center" appears in *Moly and My Sad Captains* his most recent volume of poetry, published by Farrar, Straus & Giroux, Inc.

KEN KESEY's latest book is *Garage Sale,* from Viking Press, Inc.

ED MCCLANAHAN has taught writing at Stanford. He has published in *Esquire, Playboy,* and elsewhere.

PAUL MARIENTHAL is a Southern Californian, a Stanford graduate, and most recently a Columbia grad school dropout.

SPEER MORGAN is a Stanford graduate from Arkansas who now teaches English and writing at the University of Missouri at Columbia. His first novel, *The Farm Motel,* will be published by Alfred A. Knopf, Inc., in 1973.

GURNEY NORMAN is the author of the remarkable first novel *Divine Right's Trip,* which originally appeared in *The Last Whole Earth Catalog* and has since been published by Dial Press and Bantam. A former editor of *The Free You,* he lives in Menlo Park.

JUDITH RASCOE has published fiction in *Atlantic, Harper's, Audience* and many other magazines. She is currently at work on an original screenplay for a film to be produced by Joseph Strick.

SPACE DAISY is, in Real Life, Judith Corcoran, who lives now in Youngstown, Ohio, with her husband and three children. Her poems are lettered and illuminated by Jon Sagen.

ROBERT STONE is a veteran of the last days of Perry Lane, a former Wallace E. Stegner Fellow in Creative Writing at Stanford, and author of the Houghton-Mifflin Prize novel *A Hall of Mirrors*. He was with Kesey and the Pranksters in Mexico for a time, and this article is excerpted from notes he kept during that venture.

TIGER THOMPSON has been a Montana copper miner, a Wobbly, a journalist (he was fired as drama editor of the San Francisco *Examiner* for helping to organize the Newspaperman's Guild during the thirties), a United Artists movie publicist, and a writer of mystery novels (*Hear Not My Steps* and *Death Stops the Show*). He has lived for many years in Menlo Park, where he is currently working on his memoirs.

RICHARD WYMAN is a Stanford graduate who taught for several years in the public high schools of Little Rock, his hometown. He is currently studying law at the University of Oregon.